Winning with *HorsePower!*

Also by Rebekah Ferran Witter

Living with *HorsePower!*
Personally Empowering Life Lessons Learned from the Horse

Winning with *HorsePower!*

Achieving Personal Success through Horses

Rebekah Ferran Witter

TRAFALGAR SQUARE PUBLISHING
North Pomfret, Vermont

First published in 1999 by Trafalgar Square Publishing, North Pomfret, Vermont 05053

Library of Congress Cataloging-in-Publication Data

Witter, Rebekah Ferran.
Winning with horsepower! : achieving personal success through horses /
Rebekah Ferran Witter.
p.   cm.
Includes bibliographical references (p.   ).
ISBN 1-57076-132-9
1. Horses.   2. Horsemanship.   3. Human-animal relationships.
I. Title.
SF285.W76   1999
798.2—dc21   99-32972
CIP

Printed in Canada

10 9 8 7 6 5 4 3 2 1

Table of Contents

Acknowledgments

I owe tremendous thanks to everyone who contributed so generously to this work. During the interview process, I made many "cold calls" that turned into wonderfully warm connections through a mutual love of horses. Contributors related many exciting experiences that define the human value of horses and illustrate the profound, personal benefits, of *HorsePower!*

Jo Abbott
Adrian Arroyo
Zaven Ayanian
Laura Bianchi
James Brady
Buck Brannaman
Octavia Brown
L.D. Burke III
Jenny Butah
Bobby Christian
Lt. Carl Clipper
Tracy Cole
Diana Starr Cooper
Kelli Cox
Helen K. Crabtree
Charlotte Dicke
Bev Doolittle
Anonymous
Bob Douglas

Phyllis A. Eifert
Dale Evans
Jimmy Fairclough
Mary Fenton
Carole Fletcher
Maxine Freitas
Carol Grant
Becky Hart
Sarah Hafner
Ron Harding
Jill Keiser Hassler
Chris Hawkins
Vicki Hearne
Bob Henry
Amy Hubbard
Jack Huyler
Allan Jamison
Martha Josey
Valerie Kanavy

Anne Kursinski
Dr. Patty Latham
Dr. Elizabeth Lawrence
Pat Lawson
Doug Lietzke
Rege Ludwig
John Lyons
Larry Mahan
Mary Mansi
Dennis Marine
Dede Marx
Dr. Robert Miller
Holly Peterson Mondavi
Tom Moore
Stagg Newman
Kelly O'Boyle
Cara O'Neill
Macella O'Neill
Rex Peterson
Irving Pettit

Mary Deringer Phelps
Michael Plumb
Monty Roberts
Roy Rogers
Sam Savitt
Jane Savoie
Tina Schuler
Richard Shrake
Penelope Smith
Curtis Steel
William Steinkraus
Genie Stewart-Spears
Susan Stovall
Carol Stratton
Sally Swift
Linda Tellington-Jones
Caroline Thompson
Diana Thompson
Camille Whitfield Vincent
René Williams
Cathy Ziffren

I am eternally thankful for the love, cheer, and support so freely given by my wonderful husband, Kip, as well as the invaluable help received from William Steinkraus, Kathy Kadash Swan, Betsy Butterfield, Lynda Paffrath, Gert Mazur, Cathy Nessier, and Peter Breakwell.

Thanks also to everyone at Trafalgar Square Publishing—especially Caroline Robbins and Martha Cook—for guiding the manuscripts (and me) along the road to publication. And I appreciate the many readers of LIVING WITH HorsePower! who sent such enthusiastic reviews and have asked for more—here it is...enjoy!

Author's Note

Like its predecessor, LIVING WITH *HORSEPOWER!*, this book employs a unique conversational format, with contributors' comments set in *italics* rather than quotation marks, so that you can easily distinguish their voices from mine.

There is a photograph and biographical information for each contributor. When that individual's name first appears in the text, a page number in parentheses tells where to find this information. Thereafter, you may refer to the index, where the listing indicated in bold will reference the biographical page.

For accuracy, I've worked directly from taped interviews and all conversations have been reported as closely to the original transcript as possible. However, occasionally it was necessary to modify spoken phrasing to wording more conducive to written text. In doing so, I was careful to preserve content, but if any oversights, mistakes, or errors occur in the text, I apologize, as they are completely unintentional.

Most of the opinions expressed are mine; those that come from the individual contributors were given freely. I attempted to reference and verify all pertinent information; however, due to the very nature of conversational anecdotes, total verification is not possible.

Dedication

This book is dedicated to all true horsemen—individuals who realize personal growth, compassion, strength, and success through *HorsePower!*

FROM HORSEPOWER!
TO HUMAN POWER

It's not what you learn about horses that makes them important;
it's what they teach you about people.
—Bill Wyman, former Headmaster of The Thacher School

The narrow trail switched back sharply up the canyon wall. The horses scrambled to gain purchase on the shards of shale that crumbled beneath their hooves and fell away. The precipitous climb rewarded us with a rush of adrenalin and a spectacular view of patchwork ranch lands, orange groves, and Lake Casitas in the Ojai Valley below. Our guide, Jack Huyler (p.6), had been riding these steep trails for so long that he hardly considered that those with fainter hearts might be saying their prayers. He knew the horses could handle it all and that the riders not only would survive, but ultimately revel in the thrill and grow from the ordeal.

At Jack's invitation, my husband, Kip, and I were experiencing life at The Thacher School, east of Santa Barbara, California. Kip had attended Thacher in the 1960s, but this was my first visit to the fabled school where Jack and his wife, Margaret, now enjoy an eventful retirement after more than fifty years of teaching, coaching, and administrative duties. A renowned horseman who reset the standard for gymkhana competition in 1969 when he and his gifted stallion, El Paso Gap, won the state championship, Jack—now approaching his ninth energetic decade—still contributes enthusiastically to Thacher's riding program.

Founded in 1889, The Thacher School has earned a national reputation that affords its 240 students access to, and active recruitment by, the best colleges and universities. A large part of Thacher's success stems from its unique horse program, in which every freshman is assigned a horse to ride and take care of for at least one year...and longer if they desire. This equestrian experience gives Thacher students an exceptional advantage, since they gain personal empowerment from the many valuable lessons inherent in working with horses—what I call *HorsePower!*

This concept of personally empowering life lessons learned from the horse was first introduced in LIVING WITH *HORSEPOWER!*, which explores such benefits as compassion, honesty, communication skills, awareness, deductive reasoning, self-confidence, and coping with loss—personal rewards of *HorsePower!* that enhance the body, mind, and soul, and improve our daily lives.

Once you become attuned to the many empowering benefits of *HorsePower!* and begin applying them to your life with intent, you can generate tremendous success. It is at this point of consciously incorporating lessons for individual improvement and success that you move from *living* with *HorsePower!* to *winning* with *HorsePower!*

Through stories and insights of more than seventy of the horse industry's most renowned members, WINNING WITH *HORSEPOWER!* explores the *proactive* lessons of *HorsePower!* that foster personal success: living into your future, overcoming fears, controlling anger, developing partnership, parenting, and sportsmanship skills, prioritizing time and money, and gaining the ability to transform life's toughest trials into individual triumphs. It also identifies the four cornerstones of *HorsePower!*: simplicity, balance, spiritual nourishment, and personal growth.

The benefits of living and winning with *HorsePower!* allow you to define and lead a more fulfilled, dynamic life by providing the strength, knowledge, and coping mechanisms needed to navigate the challenges of your chosen life's path. This is a powerful education to have.

While most schools acknowledge the value of education's traditional "Three-R's: reading, writing and 'rithmetic," schools with equestrian programs, such as Thacher, also recognize the human value of *HorsePower!* and offer their students an enhanced curriculum—the *four* R's: reading, writing, 'rithmetic, and *riding*. The traditional three R's strengthen the mind, while the fourth—riding—also strengthens the body and the spirit. As a result, Thacher students exhibit a self confidence, a respect for faculty, and a love of their school that is obvious even to a casual observer. It was enlivening just being among them because, with the assistance of their "equine faculty," Thacher fosters individuals who relish living—and winning—with *HorsePower!*

An education enhanced with *HorsePower!* would be an asset at any stage of life, but having the opportunity to gain that in your youth provides the distinct advantage of a stronger foundation for the future. Thankfully, *HorsePower!* is available to enrich your personal curriculum at any age—just get involved with horses and be open to the lessons of your very own "equine faculty." I say "be open to the lessons" because even though the rewards of *HorsePower!* flow naturally from equine experiences, *you need to be open to receiving them.* To maximize the benefits, you need to be aware of the educational potential and power available to you through your equine experience.

In light of that need, I composed the following affirmation for myself as a daily reminder to remain openly receptive to the many personal lessons of *HorsePower!*

Grant me the knowledge to keep them well,
Grant me the awareness to honor their unique nature,
Grant me the ability to hear their side of the conversation,
Grant me the insight to respond appropriately,

Grant me the skills to enjoy their company,
Grant me the courage to share their free spirit,
Grant me the love to celebrate their soul,
Grant me a sense of humor open to their fun—and folly,
Grant me a mind open to adjusting—and to being just,
Grant me a heart open to the lessons they have to teach...
Grant me a life with horses.

Obviously, the above could be referring to relationships other than with horses—friends, family, children—most any other being you care to interact with. Within that parallel lies the fundamental point of *HorsePower!* By incorporating the personal lessons of *HorsePower!,* you develop strengths, skills, processes, perceptions and attitudes that improve your ability to handle circumstances and relationships throughout life. The many rewards of *HorsePower!* infuse your life, as well as your being, with a centered wisdom and coping skills that promote more effective living. But first, *you* must become aware of the rich education available to you through horses, then remain open to learning from them.

Today there are hundreds of horse-training manuals on the market, but the *HorsePower!* books are the only horse-to-human training manuals available. LIVING WITH *HORSEPOWER!* not only introduces the concept of *HorsePower!,* it presents horse nature in terms that must be understood for a successful relationship: that horses are prey animals with acute sensitivities, visual perceptions, social structures, and mental processes that make them vitally reactive until they are desensitized to stimuli through experience, or training. As with any successful relationships, it is essential that you come to know your partners in light of their unique nature, inherent abilities and talents, and communication requirements.

WINNING WITH *HORSEPOWER!* demonstrates the unlimited success available once you realize the empowerment through horses, then consciously apply those personal lessons to your life. For within those individual lessons of *HorsePower!* lie keys to success for all the relationships and circumstances in your life.

So, I invite you to explore the equine relationship in this new light—that of being a student of the horse. Whenever you enter its classroom, be open to the many exciting, powerful, profound lessons of equine experience, and you will find yourself living with *HorsePower!*. Then, actively apply those lessons, benefits, and strengths to bolster your personal goals and you will discover the success of *winning* with *HorsePower!*. Through this process, the personal strengths and success inherent in *HorsePower!* help you establish a more solid foundation in life, and effect even greater *human* power.

JACK HUYLER, b. 1920, has been a mainstay at the Thacher School in Ojai, California, for more than fifty years, teaching English, coaching sports and imparting horsemanship. He was the 1969 California State All-Around Gymkhana Champion, and has served on the American Horse Show Association rules committee and as President of the National Horse and Pony Youth Activities Council. This shot captures Jack and his Quarter Horse stallion, El Paso Gap, making the end turn while breaking the California record in pole bending in 1969.

CHAPTER ONE

PICKING UP THE REINS

Live the Present and Design Your Future

It's called the present because it's a gift.

"Helen, honey, get off that pig!" Edna Kitner called as she ran to retrieve her errant toddler. "I swear, child, you will be the death of me...climbing on the back of anything with four legs!" she chided, plucking the three-year-old off the squealing animal. "You've about got the calf broke to saddle, and now you're trotting off to town on the back of Pop's sow!"

Helen Crabtree's (p.22) youth was filled with all kinds of riding on her family's Illinois farm, but it wasn't until she was nine, when her father bought a mare named Lady, that she began riding *horses*. Soon Helen's ability to "ride anything" earned her a job at the nearby fairground's weekly horse sales and she was hired to ride green-broke horses into the sales arena to show that they were "kid proof." Upon learning of this exploitative, unethical and potentially dangerous calling, Helen's mother quickly terminated her "sales career." Nonetheless, Helen spent almost every weekend at the fairgrounds, shadowing a local trainer and riding young horses. (Crabtree, 16–17)

During a local horse show, an owner asked Helen to show his five-gaited mare in the ladies' class. She agreed to ride for one dollar—two, if she managed to place in the ribbons. His only instruction was, "When the judge asks you to back up, pretend you don't hear him."

She may have been only twelve, but Helen knew enough to realize he was all but saying the mare would probably rear over backward rather than back up. And, being twelve, this also posed an intriguing challenge.... So, when the judge asked her to back the horse...it wasn't pretty, but she did it. The delighted owner took the ribbon and handed Helen three dollars. Noting his error, she returned the extra dollar, but he waved it off, saying "Little lady, you earned it—that's the first time this mare has ever backed up!" (Crabtree, 17)

With that payment, Helen began her career as a "professional" horse trainer. Now, that statement does not sound extraordinary, until you put it in perspective of the times—Helen was born in 1915. In that restrictive era of protected womanhood, it was not considered proper for a woman even to be in a stable unescorted, yet Helen picked up the reins to her life and set off on the uncharted career path she came to love—training gaited horses.

With all the professional and social challenges that unorthodox path presented, Helen learned to create her own good fortune in life—becoming not only the first, but the most successful female saddle horse trainer in the world! By quiet and consistent excellence in the show ring, Helen has won the highest regard and the most prestigious awards the horse industry has to offer. When asked how she was able to scale the heights of that male-dominated world, Helen replies simply, "I kept my mouth shut and I beat the hell out of them."

Like this book, Helen's story is about winning—not just winning in the show ring, but in life—for Helen's professional eminence was not her first, or necessarily most important victory against the odds. As a junior at Illinois College, Helen contracted scarlet fever and was forced to drop out of school to fight the disease that was taking a perilous toll on her heart. The family doctor told her mother, "I think we can save her, but she may be an armchair invalid." Overhearing the doctor's dire prognosis, Helen vowed, "I can't settle for that...I will *not* settle for that!"

And she didn't settle for it. Just nineteen months after falling so desperately ill, Helen returned to college—whole and healthy. Helen attributes her full recovery to the focus, persistence, and physical conditioning that she'd gained through years of riding. "It all came from my riding," she claims. "It just never entered my mind that I wouldn't get well—I wouldn't permit it. That strength and resolve came from riding."

Five years out of college, Helen found a man with as deep a commitment to the saddle horse as hers—Charles Crabtree. They married, and have been a team sharing their mutual love, respect, and knowledge of horses for more than fifty years now. Between them, they have trained and shown more champion saddle horses and saddle seat riders than anyone else.

While working in Little Rock, Arkansas, Helen's elegant horses attracted eager visitors from a neighboring children's home to her training barn. Among them was a youngster with wonderful maroon hair and brown-flecked eyes, named "Redd." As soon as Helen saw him, she was in love. Realizing that life with the Crabtrees offered precious opportunities, the home's director recommended they adopt Redd. He moved in just five days before his eleventh birthday.

Redd grew to be more than a son to Helen and Charlie; he became a valuable partner in their business, then shaped a remarkable training career on his own and now carries on the Crabtree family tradition. If it had not been for his childhood interest in their horses, they might not have met. Their son is one more benefit Helen and Charlie have gained from a life with horses.

Helen's winning career began with coaching undefeated riding teams four years running at MacMurray College. Between 1958 and 1981 she produced 22 national equitation champions and from 1979 to 1981 trained over 75 saddle horses and ponies to world championships. For nine years she served as Chairman of the American Horse Shows Equitation Committee and was inducted into the Saddle Horse Hall of Fame. The awards she has received include the United Professional Horsemen's Association's Trainer of the Year and Instructor's Awards; Horsewoman of the Year and Lifetime Achievement Award from the American Horse Shows Association; and the coveted Jimmy Williams Trophy. Helen notes gratefully, "I've received every honor that's given in this business—yet I didn't set out to get any of them; they're just the by-product of a love affair with the horse."

For decades Helen wrote a monthly column for SADDLE & BRIDLE magazine, then authored the SPORTS ILLUSTRATED BOOK OF GAITED RIDING. In the late sixties, she wrote SADDLE SEAT EQUITATION—it's among the longest-running instructional books ever published by Doubleday and is still considered the "bible" of saddle seat equitation.

"At the Midway College American Saddle Horse Association clinic a few years ago, I was told a wonderful story," reports Helen. "One of the riding instructors stopped me saying, 'I've just got to tell you this.' She said that her seven-year-old daughter was in Sunday school when the teacher asked, 'Who wrote the Bible?' Not knowing the answer, the class remained uncomfortably silent until this riding instructor's youngster held up her hand and said, 'I think it was Helen K. Crabtree.'

"Isn't that charming?" Helen asks, smiling with delight. I sat on that story for a year afraid people would think, 'Oh, get Helen—now she thinks she's God!'"

In her quest for success Helen takes little for granted and is constantly looking to improve her craft. Turning her attention to riding equipment, she instituted the first major change in saddle construction in over seventy-five years. Helen's adjustable stirrup bar allows riders of differing builds to change the stirrup position to accommodate their personal balance points. The Crabtree Saddle also uses a softer bridle leather, allowing for increased contact with the horse—simple, logical, effective, yet revolutionary improvements.

Now, in her later years, Helen is once again facing medical challenges. She's lost one eye to cancer, and sight in the other is fading. When told she needed an artificial eye due to the cancer surgery, she chuckled, remembering Warlock, the remarkable Saddlebred that was a champion despite having lost an eye in a barn accident. "I know where to get one, and I already know how to put them in, because I tended Warlock's artificial eye for four years." It's amazing how horses prepare you for life!

Lately, Helen's personal trials have been piling up: "Recently we've been tested," she sighs. "I almost lost Charlie in an accident when he fell at home and crushed four ribs; then he had three crises in the hospital. Five days after getting out of the hospital, we were in a head-on collision that totaled our El Dorado. If we hadn't had our seat belts on we would be dead! And now my encroaching blindness has gotten so rapid in the last six weeks...well, we've had a time!

"One day, I almost gave in to it. I've been such an optimist all my life...but I'd almost given up. I was sitting on the side of the bed, my legs jerking around with this restless leg syndrome, taking pills that were not helping—I was just a mess. I sat thinking, 'Why me?' when all of a sudden I thought, 'Why not me?' Why did I expect special favors? It's up to me to get out of this mess, not to rail against fate.

"I realized the road goes both ways—the Lord's piling it on a little bit, but I'm so lucky that I have such a wonderful interest as the horses that keeps me going."

When Midway College recently decided to add a saddle horse program to their existing hunter/jumper and western horse programs—including a new forty-stall barn—they called on Helen to create the project.

"To think that at this age I can still be filled with excitement. So many women, when they get fifty-five or sixty years old, sit down and retire—men do too. But I'm so lucky to have this passion—and that's the right word for it—it transcends compulsion; it is a passion that serves us so well. What a blessing it is for all of your life. Here life's beginning at eighty all over again and it's just wonderful. Isn't it a full life?"

Helen's love affair with horses has brought a great deal to her life: riding gave her the physical strength and determination to fight and win the battle against scarlet fever, heart disease and cancer; horses provided a revolutionary career path for herself and her sex. Horses attracted her husband and her son to a lifetime's working partnership; they are the vehicle by which she became a celebrated trainer, instructor and author of "biblical proportion"; they taught her to cope with an artificial eye; brought her lasting friendships and exciting travel; and earned her the most prestigious awards of her profession. All these gifts from the horse were not simply given outright—Helen's abilities, hard work and genius made them merited prizes of mastery. By actively applying the inherent benefits, lessons and gifts she received from horses, Helen dared to follow her unorthodox dream, live into an improbable future, create an incredible family, and a dynamic life of accomplishment. She confidently picked up the reins of her life, struck out on her own path, and showed the world what winning with *HorsePower!* is all about.

Proactive Dreaming

Riding is a natural metaphor for one's journey through life. You can get on a horse and just hang on—letting the animal carry you where it wants to go at its own speed—or, you can pick up the reins and direct the journey, arriving at your desired destination by taking control.

Some people go through life unconscious—just not with it, notes international jumping champion and Olympic Silver medalist, Anne Kursinski (p.23). *But to me, riding and life are almost totally about awareness. With riding, you have to be conscious: constantly having to read your horse, yourself, and the environment to be tuned in to what's happening for safety's sake and for the sake of good riding. First this general awareness has to happen, then you can see what needs to change and what's going well. That's life—being in the present—aware of what's going on, coupled with an honest awareness of who you are and what it is that you're after.*

Until recently I was one of those living unconsciously—I'd wake up every morning ready to cope with what life had in store for me, but I didn't really understand that I could design my future. I was living *reactively* not *proactively.* I had never invested in a dream of what my life could be. This may sound incredibly naive, but I didn't truly understand the power of dreaming until I was forty-four and read THAT WINNING FEELING! by dressage champion and 1992 Olympic alternate, Jane Savoie (p.22).

When I read Jane's book in hopes of improving my riding, I learned that dreams are an inspiring catalyst for proactive living. Add passion and persistence to dreaming, and you've got a powerful recipe for success.

That is the beginning: you have to dream, says Jane Savoie. *Some people think, "Okay, I'm a dreamer," and think it's enough to just dream. It isn't. You start with a dream, but you have to back it up with hard work.*

Kids are great dreamers: "I'm going to be President of the United States." Then, as they grow up, friends, parents, boyfriends or girlfriends—whomever—start telling them they can't do it, and they start to doubt. Then they may experience a failure or two and get caught up in the distractions of daily life…little by little the dreams get smaller and smaller until they're gone. But the thing is, it doesn't take much to get the whole process going again. But it all starts with a dream….

Through psychocybernetics, Jane showed me how to use dreaming and visualization to live proactively toward my future goals: *You have to conceive it, and believe it before you can achieve it.*

Innovative trainer and clinician Linda Tellington-Jones (p.24) has also discovered the strength of proactive dreaming: *I've learned that the ability to create our own potential goes beyond daydreaming—you need awareness, clarity and intent. In 1976, Gwen Stockbrand was on the U.S. Dressage Team that went to Goodwood in England. I had Gwen sit in her stall and go over the whole course with her horse as though the horse could see the course with her. She did that, and became the first American in many years to win the Bronze Medal. I've had so many successes in this way.*

As powerful as psycho-cybernetics and proactive living may be, it is obvious that no mortal truly "controls" life. As cowboy artist and philosopher L.D. Burke (p.26) jokes, *Know how to make God laugh?…Tell Him your plans.*

Many would scoff at a young artist's intention to concentrate on a career of drawing horses, but Bev Doolittle's (p.25) international success was based on a career of that simple dream. *The horse captured me and started me on the path to my art. I just had that narrow, focused path, "I want to be an artist, and I want to paint horses." You just have to do what you feel is important and hang onto your integrity. Do what you really love, and do it for yourself; do it because you really enjoy it, and that work comes from you and nobody else. This applies to any job—it doesn't matter whether you're an artist or a bricklayer—if you enjoy doing it, you should be doing it. If you do it because you love it, you're going to do it well, and you're going to do it better than someone else because you like doing it; you'll get better at it, and pretty soon a door that you hadn't thought of opens.*

Almost any dream, when lived with intent, integrity, determination, drive, and ability, transforms into a wonderfully fulfilling reality for the dream weaver.

Real Time

When I started riding lessons, I discovered the importance of living in "real time." Real time—the present—is the only actual time we have. We may remember the past and anticipate the future, but we exist only in the present. Horses, like all animals, are very present beings—the moment of import with them is what's happening *now*.

Horses constantly encourage me to savor life at the very moment I'm living it with them, says hunter/jumper trainer Macella O'Neill (p.26). *I always try to return them that magnificent compliment of paying attention, give them the best of me that there is and be as they are: generous, patient, kind, and obliging.*

Horses have good memories, so they do remember events in the past; however, their concept of future is anyone's guess since the future exists only in imagination. Humans waste a great deal of time and energy decrying their past and wishing for a better future. Since we cannot change the past, and the only way to affect the future is through the way we live in real time, it's obvious how vital living in the moment actually is—it's the only time in which living takes place.

Often when I'm working in the ring, my instructor will call out, "Ride every stride!" That little mantra puts me in step with my horse and prompts me to stay present with her. Ride every stride—not *control* every stride—but ride it well: be aware, feel the rhythm, the action, then adjust to it or correct it. With that, a ride suddenly becomes an exciting dance.

Loving the Moment

We've all had the feeling of wanting to freeze time when we're involved in an activity that we truly enjoy. "Time flies when you're having fun" is all too true. Yet, when doing something that doesn't spark our interest, time drags along like an anemic snail. It is this phenomenon that is often misconstrued as patience: *I am always told that I'm incredibly patient*, muses trainer and author Diana Cooper (p.27). *When I'm training, owners often comment that I have the patience to work with their horses and they don't. But I know I'm not a patient person. I started asking other trainers, "Are you a patient person?" I have never heard anybody say they were patient.*

Here's what I think happens: when you're really enjoying what you're doing, you're able to go into a place where time "stops." Forward time, linear time seems suspended, and you go "sideways" because you're in- credibly, intently focused in that moment. So it's not what most of us think of as being patient, where people are calm and graciously tolerant....When you're really working well with an animal, there's this extraordinary op- posite to that kind of feeling. There's an intensity and aliveness in that moment. And it's in that moment—when time stops—that you sense be- ing alive.

I know a woman who's a quilter and does these incredibly tiny stitches...I said, "Gee, you must be really patient." She said, "I'm not!" She just realizes there are no shortcuts in the art of making a good quilt.

You have to love *what you're doing so much that you're not think- ing of it as "Oh God, I've got to spend two hours making $^{1}/_{16}$th-of- an-inch stitches...." You're so focused on the beauty of those tiny stitches that you just keep on making them.*

People who are not interested enough to invest in an activity look for short cuts to the end result. They want the horse trained *now* or want the quilt on the bed *tonight*. They don't want to have to teach all those tedious training steps, or make all those tiny, even stitches. They're seeking a quick fix where there are no quick fixes. Hence, a trainer or quilter is considered "patient" simply because they value the activity enough to dedicate themselves to the com- plete process.

As Diana Cooper explains, *I asked the Big Apple Circus horse trainer, Katja Schumann, what was the most important thing she'd learned from horses. She replied simply, "Festina lente," which means, "Make haste slowly." That's a very complicated concept. That's what I was trying to describe as that moment when you're in the absolutely endless, expansive present—time is not going forward or backward— it's going sideways, and you learn to trust that and stay in that. That happens when you are fully involved in what you're doing: training a horse, or writing a book, or making a quilt. It's crucial to doing any-thing worthwhile.*

Mankind used to make haste slowly, for horses set the speed of travel for millennia—until combustion engines blew us through the sound barrier. With technologies of the modern age, we rou-tinely cruise along at 65 miles an hour just running errands.

A return to the pace of hoof beats offers a welcome respite from the supersonic speed and frenetic complexities of contem-porary life: *The one thing I really, really enjoy and appreciate as much as anything about dealing with horses is the moment,* relates rodeo Hall-of-Famer Larry Mahan (p.28). *So few things, in this day and age, do we really do for the moment—that instant where we have to totally concentrate on what we're doing. I've always lived on a pretty fast track and expected things to happen right now. I can gear up when things go fast, and I really have to get out there and cover a lot of terri-tory in a short period of time. But I don't want to lose perspective of the idea that the moment is the key. That helps me to get the most enjoyment out of the things I do.*

Living the Moment

The more present we are, the more aware we can be in real time, the more sensitive and responsive we become in life: *When you're riding, you get to focus on physical rather than mental problems,* notes therapeutic riding instructor Octavia Brown (p.27). *When you're on a horse, you can fantasize all you'd like, but if the horse bolts, you've got to be ready. So it teaches you to separate reality from fiction, to be present, and keep one foot in the now and what really is.*

Being present to an activity can also trigger physical response and enliven our state of being: *I ride with friends every week, and I still get a little surge of adrenaline,* says L.D. Burke. *I'm into adrenaline—it's a great feeling—a wonderful, warm, alive feeling. Adrenaline snaps me directly into the present. Horses are in the present; all animals are. For me that's the singular greatest reward of riding, the totally here and now. Like a lot of people, I have a tendency to think about what's going to happen next, or what happened yesterday, but riding horses makes me totally present. It's been said that the devil's playground is the past and the future, so if I can stay in the present— hey, no problem!*

Relinquish the Past

One of the cardinal rules in jumping a horse is, "Don't look back." When riding a course, you may come off a jump with rails crashing behind you—don't look back at the commotion—continue on with the job at hand. Looking back is detrimental; it throws you off balance, breaks concentration, creates doubts, anxiety, or anger, and steals time from preparation for the next fast-approaching obstacle. Once over a jump, it is far better to stay on course physically, mentally, and emotionally. After completing the course, there may be benefit in analyzing what caused the rails to fall, in hopes of gaining insight to improve future performance; but when in action, stay present. As past actions are unalterable, staying present offers the only opportunity to improve results. The only benefit gained from revisiting the past is a lesson learned, not a history lamented.

Step Into Your Future

As the strength of recalling the past is lessons learned, the benefit of contemplating the future is to find direction. The future exists only in imagination, which holds a mighty force for positives, or negatives. Contemplating the future through wistful hope or unfounded worries sows fear and intimidation, while contemplating the future through dedication to a dream reaps possibilities and direction.

I heard that 2% of athletes write down their goals, 48% know what their goals are in their head, and 50% don't have goals, notes endurance rider and sports psychologist Doug Lietzke (p.28). *It's very hard to get satisfaction and to do well when you don't know where you're going. There are lots of people who are comfortable not dreaming, and with tomorrow being the same as today; that's fine. But there are also a lot of people who like to dream, who desire growth, who want the excitement of their fantasy future, but don't realize that it's within their grasp to achieve.*

When I counsel clients, I ask, "What do you want to do? What are your goals?" Then I ask them to put it down in writing. As they write, they discover what their long- and short-term goals are and define necessary daily activities. That simple act of writing it down forces them to clarify in their own mind what they want to do. So I tell them, "If you think it, ink it."

Individuals who are fortunate enough to be living their future fantasy often become the envy of those who have no direction in life: *I've heard plenty of people say, "Well, dang, look at you. You get to ride and travel all over and meet all kinds of fun people and do all kinds of fun stuff with your clinics,"* declares trainer and clinician Buck Brannaman (p.29). *They almost make it sound like it fell out of the sky and landed in my lap. One thing I can say is, I did it myself. A lot of folks cop out and say, "Well, I didn't get the breaks. I didn't grow up with the opportunities." Well, neither did I. You make your own luck. I believe you can create whatever you want to create—it's just easier to create a failure.*

Another who didn't have it fall from the sky for her is microfilm technician Tracy Cole (p.29). Being born with cerebral palsy would defeat many, but Tracy has never let it even slow her down. When her future posed the threat of having to give up riding, she took action and opened up a whole new world for herself: *It's a forty-five minute trip each way to the barn, every week for thirty-some weeks a year. After fourteen years, I could see my mom was getting tired of driving me. I wasn't comfortable with the idea of driving—not because of the physical difficulty—it was more my nerves questioning whether I wanted to be on the road with maniacs doing seventy-five in a fifty-five zone.*

The better I got at riding, the more self-confidence I got, and the more willing I became to try new things. It was like, "Wow, I can really do this! Now let's give this a try, and give that a shot." Since I've learned to drive, I've become more independent. But if it hadn't been for my riding, I would never have learned to drive. And if I hadn't learned to drive, I wouldn't feel independent, and if I didn't feel independent, I wouldn't be doing things on my own. Now I'm taking vacations on my own—I even went to Hawaii!

A future without riding was inconceivable to Tracy, so she faced her fear of driving and reaped the rewards: increased independence, greater confidence, and a fuller life.

You are the only person who can live your life and make your own choices, states Olympic Gold Medalist, William Steinkraus (p. 30). *The ultimate goal of all this riding training is a very high degree of self-reliance. You can't expect your coach to ride the round for you; you're the only one on the back of the horse. At some point, you have to decide where gurus or technical analysts fit and use them in the way that's best for you. But if you never cast away the pilot, you will never achieve the highest level of success.*

Skills for Success

Dealing with horses has taught me the value of living in the moment because that's the only real time we have. The past exists only in memory; the future exists only in imagination; life exists only in the present—it's vital to *be there!* When you live consciously and fully in the moment, you can focus on doing your best without being distracted by doubts of the future or regrets of the past. By being purposefully present, we gain the greatest awareness and control over our own fate.

In order to live your own life, you must first dream your own dream, plan your own course, then ride your own ride. To live a life of passionate purpose and personal success, such as Helen Crabtree's, is rare and tremendously rewarding. First, you must identify what your dream is, then develop the talent and heart to pursue it, and the confidence to accept the risks.

Before becoming aware of real time and the power of dreaming, I just let life happen, then I'd react to circumstances—not realizing I had much say in it. Now I'm *proactive*—creating my future by living into my dream every day. No longer a spectator watching my life go by, I'm deliberately inventing my future by living it moment by moment in the present—a much more dynamic and exhilarating way to live.

Taking charge of your life is both inspiring and intimidating, for when you pick up the reins, intent on directing the action, it is apparent to all that the choices are yours alone. Many people would rather remain a passenger; then if they crash, the blame will fall on something other than their actions. That is a choice as well. So, whether you're consciously directing your life with intent, or just going along for the ride, you are still ultimately responsible for your choices.

Since you control the reins to your life's plan, why not start riding into the future of your dreams today by envisioning your future, learning from the past, living in the moment and succeeding with *HorsePower!*

HELEN CRABTREE, b. 1915, has most of the equestrian world's prestigious awards to her credit. The first female saddle horse trainer, Helen trained hundreds of world champion horses and riders over the course of her exceptional career and wrote the definitive work on saddle seat equitation. Now retired, she continues actively contributing to the horse world through writing and consulting in Kentucky. This 1978 photo pictures Helen on the elegant saddle horse, Barbados Exit.

JANE SAVOIE, b. 1949, is a trainer, writer and motivational speaker who has created her own success of Olympic proportions. Through dreams and determination, Jane became reserve rider to the United States Dressage Team for the 1992 Olympics in Barcelona, Spain and dressage coach for the Canadian Olympic Eventing Team at the 1996 Olympics in Atlanta. She is pictured on Zapatero in Orlando, Florida, after they won final selection to the 1992 Olympic team.

ANNE KURSINSKI, b. 1959, has competed in more than thirty USET Nations' Cup teams, nine World Cup Finals and four Olympics—returning home with Silver Medals in 1988 and 1996. Her stellar record also includes Gold team and individual medals from the 1983 Pan American Games, plus prestigious awards: 1988 AHSA Horsewoman of the Year, 1991 U.S. Olympic Committee Female Equestrian of the Year, 1996 USET Whitney Stone Cup and more. Anne is pictured on Cannonball as they clear an Olympic oxer on their way to the Team Silver at Barcelona, Spain, in 1992.

LINDA TELLINGTON-JONES, b.1937, is an innovative trainer and master teacher who achieved international acclaim for creating TEAM Training (Tellington-Jones Equine Awareness Method) and The Tellington TTouch techniques: holistic methods for training, healing and interacting with animals. A record-setting equestrian in many disciplines, Linda has worked with a variety of international Olympic teams, basing her success on aiding both horse and rider to maximize their potential. In addition to her clinics, many articles, books and videos chronicle her techniques. Linda and Honey enjoy a bridleless trail ride in 1994.

BEV DOOLITTLE, b. 1947, is an internationally renowned watercolorist famous for her unique camouflage technique, in which multiple images are ingeniously woven into the fabric of the main composition. Bev seems to capture the individual spirit of each horse she depicts. The varied markings of Pintos offer a myriad of possible interpretations for her camouflage art. Bev is shown in a beautiful desert meadow surrounded by a number of splashy "paints."

L.D. "DOC" BURKE III, b. 1934, may have been born a New England Yankee, but his soul is that of a cowboy philosopher. L.D. moved west and bought a ranch on which he ran cows and horses for a number of years, then began his successful career designing cowboy furniture and apparel. Perhaps a bit of his New England heritage is showing through in this 1994 shot taken with Saltamontes (Grasshopper), his borrowed sure-footed hunter, after a challenging hunt for red stag across rugged terrain in Argentina. L.D. proclaims riding to the hounds is "the absolute grandest high!"

MACELLA O'NEILL, b. 1963, shows a winning style aboard Luminous as they capture the 1996 Gambler's Choice in Reno, Nevada. Macella began her riding career on Sultan, the donkey her parents gave her for her third brithday. Years in the saddle ensued and after graduating from the University of California at San Diego, she and partner Charlie White founded Diamond Mt. Stables, a successful hunter/jumper training stable, in 1983. In 1997 she was the leading Northern California Jumper rider.

DIANA COOPER, b. 1946, is a trainer and writer who has authored a book on circus life. She is pictured with her Welsh Corgi, Gaddis at home in Connecticut.

OCTAVIA BROWN, b. 1942, is Assistant Professor of Equine Studies at Centenary College, a master therapeutic riding instructor and breeder of sport horses. She was a founding board member of the North American Riding for the Handicapped Association in 1969, began the first NARHA program in New Jersey, was New Jersey Horseperson of the Year in 1981, and has recently published two books on therapeutic riding. Octavia is pictured with a young Somerset Hills Handicapped Riders, Inc. client taking part in a field trip for preschoolers with disabilities in the 1980's.

LARRY MAHAN, b. 1944, is a world champion bronc and bull rider, rodeo stockman, Western clothing retailer, host of HORSE WORLD television program and Rodeo Hall of Famer. Larry is seen giving Australian fans an exciting show of his winning style in Sydney, 1978.

DOUG LIETZKE, b. 1944, psychologist, is a National Top Ten Competitive Rider specializing in equestrian sports psychology through his many articles, tapes and seminars. He is a winner of the Solo Divisions (riding one hundred miles in one day without any support crew) for the Old Dominion and Race of Champions endurance rides. Doug is shown with his Arabian mare, TDA Lannerette, as they win the Bucks County 25 mile Competitive Trail Ride.

BUCK BRANNAMAN, b. 1961, is a cowboy whose colorful career has included being a child roping star, which won him rodeo credits as well as a stint with his brother as the rope-twirling "Sugar Pops kids" in the sixties. Since then Buck has turned his talents to horses, where his abilities at starting colts and training horses developed into a very successful clinic practice and led to his becoming the technical advisor for Robert Redford's production of THE HORSE WHISPERER. Buck is shown on his horse Rambo (who was Redford's movie mount, "Rimrock") lending a hand at branding time on his foster parents' Montana ranch.

TRACY COLE, b. 1965, is a principal microfilm machine operator who began riding with the Somerset Hills Handicapped Riders Club in 1972 as therapy to combat the effects of cerebral palsy. She competed in a national horse show for disabled riders in 1989 and in the Victory Games in 1991. A victorious Tracy is pictured with her blue ribbon partner, Freckles, after they took first place honors in their equitation class for the first time in five years.

WILLIAM STEINKRAUS, b. 1925, editor and legendary equestrian, is a
six-time Olympian who shared a team bronze in 1952, team silver
medals in 1960 and 1972, and in 1968 on Snowbound, Bill became the
first American to win an individual gold medal in equestrian sports.
He has served as U.S. Equestrian Team President, Chairman and
Chairman Emeritus, been a Director of AHSA, and received both its
Horseman of the Year and Lifetime Achievement Award. He has served
as international judge and also as television commentator for the
Olympics and World Championships, been elected to the Madison Sq.
Garden, National Horse Show, N.Y. Sports and Show Jumping Halls of
Fame, has served in many executive positions for the Fédération
Equestre Internationale, and is President of its World Cup Committee.
He has authored several equestrian books, is married to a noted
dressage judge, has three sons, is a scratch golfer, plays concert level
violin, and still enjoys riding. Bill clears a brush jump aboard the
Princess de la Tour d'Auvergne's Snowbound at Hickstead, England in
1967, a year before this pair won the Olympic Gold Medal at the 1968
Mexico City Games.

CHAPTER TWO

NIGHTMARES

Overcoming Fear and Expectations

You can't ride with fear and reach the top. —Valerie Kanavy

"Daddy! DADDY! *DAD -DYYYY!*" Screams shattered the stillness and yanked a father from the depths of midnight slumber. He ran down the dark hall to his five-year-old's bedroom envisioning a fire, a burglar, a fall....As he reached the open door, the family cat shot out of the room; the boy was sitting bolt upright, wide-eyed, rigid with fright. Salty tears washed his small face as his father's arms encircled him and hugged him securely. The boy sobbed into his father's chest, telling him all about the fearsome monsters that had been threatening just moments before.

Hearing what had caused the alarm, the father immediately relaxed, then grabbed his son by the shoulders and shook him.

"Don't you EVER do that again! You scared me to death! There are no monsters in this room. It was just the cat."

He pushed the petrified child down on the bed, gave him a spank, tucked the bed clothes in tight and snarled, "Now, no more nonsense! Quit crying and go to sleep. You're acting like a wimp, and no son of mine's gonna be a coward!" He stormed out, leaving his son sobbing, confused, and more terrified in the dark.

Winning with *HorsePower!*

Many would describe this father as callous or even abusive, yet compare his actions to those of the person in the following scene: The autumn sky was brilliantly clear with only a few cotton clouds scudding across its expanse. A horse and rider walked lazily along a trail, listening to the whisper of trees, as dying leaves shook loose in the soft breeze. Suddenly the gelding snorted fearfully and lurched sideways, throwing the startled rider to one side. The rider grabbed mane, and with one foot still in the stirrup, managed to pull back into the saddle, sit up, and regain control of the shaking animal. "Easy boy, easy...what was that about?" The rider looked back along the path and caught sight of a doe disappearing into the brush. "A deer? You almost dump me because of a *doe*?!! You idiot!" He raised his crop and flailed at the still frightened horse, while clamping spurred heels into its flanks until the animal was white-eyed with panic and confusion. "You're bigger than any deer in the country, you idiot!" Whack! "I'll teach you to jump from a harmless doe! You stupid wimp!" Whap! Whack!

The first scenario elicits a feeling of shock at a parent's insensitivity, while the second demonstrates a common horse-training method. In both instances, however, an innocent being is genuinely scared, yet the guardian's concern turns to scorn and anger when he identifies the source of the fear and judges it to be irrational.

Yet, fear is often irrational. Anger and punishment aren't effective in allaying fear, for they compound anxieties by adding the fear of reprisal to the original fright. A parent, rider, partner, or guardian must alleviate fears through compassionate trust and empathetic education.

Part of the attraction of horses is their childlike qualities: large, inquisitive eyes; a busy nose that pokes and pleads for a sweet treat; the chuckling hello of a buddy eager for adventure. Along with these many endearing qualities come equine fears of the monsters of the horse world.

"Monsters" come in all sizes and shapes—real and imagined—seen and unseen, from the real threat of a bear to the innocuous fluttering of a newspaper. Fear engendered by "horse monsters" is always justified in the mind of a horse who operates from the equine "better safe than sorry" wariness of self-preservation. When associating with horses, people are forced to deal with fear—their own as well as their horses'.

Comfort Zones

Normally we go about our lives in relatively safe and secure comfort zones, where a certain level of comprehension and competency assures us we can cope; things are under control. As consoling as comfort zones are, they are also confining—limiting personal growth, challenge, learning, and maturity: *People are often reluctant to go beyond their comfort zone,* observes Jane Savoie. *That's why they'll stay in a job they hate. They're afraid to go out, pound the pavement and face the unknown. I've found it's exciting to stretch beyond my comfort zones—like writing my book, then doing the videos, and now public lectures. Sometimes I think I must be nuts, but that's all been part of my growth, and it is exciting. Sure, there's something to be said for living in comfort zones—you're safe and secure—but you don't get to live your life with passion, and that's boring. A life lived in fear is half-lived; I would not want my epitaph to read: "Dead at thirty, buried at seventy." If you don't dream and just stay within your comfort zone, you might as well be dead.*

Some people never actually break out of the comfort zone surrounding a specific fear, but instead work from within to expand its boundaries: *I had a student that as soon as his horse went beyond a walk, he'd tighten up and stop breathing,* reports polo coach Rege Ludwig (p. 58). *Through extreme diligence on his part and mine, he now runs up and down a polo field on his horse, very fast. He can run almost wide open before he starts locking up now, where four years ago a trot made him panic. He still has a fear of speed, and that dimin-*

ishes what he can put out as far as being a good polo player goes. He has taken his "speed comfort zone" and expanded it tremendously.

In other situations, the walls of a comfort zone are torn down as a result of the individual's desire to grow, to learn, or to participate: *There's a young girl here, Karen, whose grandfather had a breeding farm,* relates Helen Crabtree. *When Karen was three years old, she was in the pasture with a bunch of yearlings. On her way back to the barn, the colts started to chase her. She ran, fell down, and they all leaped over her, so she had a tremendous fear of horses. After her sister started taking riding lessons, Karen finally got up the nerve to come and watch. I have a teaching booth in the corner of the arena, so I brought Karen in there to sit with me, and she got comfortable with that.*

One day her mother phoned and said, "Karen wants to ride." I asked, "Is she begging?" She said, "No, but she thinks she'd like to ride." I said, "Let's wait until she begs and really, really wants to." When Karen was finally begging to ride, we started her lessons because by then it was a privilege for Karen to ride, and she would be learning through desire rather than fear. Waiting until Karen was begging to break out of her comfort zone changed her motivation from fearful dread of the horse to eager anticipation of lessons that she had come to view as a privilege earned.

Comfort zones can be valuable cocoons of learning, since the security they provide allows us to focus attention on the lesson at hand without fear. At our barn, some people ride only in the arena because that's their protected comfort zone. Other riders start in the arena, then go out on the trail. After enjoying the trail, they may decide to start showing. When showing proves to be fun, they move on to jumping. Jumping's a thrill that leads them to compete in point-to-points, fox hunt, or event. Through this process, using each comfort zone as a stepping stone to the next challenge, their world of experience continually expands. The very act of growing beyond an established comfort zone is rewarding, strengthening, and liberating.

Fear sets the limits of a comfort zone. Each new activity or perilous situation that yanks us out of a comfort zone creates a certain level of fright: from vague concern to physical fear indicators such as sweaty palms, racing heart and constricted breathing, to all-out panic and hysteria. Fears grow out of instinct, experience, or imagination and can be as real as dirt or as illusory as a nightmare. Fears are found in the physical, mental, emotional, and spiritual realms and differ greatly from one person to another— one individual's worst fear may actually be another's idea of fun: bronc-riding and hang-gliding are examples of this.

When our fear alerts us to potential danger, we must choose— through instinct or rational analysis of the situation—to pay heed or cast it off. Hence, we are able to control almost all fear short of blind panic. I have a personal horror of heights, yet I've gone parachuting and bungy jumping. In both instances, as I stepped to the edge of the wind-whipped platforms, all my physical and mental systems were screaming "Danger! Go back! Red alert!" My heart was pounding, my breath almost nonexistent, and my circulation had pretty well shut down. Normally, I would have retreated from the ledge and attached myself to anything of substance. However, since I had faith in the training, equipment, and safety records of the companies I was dealing with and had made the conscious decision to jump, my mind overcame my fear mechanism. That mental override allowed me to leap into space, yell "Geronimo!" and enjoy the ensuing rush.

Vital Alarm System

We must be prudent, however, when overriding a fear response, since fear is a vital, genetically wired warning system whose core function is our protection and preservation.

There's always going to be a little fear when you're learning something new: a first time to canter, a first time to take a jump, or a first time out on a trail, notes holistic equine therapist and journalist

Diana Thompson (p.60). *But if you feel strong fear—or terror—your body's warning you: danger ahead! A young horse was having trouble adjusting to being on the trail and his rider said to me, "I'm very frightened!" She wasn't just being chicken; her horse had thrown her two months before. Now he was on the muscle: he was prancing, his breathing was fast, his flight reflex was right at the top of his throat. Anything could set him off, and she knew it. So we stopped, and I said, "Here's a nice field; take him in a big circle, and see if you can get him to walk instead of jigging. We can do circles until you feel okay, or we can get off and walk." She chose to circle, and they both calmed down after a while. I don't ever, ever override my student's fear. When people tell me that they are afraid, I respect that; then I see how we can build their confidence up. Everything has its time. I would rather go forward in tiny steps than force dangerous fear situations. Fear needs to be understood in order to feel safe.*

When horses are panicked, they are a thousand pounds of instinct totally out of control, and you don't have a lot to say about it, Diana Thompson continues. *On a horse like that, your life is in danger no matter how much skill you have. The horse that hurt me the most spooked and bolted. I thought, "No big deal, he's bolting and bucking, but I'm up there feeling pretty secure in the saddle." All of a sudden I realize his eyes are closed! He's in a blind panic and going right for the end of the arena—a straight wall of metal. I have his head, but I can't turn him, and he's not looking where he's going! Luckily, I turned his head loose, and he opened his eyes at the last minute and shied away. We made it through that turn. Then he headed for a big fence to jump, but at the last minute ducked out and threw me into the fence. I was in bed for two weeks with a concussion.*

I learned from that what a horse will do in a panic. Now I do not get on fearful horses until their bodies are calm and they can think. I don't try and ride through panic. That's where people really get hurt or where tremendous fear gets created. I may sound like a chicken, but other than that one incident, I have never, ever been hurt by a horse in my entire career—and I've taken on some pretty tough horses. When I see an old trainer bent over and limping, I'm not excited about that. Not at all.

Patronizing a frightened individual by belittling or denying his fear tells him he's wrong for tuning in to himself, his horse, and his situation, and invalidates his vital sensory system. It's important to respect fear indicators, identify specific concerns, then work through the fear at a manageable pace.

Arbitrarily overriding fear indicators can lead to a disturbing and dangerous condition of total denial. Denying fear results not in bravery, but in vulnerability, by willfully disarming the entire warning system: *As a child, I had been taught not to display fear, so I didn't know what fear was and didn't recognize it as an emotion,* says L.D. Burke. *I'm sure I had it, but I didn't recognize it as fear and just walked right on through. That's not to say I was brave; it's more to say I was ignorant…or numb.*

In today's power-based society, many people condemn any and all fear, disregarding its vital function as a defensive alert. Fear may be a four-letter word, but there's no shame in it unless it turns to mindless cowardice. Fear is a critical indicator we must read and deal with—not deny or ignore—for it enables us to take care of ourselves. As Buck Brannaman explains: *There are times when I'll get someone in a clinic that I tell flat out, "My first goal is to get you afraid because you don't even have sense enough to be afraid, and you should be!" When I see that it's necessary for their longevity, that's exactly what I'll do. Then, once they're afraid, I'll help them from a basis of reality. But it's got to be a real thing rather than some pipe dream that they've had.* You cannot learn about fear, or any subject, by denying its existence.

Seasoned horsemen recognize and value the level of respect that fear instills and helps to keep us out of harm's way: *I have a definite fear of horses,* states popular trainer and clinician John Lyons (p. 59), *You bet! Fear is common sense in disguise telling us, "Hey, we can get hurt in this." Fear is extremely important; we just need to keep it in balance.* Keeping fear in balance with knowledge teaches us to respect the danger, not shrink from it.

Invoking Fear

Instinctive fear is triggered by real threat or experience, while imagined fear is triggered by a state of mind. Both types of fear can be equally compelling, since the mind cannot always distinguish between actual and vividly imagined information. Old-time radio horror shows are proof that imagined circumstances can elicit fear reactions ranging from worry to full-scale hysteria. Likewise, the anticipation that something terrible will happen is often worse than the actuality: *When my ex-race horse, Lady, was first learning to go under saddle, I had a recurring dream that she was going to blast out of the arena with me, take off through the fields, and I'd be killed,* recalls dressage instructor Kelly O'Boyle (p.60). *One day, I was taking a lesson from a woman who has an old airplane hangar for an indoor arena—big and beautiful and wide—open at both ends. We were working on my problem of not being able to relax at a canter, so she had me canter a straight-line, from one end of the arena to the other. Well, Lady took off, and out we went—into the field! Suddenly I was living my worst nightmare of having to ditch off of this racehorse, but I was able to make her stop. After that, the dream went away, which was really cool.*

I think my fearful dream actually created that incident. If you can create your best outcome by imaging it, you can create your worst outcome by focusing on it as well! That taught me anticipating and concentrating on a problem can make it occur. Once Kelly had identified the problem, she needed to refocus her thinking to find a solution. Instead, she continued dwelling on the problem and discovered how effectively imaging can invoke negative results as well as positive ones.

Beyond imaging, the very state of being scared can create a

fearful equestrian situation through the sensitivity of the horse and the actions of the rider: *When people say, "The horse knows I'm afraid and takes advantage," I disagree,* declares acclaimed equine artist Sam Savitt (p.61). *The horse isn't taking advantage. When riders are afraid, we do the wrong thing. For instance, when you tighten up because you're afraid, that tightening tells your horse, "Move on, faster." Then when he does, you grab the reins to hold him back. You're giving "clashing controls" by asking him to go and to stop at the same time. The horse is not taking advantage; your clashing controls are confusing and agitating the horse.*

This concept of clashing controls was dramatically demonstrated when our 11-year-old daughter, Allison, invited her friend, Rhoda, to vacation with us on our family's cattle ranch. Since trail riding is a favorite activity, I'd asked Rhoda's father if she had permission to ride. He said yes, Rhoda had been taking lessons and was a good rider. As soon as we arrived, the girls were begging for horses; so we saddled Deuce and Marigold and let the girls ride around the driveway while we unloaded the car. After a while, Allison asked if Rhoda wanted to trot; she gave an enthusiastic "Sure!" and off they jogged toward the bunkhouse.

The action of the trot quickly unsettled Rhoda, and she leaned forward to grab the saddle horn with both hands, slacking the reins. Then, with each bounce of the trot, Rhoda's legs kicked Deuce's sides. Feeling her forward weight, persistent kicks, and slack reins, Deuce obediently broke into a lope. With that, Rhoda began screaming, and Deuce dutifully picked up the pace a little more. I called to Rhoda to sit up and pull back on the reins, but she could not hear through her terror.

I watched helplessly as the scene snowballed toward disaster. Deuce lunged up the hill, then circled toward the barn with Rhoda's kicks and screams sending him evermore forward. As the two flew back down the hill, Rhoda bailed out—into a tree. Now riderless, Deuce slowed to a trot, then stopped, and began to graze

39

calmly beside the driveway. When I reached her, Rhoda was hysterical, but luckily had hurt only her hand on the tree. She refused to ride the next day, but did eventually climb back in the saddle with a greater appreciation of correct riding cues.

When out of control with fear, Rhoda had given Deuce every command to run: she leaned forward, gave him his head, kicked his flanks, and hollered. With all that, they could have won the Kentucky Derby!

Although fear is a vital factor in assessing situations, surrendering to it and losing all control can be dangerously counterproductive. After a point, we must calm down, take a deep breath, and regain control.

Individual Nightmares

Fears normally change with age, experience, and circumstance. The childhood fear of separation may ironically be offset with the adult fear of long-term commitment, as if Mother Nature wants to be sure we experience the entire spectrum of fears in a lifetime: *As an adult, I've developed a whole different set of fears,* notes Pat Lawson (p.61), founder of an urban riding group, Ebony Horsewomen. *Suddenly I'm thinking, "I can't afford to be hurt now. If I'm laid up, what would happen to my kids?" And then you get this thing in your head about age—that bones are more brittle now and recuperation is slow…I know I didn't begin to fear all this until I was an adult.*

Fear is not restricted to personal injury or death—it may center around concern for others you care about: *I've never been scared about physical injury, but I'm always afraid of mistakes,* says Macella O'Neill. *Horses are total innocents. They are so much heart; they're so magnanimous, and they try so hard for us that I can't hardly stand making mistakes on them. I hate to let them down, and yet I know I do make a lot of mistakes. I look back at my riding six months ago, nine months ago, and I can't believe some of the things I was doing wrong. It's like rereading my diary. "I can't believe I did that. Ooh, no! Was that me?" I've never been scared by the physical danger, but I do fear making mistakes for the horse's sake.*

Being afraid to make a mistake is a common fear for a variety of reasons. Macella was concerned for her mount, while others might be afraid of failure or looking foolish. At any rate, this attitude is limiting, for being afraid of making a mistake dilutes the learning process by removing two of its most effective tools—risk and error.

For policewoman Laura Bianchi (p.62), a job change to the mounted unit highlighted an unexpected fear for her; not of her new horse, but of her new exposure: *I'd worked for five years in the Mission Station, a busy and often volatile section of San Francisco. At Mission, we always thought about officer safety and immediate cover. You get out of the cruiser and think, "What am I going to stand behind?" So for me, the shock of the Mounted Patrol was suddenly I'm the biggest target in history! In the beginning I found myself crouching down on the horse or standing behind trees. But after a few weeks, I realized that none of the other mounted patrolmen were trying to make themselves invisible, and nobody had taken a shot at me, so I got over it. I learned to balance it out—not so afraid of being a target and yet not too relaxed either. Sort of a calm vigilance.*

After adjusting to her new visibility, Laura began having to deal with the fears of confrontation that come with the job of the Mounted Patrol: *It was the 1982 Super Bowl parade when all the fans went crazy because they thought the Forty-Niners were on the stairs of the San Francisco City Hall. Suddenly surrounded by maniacs, my horse and I were being crushed into a small corner. Since I was pretty new to the Mounted Unit, I became extremely afraid, thinking, "My God, what if this horse blows up and tears apart all these people standing in front of me?" But with that small squad of horses, we were able to move the crowd back and re-establish a fairly safe position. All the horses did what the officers asked of them—even with having beer* cans hitting them in the head, getting hit with signs...all kinds of violence! That experience showed me that even in the face of fear I can still get the job done. That was a changing point for me.

Equine Desensitization

As noted earlier, horses naturally flee from fearful objects and situations. However, domestic horses are trained to cope with many of the unnatural, often outrageous demands humans concoct: *Horses are not naturally courageous, but they can be desensitized to frightening stimuli,* explains veterinarian Robert Miller (p.62). *After all, they've been taught to charge into artillery fire, which is about as extreme as one can imagine. That's not a question of courage per se, it's a question of being successfully desensitized.*

In the United States today the mounted police patrol is as close to "artillery fire" as a horse will get. These horses face the daily pandemonium of city traffic, flashing lights, screaming sirens, angry mobs, rushing tramways—all the chaos and violence of contemporary life: *We ask our police mounts to do things that a horse just isn't supposed to do, and you can feel his heart beating right through the saddle,* marvels National Park Service Patrol Officer Lt. Carl Clipper (p.63). *You know he's scared to death, but he's doing it because you're asking him to—it's really something. Every time in crowd control, emotions are high; people are throwing rocks and bottles at him and hitting him with sticks. I'd hate to see him get cut up. He's in it because I've put him there. I've got to protect him.*

Horses are innocents that humans often put in harm's way, and yet they comply, which is amazing when you consider how far out of their natural comfort zones we take them: *I was on my police mount, Doc, at a rowdy New Year's Eve celebration,* reports Officer Laura Bianchi, *when somebody in the crowd stuck a cigarette on him—almost burning straight through his hide. Doc's ass went up in the air, but he didn't blow up. I turned and saw that the guy was doing it on purpose. Just then, another officer, on the ground, grabbed the guy with the cigarette, pulled him over the barricade, and arrested him for injuring a police horse on duty.*

Equine desensitization requires trust, training, and patience, for it means reprogramming their natural alarm system. Just as you continually educate a child to the world around him, you have to build a working "vocabulary" of experience that your horse can accept. Through gradual and repeated exposure to fearful stimuli, desensitization redefines what is feared to what is familiar by expanding a horse's "experiential vocabulary" of its environment. The photo of John Lyons and his Appaloosa stallion, Zip, on page 59 is a good illustration of desensitization to the alarming commotion of a hovering helicopter.

Overcoming Human Fears

Desensitization is an effective method of countering instinctive fears based on physical stimuli such as movements, sounds, and odors. However, unlike our equine partners who deal primarily with instinctive reactions to physical stimuli, most human anxieties are products of our inventive imaginations and therefore require techniques beyond physical desensitization. Because of their work with horses, many of the people I interviewed have developed individual methods of dealing with fear—both equine and human: *Horses are so empathetically sensitive that fear transmits to them like a lightning rod,* says Macella O'Neill. *You can't simply mask fear because that will not fool the horse. You honestly have to eliminate the fear. Get rid of it. No one rides to their fullest potential when there's an element of fear involved. I'm not saying it's wrong to ride when you're scared, but you're not going to be riding to your ultimate until you've mastered the fear. That means not having fear of anything, not of a mistake, not of an injury, not of your horse's unpredictable nature, not of anything.* So horses not only force us to face fears; they are the perfect vehicle on which to practice various ways to erase fears.

Immersion

As with equine desensitization, people can also be desensitized by doing a dreaded activity until they are able to relax into it and cope: *When I was four, our mule dumped me, and I banged my head on the concrete and didn't want to ride,* liberty horse trainer Rex Peterson (p.63) remembers. *My dad let it go for two or three years, but then one day he put me on a horse and said, "Don't get off until I come back." Then he started doing other things and forgot about me. I sat on that horse five hours. Mom said, "You can get off the horse." I said, "No, Dad said not to." You didn't cross him; so I didn't. My dad was very, very good to us, but he also realized that I had a problem and that was his way of dealing with it. I was raised in ranch country where riding horses was a necessity; we worked cattle and stuff in the Sand Hills, in Ogallala, Nebraska. I don't condemn him for it one ounce. I'm glad he did it. The first thirty minutes I sat on that horse I didn't understand why he did it, but by the next morning I knew why, and it was the best thing that ever happened to me. From that day on,* Rex jokes, *I terrorized that poor brown horse to death. I wouldn't let anybody else ride it. It was **my** horse...I've been with horses ever since.* Sometimes being pushed to endure what you fear makes you realize that you can cope.

The Power of Knowledge

Confidence also comes from getting to know your subject as an expert: *When I got out of high school I cowboyed and started horses for a ranch that usually had three hundred head,* says Buck Brannaman. *These horses would buck ya' off, kick ya', strike ya' and run off. They were basically bred bucking horse on both sides; not bred for rodeo stock, just touchy horses that could really buck! If you survived starting them they made pretty good ranch horses, because they were tough as a boot. Now I'd ridden saddle broncs in high school, so it's not like I was wet behind the ears when I went to work for this*

44

ranch, but these were real dangerous horses to work with. I knew fear then. All my horses were bucking, but there was this one roan horse who was the worst in the bunch. He was treacherous! There were mornings when I'd walk into the horse barn, saddle up and sincerely pray, "God, give me one more try with this roan and I'll never ask a thing again." Then the next morning it would be, "Hey, God, it's me again...." I was afraid of some of those horses. Not so afraid I didn't ride; that was my job...it was either ride or quit...but I was afraid. It was about that time I realized the only way that you ever get over fear is to know your subject. Your biggest fear is what you don't know. Like looking into the darkness—you know something's there, but you don't know what or when it's gonna get you. You just know it's inevitable.

The more I worked with those broncs the more I learned, and the less and less I was afraid. It's been a long time now since I've been afraid of any horse. Even figuring the kind of horses people lead at me now, sometimes setting me up, just trying to humiliate you in public because you're the guy from outta town doing clinics—the hired gun. I get the worst of the worst, and I can honestly say that there's not a horse alive that I'm afraid of. I'll be cautious, and I'll respect the danger, but fear is a different thing. I don't know fear of horses any more, because I know horses. This kind of expert knowledge transforms fear into confident respect—for the animal, the challenge, and one's own abilities.

In challenging my own nightmares over the years, I've come to understand that most fears are a state of mind, not necessarily the reality of the situation. I never thought I'd have the guts to fly over a fence on the back of a Thoroughbred, but what used to be a fear is now my all-time favorite recreation. Sure my alarm system still warns, "You could get hurt doing this!" as I approach a jump, but now my response is not anchored in fear—it's anchored in the confidence of educated ability and experience. Now I acknowledge the warning, accept the risk, and take the jump—an attitude adjustment that turns fear into fun.

Learn a New Approach or Ability

Accidents and injury can shake anyone's confidence, reigniting old fears or creating entirely new anxieties. There are times when we must look beyond the immediate problem to find the necessary ability to break through a fear. *I came off a young horse, and my leg hit a rail lying on the ground and snapped my femur,* reports Diana Cooper. *They put a plate in my leg, and I couldn't get back on for six months. When I did, I was scared—no doubt about it. I wasn't afraid of horses—I was afraid of the* ground. *Now when you're riding, you can't go around being afraid of gravity. So I went back to modern dance class and learned how to fall. Then, when I got myself back in the feeling that the ground was not my enemy, I could ride again.* Diana turned to dance to learn to "fall defensively" so that she would react more protectively in the future. This new skill restored her confidence in her ability to cope, allowing her to return to riding.

Take Charge

Whether or not we're sure we can handle it, there are times when simply taking action transforms fear, as Sam Savitt explains: *Gordon Wright [eminent coach and trainer] used to tell his students, "Don't be a 'hope-to-God rider'! If you get into any kind of trouble, do something! Don't just sit there—take charge!"*

Years ago, I was doing a job at the LBJ Ranch in Texas for Random House, Sam continues. *We had a boy scout and a girl scout visiting the ranch. The girl was a very good rider, but the boy was not. Both were on horses, and I'd asked to see them out on the prairie, so they moved out. There was a young photographer with me, Randy Wolfe, an ex-steeplechase rider, who walked out with them taking pictures. I could see the boy's horse was getting more and more anxious; he's prancing and snorting. The mother of the boy is standing next to me and asked, "Do you think he's all right?" I said, "Yeah, he'll be all* right," but I'm really thinking, "Hey Randy, do something. Don't just stand there." Just then, Randy vaulted up behind the boy with all of his camera equipment on. He put his arms around the boy and picked up the reins and in a second that horse was down and was quiet. They came on back, and I thought WOW! That was close! But Randy took charge, and it all ended well.* Taking charge replaced fearful anxiety with decisive action.

Distraction

Since focusing on a fear often increases anxieties and makes matters worse, distraction techniques can be helpful. Unlike denial, distraction does not ignore a fear alert, but rather acknowledges its presence and then forces your mind to concentrate on a mental function other than the fear: sing a song, recite a poem, a prayer, or as they suggest in the musical THE KING AND I, "Whistle a Happy Tune."

As mindless as this sounds, it does work. When I was very young, I used to wake up alone in my room with terrible nightmares. This was shortly after my family had purchased our first television set, so I got in the habit of mentally "switching channels" in my mind until I found something soothing enough to induce sleep. From then on, knocking out nightmares was as easy as changing my mental channel.

Visualization

Akin to imaging and distraction is visualization, where you redirect your mental focus from the fearful image to one in which you are successfully coping. Three-time world champion endurance rider Becky Hart (p.64) explains: *I have a fear of scary, high, narrow ledges that I often encounter during endurance rides. I can't really go practice them at home, so when I'm faced with one, I visualize myself across it. I look forward (trying not to look down), stay in my center, balance as best I can so I don't interfere with my horse, and let him do it. I visualize that we're doing it easily and safely; everything is going just right; the horse's feet are nowhere near the edge, and the ground's staying sturdy. Then we're zooming right across and it's over before I know it.*

Place Your Trust in Something Outside of Yourself

Often when we cannot garner the strength to face a certain fear, we turn to artificial aids or even a magic talisman to set our resolve: *It was dark, and Dad was showing some people his roping mare, Babe,* recalls farrier Dennis Marine (p.64). *He had me sitting on her bareback—didn't have a halter on her or anything else. A car went by and backfired. Babe spooked and sold out. She ran towards the corn crib where Dad had stretched a new piece of barbed wire. She hit it, and I hit the deck. That wreck shook my five-year-old confidence and I really didn't want to ride after that. Then Dad bought a new bridle that he called an "Easy Stop" and he convinced me that it was the cure to everything. So I rode with that magic bridle and everything went well. A few days down the line, everything was still going well, and pretty soon I was back where I left off. But Dad had to do a little psychological trickery to get me conned back on Babe.*

Trust in Your Horse

Just as Dennis gave his fear up to a trust in equipment, many riders rely on their horse's abilities to get them through a frightening situation: *I ride my little mountain pony, Lorenzo, up into the hills by my home,* says scriptwriter and director Caroline Thompson (p.66). *I love going on the tiny little trails stamped out by the deer. Some are so steep we can't even follow them, or they peter out, washed out by the rains. We were going down this one little trail, when it suddenly narrowed down to ten inches with a crevasse about twenty feet deep on my right, and sheer rock wall on my left. Too narrow to turn around. My adrenaline started pumping, and I'm thinking, "Dear Lord, what am I going to do now?" Well, I just gave Lorenzo his head, betting he could take care of himself better than I could take care of us. I'll be damned if that sure-footed little guy didn't just tiptoe around and get us past that.*

Even seasoned endurance riders have to deal with overcoming new fears: *In an endurance race, when we're galloping at speed, my heart's in my throat, but I've learned to trust the horse to overcome that fear,* claims endurance rider Stagg Newman (p.65). *But when we moved out to California and started riding in the hills, we hit some really steep terrain.... I have acrophobia and back East we didn't have rides like that. When I started riding on Mt. Diablo, some of the trails made me feel like "Oh my God! get me out of here!" A couple of times I had to get off and walk until I could convince myself to put faith in knowing my horse didn't want to go down either, and he's more athletic....*

On one endurance ride, my wife and I were in a group of eight horses on a single track for eight miles—with mountain straight up on one side and straight down into a deep canyon on the other! I've had to overcome acrophobia by learning to put my faith in my mount.

Trust in Expert Authority

By trusting an authority figure, such as a trainer, you may receive back the necessary faith in yourself to attempt a fearful activity: "If my coach thinks I can do this, by gosh, I *can* do this!"

There are times when the authority figure does not even have to be physically present to be effective: *My father was a jockey in Alabama, so horses were in my blood, and I was a daddy's girl,* says Pat Lawson. *Not long after Daddy passed away, in '91, I was riding in a parade with the Ebony Horsewomen. My horse, Star, began acting up, but this time, as he kept getting worse, I was growing more afraid. I could feel that any minute Star was going to run into the crowd. I also knew that the worst thing I could do was give in to his behavior, because trying to control him after that would be near impossible. I didn't want to give in, but I knew I needed to get Star out of the parade and get off.*

Right then I saw my father walk out of the crowd. I hadn't seen him until he came through the first row of people to the street. He moved around this man and walked right up to me and said, "Stop it. You know how to ride this horse. Now ride him!" Suddenly, I felt myself relax. I was no longer tight, and the minute I relaxed, Star re-laxed.

My daughter was riding abreast of me. I looked over at her and asked, "Did you see him?" "See who?" she asked. "Granddaddy. Did you see him?" I asked. "No, Mom, I didn't."

But I saw him. I don't know how many people believe me, but it happened. Whether it actually happened or not is moot; the mere thought of her father's reassurance was enough to convince Pat she had the ability to handle the situation, and that was all she needed to allay her fear.

Trust in the Ultimate Authority

The immeasurable power of positive affirmations and prayer has been demonstrated since time immemorial: *I happen to be a very religious person and there are some principles about God Law that I believe,* continues Pat Lawson. *Fear is not the spirit that God gave man. Fear destroys, inhibits, prevents, denies, doubts. God gave man the spirit of power, love and a sound mind. When I begin to feel fear rising in me that I know Star can pick up instantly, I dispel it. I say to myself, "God does not give the spirit of fear, and it is not mine." Then I take a deep breath and blow it out. I just release it.*

In times of trial it's best to draw strength from wherever possible: inside, outside, and above. As L.D. Burke suggests, *"Let loose the reins and He'll lead you."*

Conscious Breathing

One of the most important coping mechanisms I have ac-quired through riding is that of conscious breathing. From the slow, relaxed breathing of yoga meditation to the various choreographed techniques used in natural childbirth, the impact of controlled breathing on our emotional and physical systems is evident and fascinating. Normally, we do not think about breathing or even whether we are; we take it for granted. However, if you learn to understand and control various manifestations of breathing, you can influence your physical, emotional and psychological states of being: *One of the basics of success is using and controlling breathing,* states Linda Tellington-Jones. *I've had students who, honest to God, cannot get a sound out of their mouth when the horse starts galloping, just because of fear. So I have them count out loud in rhythm with the gallop stride of the horse, which forces them to breathe, and the breathing then makes it easier for them to relax. At any level, getting in rhythm with the breathing of the horse makes an enormous difference. It's the key to success. Even when you're not on a horse, you can do the same thing—breathe in rhythm with your walking—that's another thing that I learned from my grandfather who trained racehorses.*

When frightened, our normal reaction is to suck in air, hold it and tense up—ready for fight or flight—just like horses. By taking deep, full breaths, we can release much of the tension triggered by holding our breath in fear. Recognizing this, many trainers today incorporate breathing techniques into their programs.

Centering

Deep breathing that is generated in the diaphragm involves the very center of our being so that it causes a sense of peace and relaxation that is not produced by shallower upper body breaths. Award-winning Centered Riding instructor Mary Fenton (p.65) describes the process: *Finding that center of power in your body creates a sense of peace, quietness, primal knowing, and trust. Being able to breathe your way into your center is profound. Then to be able to relate your center with the horse's center behind you, really harmonizing, gives me a feeling of stability in space....* In riding, that sense of stable harmony with your horse counteracts a basic fear of falling off.

Individually, controlled breathing and centering are effective techniques for reversing the symptoms of fear; combined together they become even more powerful: *My big fear is being out of control,* admits Mary Fenton. *I am really scared on a roller coaster because I have NO CONTROL. When you get on a roller coaster, you put your life, your body and your soul in that seat, and off you go. I always used to be afraid of that, and I'd grip the bar until I thought it would break, trying to force myself into my seat—resisting the curves, the twists, the ups and the downs. When the ride was over, I'd be shaken, sore, and exhausted from fighting the natural forces of the ride. Then one time I went to the boardwalk with a friend who's a pilot and loves the thrill machines. I thought, "By gosh, this time I'm just going to apply my centered riding techniques—center and breathe."*

We got on the roller coaster; the bar was locked in place, and I put my trust in the physics of centripetal force. As the car climbed up the first steep slope, I opened my mouth, sucked in a lungful of air, which I blew out in an incredible scream as we plummeted over the precipice. We spun this way and spun that way, and I just centered, relaxed, breathed and yelled with every massive exhale. It was amazing how much fun that ride was! My body moved with all the outrageous actions, as we whirled and swayed and extended and compressed—but it was soft and supple—not rigid and resistant. At the end of that ride I was invigorated and thrilled rather than tight and tired. It was a wonderful lesson that you can actually breathe away a lot of fear...I was the same person on the roller coaster as that initial stiff, resistant, holding-my-breath robot, but this time I had made a conscious decision to trust the experience, breathe to my center, relax, and go with the natural flow of the ride. I became a part of the roller coaster and had a ball moving with it, rather than being shaken by it—rigid in fear and resistance. Mary successfully applied techniques learned through riding to master her fear of the roller coaster.

I had the opportunity to spend a week with Mary and work on Centered Riding techniques. Much like Mary's fear of the roller coaster, I held a fear of being out of control when my horse shied. Conscious breathing and centering skills have transformed my response from tense, tight, and insecure where my mare's sudden movements could easily unseat me, to having a deeper, more relaxed seat where I move with her actions. Shying still catches me by surprise, but I can now counter her frightened response with centered, conscious breathing and my quiet response allows her to relax as well, so we work through the fright together. As a result, shying has become a spontaneous excitement instead of a paralyzing spook.

The Flip Side of Fear

Adrenaline Thrills

Noted psychologist, Fritz Pearl, once said, "Fear is excitement with a held breath," and one of the most exciting fear events around is rodeo! *Fear's something you have to be able to control when you want to go play a crazy game like I did for years—riding bulls and bucking horses,* states Larry Mahan. *The real element of danger is there, and when you're young and not sure how to deal with all the unexpected twists, an additional fear element is there as well. But if you're gonna be good at rodeo, you have to overcome the fear. You have to develop the attitude, "It never happens to me," even though you know it's inevitable. You can't go play a game like rodeo and not get hurt. So, then you have to say, "Okay, if I do get hurt, I can accept that." And then when it happens, the first thing you think is, "How long is it gonna take me to get back out there and do it again?" It's a really weird form of mental development.*

Eight seconds of fear for a lifetime's excitement. It's hard for the uninitiated to comprehend the "why" of such risk, but rodeo cowboys line up for the reward of the rush and the glory.

Rodeo contestants aren't the only ones who seek the risk, the rewards, and the rush of a ride; backyard cowboys enjoy their own brand of riding thrills as well: *Horseback riding is risky, but part of us yearns for risk and that element of risk adds adrenaline to the beauty of riding,* says L.D. Burke. *Adrenaline is cool. I love it. But there is no free lunch; to have a feeling of well being, you have to understand that you are really at risk at all times anyway. We have this thing about death being so awful. But for me, quality of life beats out quantity of life hands down!*

Even seniors are attracted to the excitement and risk of riding: *There's a really cool guy at my barn who's about eighty-five years old, who at seventy-six decided he was going to learn how to ride,* reports Kelly O'Boyle. *"What have I got to lose?" is what he says. "I've lived my life, and I can go out and take big risks again" and riding's what he chose to do. Taking risks are good because you don't rest on your laurels; you continue to challenge yourself.*

So the flip side of fear can be the charge of risk, excitement, or challenge, but first you must transform the fear: *Since fear lives in the mind, you must first acknowledge it consciously, so it can be brought up for discussion—with yourself or others,* explains Mary Fenton. *Then you can decide to change it into something else by learning skills to deal with it. The resulting understanding, ability, and familiarity bring the acceptance and confidence which disarm the fear. Then that fearful activity can become excitement, or a challenge, or even routine—I can do this! Fear that becomes familiar melts into something else...you can actually transform fear into power.* Overcoming fear generates self-confidence and adds the fun and satisfaction of another "can do" to the text of your life.

Courage

Since opposites actually define each other, courage cannot exist without fear: *I have a friend,* reports Jane Savoie, *who is a kamikaze event rider—absolutely crazy! She charges over solid advanced courses, and I'm thinking, "You're going to die!" But she has no fear of it. She probably has other fears, but for her to face an advanced three-day course brings no fear to her, so it takes no courage. It takes a lot of skill, and a lot of strength, but not real courage.*

To me, the most courageous people in life are the fearful people that do in spite of their fear. People who deal with real fear issues and say, "Okay, I'm afraid, but here goes...."

Since my book came out, I've been having to do a lot of public speaking. Recently I stood in front of five hundred people with a microphone in my hand and gave a motivational seminar. You think I wasn't scared? I was terrified! But to do it in spite of...there's the courage.

Sam Savitt relates an example of just such courage: *I was in an open class at a local horse show with a number of younger riders. Early in the class of about 25 competitors, one horse and rider took the fence wrong and the horse somersaulted. The rider was thrown clear, but the horse landed on its neck and was killed on impact. It took ten or fifteen minutes for the horse to be taken off the course. When they announced the course was ready again I watched a lot of those young kids just swallow their fear and go on. It was a terrific thing to see because they were obviously deeply affected by it, yet continued on. I watched them grow in those few minutes. Boy, they matured! Luckily, things like that don't happen very often.*

One of the most inspiring examples of competitive courage I have witnessed was delivered by Anne Kursinski and Cannonball at the 1992 Olympics in Barcelona: *Cannonball was a very careful horse; he hated to hit the jumps. There's a very fine line between too brave and too chicken. You want your horse just chicken enough so he won't hit the jumps, but if he's too chicken, he won't jump big at all. He's got to be brave, and yet if he's too brave, he'll knock down jumps and go—come hell or high water—not being careful enough. Your horse needs to have just the right balance in attitude.*

I never imagined it, but in the 1992 Olympic Games Cannonball stopped out in the first round. He'd never seen jumps like those in his life. That's the worst thing you can have in a team event because then the other three scores count entirely—no throwing out the bad score. After that first round I had the option of withdrawing or trying to place in the second round. I had to wait around for many long hours until the second round, while my mind and stomach created tight, intricate knots, wrestling with the question of whether we should go or not. I was gripped by the emotional fear of letting the team down plus the physical fear of not knowing if Cannonball and I could actually get around that Olympic course. Had it been an individual competition, I probably wouldn't have gone back in the ring. But I knew we had to try—for the United States team—we had to go! When it was finally my turn again, Frank Chapot thought I was crazy to have another go at it. But trainer George Morris thought we could do it and somehow I believed we could—it was a real sort of a spiritual knowing.

Somehow I got Cannonball around with just one rail down. I still don't know how we did it. Honest to God, I have no idea other than desire and adrenaline—here goes, we're going to do it! We went around that course—did the triple combination and just knocked one single rail down—it was really something. Listening to Melanie Smith's commentary on the television is a riot because even she's yelling, "Oh my God, she's doing it!" She's as dumbfounded as I was. Other Olympic riders that were there still talk about it to this day. That course wasn't completed with just physical strength; there was something on a much deeper level. It really was amazing. I hope I never have to do anything like that again. I lost several pounds that day. Even today—years later—when I watch that videotape, my hands get all sweaty with the very same fears.

Watching Anne's two rounds at the Barcelona Olympics is a study in unadulterated courage. Their second round was successful because Anne *willed* Cannonball to jump—she charges that course, practically hoisting him over each obstacle with inflamed determination. With that ride, Anne and Cannonball shared a mutual trust and inspired conviction that showed the world, "to be afraid and *do in spite of*...there's the courage."

Skills for Success

This chapter has shown that being on and around horses offers a myriad of opportunities to deal with fears. Equine fears are triggered by physical stimuli and perceived threats, so they can be addressed simply by removing the offending object or situation, or through desensitization training.

Human fears are more complicated. In addition to reacting to physical stimuli, creative human minds and highly developed emotions trigger fear responses to *imagined* threats, creating a much wider and more complex range of fears. However, just as the human imagination can create, invoke, and magnify fears, it also has the power to control, limit, and dispel fear. Through the horse-human relationship, we learn to identify, prevent, and diffuse fearful situations; to deal with the various reactive levels engendered by fear; and to educate against fear. We learn coping mechanisms, such as centering, conscious breathing techniques, relaxation, distraction or decisive action. Success, familiarization, and know-how then impart the necessary self-confidence and trust. By this process we transform the fear into a skill, a challenge, a thrill, or true courage—with *HorsePower!*

REGE LUDWIG, b. 1942, is a master polo coach and instructor based in Palm Desert, California. Rege started riding around the age of ten at the Pennsylvania polo club where his father worked. He loves the challenge of figuring out individual horses, then training each to its potential. One of his career highlights was coaching two different teams in the United States Open Polo Championships and winning both times. Rege is pictured going for the ball during a match at the El Dorado Polo Club in Palm Desert, California.

JOHN LYONS, b. 1947, has become one of America's most popular and trusted horsemen. This 1995 photo taken in California demonstrates the mutual trust and desensitization possible as John's Appaloosa stallion, Bright Zip, stands calmly while a helicopter hovers and roars nearby. In addition to his success as a trainer and teacher, one of the highlights of John's career was realized when Bright Zip was named to the Appaloosa Hall of Fame.

DIANA THOMPSON, b. 1956, is a horse trainer and journalist who rode ponies at age three and received her first horse as a Christmas present when she was seven. In 1985 she assisted Linda Tellington-Jones with TTeam Training the Russian Olympic team in Moscow. She is founder and editor-in-chief of THE WHOLE HORSE JOURNAL, an innovative publication dedicated to holistic equine health and gentle, effective training methods. Diana is shown with Sir Buckley, a riding horse rehabilitated under Diana's training.

KELLY O'BOYLE, b. 1963, is shown with her Thoroughbred mare, Independent Lady, whom Kelly purchased at a racing facility for one dollar. At the time Lady weighed only 650 lbs and could barely walk since she'd been confined to a stall for two years without exercise. Kelly brought her back to health and trained her in the sport they both enjoy—dressage.

SAM SAVITT is one of America's most admired equine artists and the official artist of the United States Equestrian Team. He is also an award-winning author, illustrator of more than 150 books, acclaimed teacher, and devoted equestrian. In 1998, Sam received an unprecedented honor from the North American Horseman's Association when it awarded him both its Equine Artist of Distinction and Lifetime Achievement Awards. Sam cares for his own horses and still appreciates the excitement of a cross-country gallop near his home in New York state.

PAT LAWSON, b. 1946. as the daughter of a jockey, Pat's interest in horses started at an early age and has been a source of strength and growth throughout her life. She is a successful attorney and founder of Ebony Horsewomen, Inc., a non-profit organization supporting urban youth through drug awareness, criminal justice, health and education programs. Pat and her Palomino, Rising Star, are shown with Ebony Horsewomen members, Heather Lawson, right, and Lynn Ford, left, as they enjoy an autumn canter at a Board of Education presentation in Connecticut.

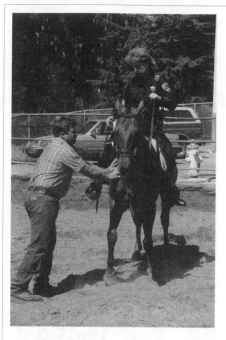

Laura Bianchi, b. 1952, was the first female officer to join the San Francisco Police Department Mounted Unit in 1981. Subsequently Laura became a trainer for the Mounted Unit, was a member of the championship Grand National Color Guard Team in 1987–1988, and has authored articles on police horse training. She is shown on her police mount, Bill, being prepped for crowd control at the police stable in San Francisco's Golden Gate Park.

Robert Miller, D.V.M. b. 1925, shown here with his Quarter Horse mare, Holly Tsunami, is a veterinarian with a lifetime's experience with horses and 25 years work with mules. An internationally recognized authority on equine behavior and author of many books, papers and videos, he is credited with popularizing the technique of imprint training foals and was the first equine practitioner to receive the Bustad Companion Animal Veterinarian-of-the-Year Award in 1995.

LT. CARL CLIPPER, b. 1946, Commander of the Horse Mounted Patrol of the United States Park Police in Washington D.C., transferred to the mounted unit from the motorcycle division of police work. On duty for many memorable park and presidential occasions in the nation's capital, a stand-out event for Lt. Clipper was commanding the Horse Mounted Patrol at the 1996 Olympics in Atlanta. Lt. Clipper and his 18.1 hand Cleveland Bay police mount, Big John, emerge from a barrage of smoke during crowd-control training at the Park Police Training Barn in Washington.

REX PETERSON, b. 1954, is an award-winning trainer for the movie industry specializing in liberty horses (horses that obey verbal and visual commands without a rider). Raised in the Sand Hills of Nebraska, Rex learned to trick- and Roman-ride as part of his family's rodeo act, thrilling crowds at Wild West Shows. He trained for many years with legendary Hollywood trainer Glenn Randall, Sr. Rex and his Quarter Horse stallion, Doc's Keepin' Time, star of the 1994 production of BLACK BEAUTY, salute the crowd at the American Quarter Horse World Show in Oklahoma.

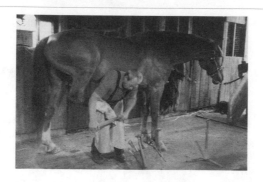

DENNIS MARINE, b. 1951, is a farrier and cattleman who grew up on a Nebraska ranch helping his dad with a boarding barn and starting colts. Since getting his degree from Oregon State University in horse shoeing, Dennis has logged more than 20 years in the trade. He has recently returned to the cattle business where he's able to use all his knowledge and skills doing jobs that he truly enjoys. Dennis attends a horse at a hunter/jumper barn in 1996.

BECKY HART, b. 1954, is a three-time World Champion who exemplifies success in endurance riding. She has won both the Tevis Cup and the Race of Champions—twice, been North American Champion, American Horse Shows Association (AHSA)/Hertz Equestrian of the year (1990), CHRONICLE OF THE HORSE Rider of the Year in 1990, American Endurance Ride Conference (AERC) Hall of Fame, 1992 and United States Equestrian Team (USET) Master Rider in 1994. Becky and her champion Arab gelding, R. O. Grand Sultan, aka "Rio," enjoy a victory gallop after being presented with their individual gold medal at the 1990 World Equestrian Games in Stockholm, Sweden.

STAGG NEWMAN, b. 1948, is a record-setting endurance rider and engineering technologist. He was the 1992 National 100 Mile Champion and took the individual bronze and a team gold medal at the Fédération Equestre Internationale North American Championship in 1993. Selected for the 1994 USET World Championship Team, Stagg completed his 25th 1-day 100 mile ride in 1997. Stagg and his champion Arabian gelding, Ramegwa Drubin, make an early morning ford across the Shenandoah River during the 1993 Old Dominion One Hundred Mile Ride.

MARY FENTON, b. 1938, Mary has enjoyed lifelong riding, teaching and coaching success from Pony Club instruction to director of a large riding school. After studying with Sally Swift, she became a certified Centered Riding Instructor. She has coached World Champion Endurance rider Becky Hart, and in 1992, was named Riding Instructor of the Year by the American Riding Instructor Certification Program. Mary is shown schooling her homebred Thoroughbred gelding, Eyptian Hemp, aka Tempo, at the canter.

CAROLINE THOMPSON, b. 1956, is a talented screenwriter and director with many major films to her credit, including the 1994 Warner Brothers' production of BLACK BEAUTY. Caroline studies dressage and delights in taking care of her own horses. She is shown with Eve, her two-year-old Welsh Pony, while Eve's dam, Maxine, looks on.

CHAPTER THREE

HOLD YOUR HORSES

Anger and Accountability

*Anger is the wind that blows out the candle of light in
a person's mind. —Richard Shrake*

"Uh oh...trouble; I must be in trouble," the eight-year-old fretted when he saw his foster father, Monty Roberts, (p.83) waiting by the mailbox at the driveway of Flag Is Up Farms. The dry Santa Ana winds blasted heat and dust through the school bus doors as he got out.

"I came to walk you in so we could talk," Monty said.

The boy studied the ground..."About what?" he asked.

"About our contract on that horse you begged me for last month," Monty replied. "You got the whole horse, remember? That means you take care of all his needs: feeding, watering, cleaning, exercising...right?"

"Yes, sir," the boy mumbled. He remembered the contract well, for it was the first time anyone had given him anything in trust.

"Well, I hate to tell you, but you didn't water this morning. And you know, this wind can suck a body dry quicker than you can wring out a sponge." Monty pointed to the horse's paddock. "That pawing hole in front of his trough is evidence that Buster was dying of thirst, so I watered him."

Dread choked the boy's heart—he'd been late for the bus and forgot to water Buster. How could he be so stupid!? He knew the kind of punishment he'd get from his real father, but he'd only been with the Roberts family a short time and couldn't guess what his foster father had in mind. Tears welled up at the thought of losing Buster, but he kept his head down so Monty would not read his fears.

Monty continued, "Now we don't have any consequences for failing to water in our contract, but I've been thinking.... This lapse isn't going to cost you anything today except the lesson it- self." The boy eyed him suspiciously as Monty reached in his pocket.

"You see this water glass? I want you to put this on the shelf in the tack room. This is your reminder. If you ever forget to wa- ter that horse again, you're to fill his trough from that hoseless fau- cet, fifty feet from the paddock, with this water glass. Now re- member, *you never have to do this*, unless, for some crazy reason, you forget to water this horse again. I will not water him; you will just do it automatically. Is that agreed?"

"Agreed!" he said shaking his head in wide-eyed disbelief at his unexpected reprieve. They both initialed the amended con- tract....

Five weeks later, the boy rushed out and failed to water Buster again. An even hotter day, but Monty left the horse until the boy got home from school. Monty greeted the boy almost apologeti- cally, "Daaamn! I hate it! You forgot to water, and I hate it!"

The boy's shoulders slumped in recognition of his offense. He set down his books, changed his clothes, and without a word, be- gan to fill the trough—with the water glass.

Around midnight, Monty's wife, Pat, woke Monty saying, "That boy's gonna die out there. He's so tired he can hardly climb the fence any more. You could have given him a bigger glass!"

Monty got dressed, went out to the paddock, sat down on the bench and asked, "If I told you you could stop short of filling that trough up, would you do it?"

"No." said the boy, climbing the fence with yet another glass of water.

"Why?"

"Because we made a deal."

"Well, what if I want to break the deal?"

"No!" said the boy, "'Cuz I don't want you to break any of our other deals and I'm willin' to fill this up."

Monty smiled and sat quietly for the final half-hour as the boy completed his sentence. Walking back to the house, Monty put his arm around the boy and said, "You know, I am so proud of you. You just took this up and I didn't have to hammer on you. I didn't want this to happen and I don't want you to ever suffer any negative consequences again. I want all of our contracts to be such that you get good things from them."

"That's good," said the boy, "I understand."

Today, that boy is a corporate attorney dealing with tax law— he's filling buckets with glasses of water everyday now—doing methodical and meticulous work. He learned a lot about personal responsibility, contracts, and consequences from a thirsty horse, a water glass, and a foster father who disciplined without anger.

Responsibility

Perhaps the most universal lesson learned from working with horses is responsibility: *We have taken the horse out of nature and locked him in a false environment, so we're responsible for his complete maintenance,* notes hunter/jumper coach Mary Deringer Phelps (p.84). *If his feet rot, it's our fault; if he loses weight, it's our fault; if he's overweight, it's our fault. Owning a horse is a full-time job. You can't pull it out of the water and put a canvas cover on it and say, "I'll see you in six months."* It's twenty-four hours a day, every day of the *week. And even when you have one day off, I'll bet you check him. Because even though you trust your replacement, you just sleep a little bit better when you're the last one who's laid the eyes on him.* Such full-time responsibility instills concern for others, dependability, and a knowledge of the routines and skills necessary to provide well for our charges. Youngsters taking on the care of a pony or horse learn to weigh personal choices and decisions, as well as make compromises and even sacrifices. They must get up early to feed, water, groom, and muck stalls; forgo after-school activities to exercise the horse; and miss important social activities in order to meet the ongoing obligations of a show schedule. By attending to the demands of a dependent, young horse owners experience the selfless concerns and considerate actions of a full-time caretaker.

To be successful in such a comprehensive commitment, you must be heavily invested in it—you need to care about the animal and the results of your caretaking.

Personal Commitment

The promise or reality of a horse can be a tremendous motivator: *My sister and I worked on our parents for about three years before they finally gave in and agreed to buy us horses,* recalls chef and avid rider Holly Peterson Mondavi (p.84). *The deal was, we had to work off their cost by doing yard work, or whatever chores they asked. My first horse was $250 and my sister's horse was given to us free, so we split the $250, and each had to pitch in $125 of hard work and ironing. That was a big deal for two young kids! When we finally got them, we felt that we really earned those horses, so we took great care of them. These were big animals and a really big responsibility for us. Mom would always say, "Horses can't just go catch mice like the cat. If you forget to feed them, they're stuck without food, so they depend on you...."* We were extremely responsible, or they were going, and we knew that. By having a personal stake in earning and keeping their horses, these girls developed a naturally enthusiastic commitment to the ensuing responsibilities of ownership.

That kind of personal investment often yields more value than an outright gift: *When we started our therapeutic program, we were not charging fees for lessons,* notes Octavia Brown. *As a charity, we felt this was a good idea. But parents came to us and said, "We should be paying for this, because keeping horses is not cheap. This should not be free to us; don't treat us any differently than you would others." So we now charge a nominal amount.* Those parents recognized the value of the program and felt an obligation to contribute to its ongoing success. Their reciprocal involvement generates an allegiance and appreciation that may not evolve from charity. "Gift horses" are wonderful, but their true value is found in the ensuing investment of commitment.

Frustration: the Road to Lost Tempers

Taking on a responsibility the size of a horse generates a multitude of new tasks necessitating the acquisition of alien skills and peculiar equipment. This can be an exciting time for the novice horse owner. It can also be a frustrating time if one's learning curve does not keep pace with the required abilities: *When someone rides, their personality shows in how they treat their horse…and how they deal with frustration,* notes realtor and recreational rider Zaven Ayanian (p.85). *We all fail; no one is 100% right every time. Success and failure are brother and sister—they go together. When a rider fails, many times it's not the horse's fault, and the rider must try hard to control his own emotions.* The novel, varied, and complex world of horses and riding offers many opportunities to learn, apply, and practice methods to counteract emotional reactions to setbacks, disappointments, and frustrations.

A lot of times, a lack of knowledge and a lack of feel turn people into bullies on animals, says Jane Savoie. *When I'm frustrated because I can't do something on a horse, it's not the horse's fault; it's because I'm at the limit of my knowledge and need to learn more. If I knew more, or had more skill, then I would know how to get this horse to do what I wanted him to do rather than have to force it out of him or beat it out of him. It is from this understanding that I've developed my training and teaching philosophy.*

I've had a couple of screamers as teachers—one really bad screamer—and I remember how that made me feel. When I was being screamed at, I got really up tight and realized, "This is crazy; I'm getting screamed at; I get tight, then I ride badly, and get screamed at some more. If this person's job is to educate me and help me, screaming is counterproductive." So, I vowed never to get angry or raise my voice in a lesson because I hated it and it was counterproductive.

However, I am a human being, and there are times when I'm feeling a little short-tempered or a little frustrated. Whenever I get to that point, which really isn't very often, rather than think, "What is the matter with this student that he doesn't get this? You're stupid, you're uncoordinated...what is the matter with you?" I turn it around and make the responsibility my own. I repeat this little mantra to myself, "If I were a better teacher, I would find a way to reach this student." Then I look for a new way to explain it. I don't make it the student's responsibility that they're not getting something—that's my responsibility. There's no reason for me to raise my voice because it's not their fault; I have to find another way to reach them.

It's the same with the horses; rather than get angry at a horse or a student for not doing what I wanted, I've realized it's my job to grow and learn more so that I will have the tools to achieve what I want with them.

By looking to herself to address frustration, Jane is always adding to her repertoire of training and teaching aids. This ever-expanding base of expertise naturally counteracts failures and increases successes, thereby reducing the frustration of not being able to accomplish objectives.

Knowledge is an antidote for frustration, and according to John Lyons, it is also an effective substitute for patience: *People say that I'm really patient with horses, but I think my knowledge looks like patience in disguise. I don't think there's a place for patience or for power in training. It takes determination—which sometimes looks like strength or power—and knowledge to train horses. When I know there's say, twenty steps that need to be taken before the horse is going to put his first foot in the trailer, and we're only on step five, then I'm not mad at the horse because he's not stepping in the trailer.*

Usually when we lose our temper with a horse, for example getting them in a trailer, it's when this thought comes into our mind, "I'm not going to be able to get this horse into the trailer." We don't know what else to do; we're exasperated, and we lose our temper as a last resort.

So people who lose their temper while training their horses have lost their lesson plan and don't know where they are in the scheme of things. They don't know if they're on step three or step eleven; they may not have a lesson plan at all, so they're just shooting in the dark. To continue working until we learn how to communicate, and the horse learns how to do it, takes determination and knowledge—not patience.

By following a lesson plan, you can proceed step-by-step without being frustrated by ignorance. But what happens when your horse just isn't following the same lesson plan? That's when you're faced with one of the most creative equine coping mechanisms—flexibility.

Flexible Approaches

If frustrations are born out of not knowing what to do next, having a single, rigid lesson plan may not suffice. For if one of those steps fails, we are once again left with frustration. In working with horses, you learn to create new approaches to old problems: *There are a lot ways to accomplish almost the same thing on a horse,* explains Sam Savitt. *For instance, we're riding down the road; there's a glitter on a fence that has made him unsure whether to go by, so he stops and wants to turn around. Rather than battling with this horse to go by that thing, getting him all revved up, where I might get thrown or anything can happen, I just turn him around, and we'll back down the road. Pretty soon the object's in front of us, and we've passed it.*

In teaching a horse to stand when I'm mounting, since some horses like to move off, I take them and stick them in the corner of a ring facing into the corner. Then I get on. He has nowhere to go. I try to think of very easy, soft ways of accomplishing the same objective. Keeping "a bag full" of innovative responses to draw upon increases your chances of success and avoids frustrations and disappointments, which can trigger anger.

When a problem comes up with one of my horses, I know in order to change the problem, I need to change his mind, notes Larry Mahan. *The biggest problem that people have in dealing with horses is that the humans won't change their own mind and come at the problem from a different angle. If we can change our mind to the point of "Forget about that, let's do something else," then we have a chance to change the horse's mind. And when you can change their mind, you can change anything. I never feel that I'm going to make them do anything; I want them to want to do what I'm asking them to do. So, it comes down to how I present the request to them that's going to make the difference; that is the determining factor.*

A hardheaded, belligerent attitude of, "Do it this way, or else..." can be an invitation to battle if "this way" fails. Since battles between horse and human are literally weighted to the equine side, it is important that the human learn to curb frustrations, anger and rage. Daily exposure to the many mental and emotional challenges of working with horses provides an effective schooling ground for developing a flexible attitude that can derail frustrations by providing alternate routes to success.

Dealing with Anger

A counselor once told me, "Anger results when things don't go the way you want." If not a universal definition, that seems to cover my flashpoints. Since anger is neither desirable or effective around horses, how do horse people handle it?

When I first came to work with Glenn Randall [renowned trainer of Trigger and other horses for movies], I had a very, very bad temper, admits horse trainer, Rex Peterson. *Between him and horses, they taught me to control my temper. Getting mad doesn't fix anything. It doesn't make anything work because you don't even think straight when you're mad. That's the biggest problem; you lose your common sense. I've seen people lose their temper and do things to horses that when you finally get them to stop and ask, "What in the hell did you do that for?" They say, "I don't know; I just lost my temper."*

Glenn always said, if you get mad, get off! Go in the house, get a big glass of iced tea and ask, "What did he do that made me mad? What caused him to do it? How can I take that cause away, and how can I keep him from doing it again?" and then really think about the answers to those questions. I'm not bigger and stronger than a horse, but I am smarter. I tell everybody who comes around here, **You must not get mad.** *Do not lose your temper. If you get mad, get off. If you don't, I will probably pull you off. Most problem horses derive from people with bad tempers. Most of them are man-made.*

If there's a problem, and I lose my cool with a horse, I now talk it out in a sort of friendly verbal assault. I go, "God, you made me mad when you did that! Why did you do that?" I sit there and talk to them. That's how I control my temper now, but I won't spur him, or whip on him....

The iced tea habit works in a variety of situations—getting mad at neighbors or whatever. Go in the house and ask yourself, "What did he do that made me mad? Why do I want to go out and strangle him?" Nine times out of ten when you sit down and think about it, it's not really that bad. All you've gotta do is this, this, or this, and that will resolve that. No more problem. However, it's more than just time out— you must think about what happened between you and the horse or the other guy in order to resolve it and learn from it. Otherwise you may calm down, but still be mad because you haven't thought it out to a point of understanding and resolving.

There's a gallon of iced tea in my refrigerator at all times... summer-time there's two gallons in there. The biggest thing horses taught me was to control my temper.

Accepting Authority

Since we live in a regulated society, it is often beneficial to learn to accept rules and judgments without railing against figures of authority. Equestrians can learn this lesson in controlling anger through the many disciplines that entail subjective judgment and require sportsmanship: *In order to survive polo, you learn to accept umpires,* states Rege Ludwig. *The guy has the whistle; he has the shirt; he has the responsibility and the authority behind it, so all I'm going to do is make life worse for myself by crossing him. He may be blind, but I've got to accept his decision and just go on with the game. If you want to fight and confront the umpire, you're going to make life harder on yourself and your team. Life's a game. If you go against the rules, somebody is going to make you pay the price.* Whether the judgment is fair or not, controlling your temper allows you to accept the results or discuss them rationally, while ranting simply makes matters worse.

Change the Subject

When communication breaks down to the point of anger, turn away from the volatile subject: *I've learned that when a horse really upsets me, I can't just blow up,* says Peruvian Paso competitor Charlotte Dicke (p.85). *It's not going to do any good, because then I'm no longer communicating; I'm just fighting. I have to take a deep breath and move on to try something different. With people, I have to do the same thing, because as soon as you start screaming at each other, you're not communicating.*

Walk Away

There are times when controlling your anger is just not possible. Under those circumstances, removing yourself from the scene may be the best solution: *When I get to the point where I'm losing my temper…I walk away,* states Quarter Horse breeder Chris Hawkins (p.86). *You lose your temper, you lose your horse. When you see that horse's eyes getting wide and startled looking, walk off, because you may find yourself doing things you shouldn't. Many people can't seem to do that—they MUST make the horse do it RIGHT NOW! They can't wait until tomorrow. A horse will teach you patience. I have a lot more patience with horses than I do with anything else.*

Vent

When all else fails, physically venting pent-up anger may be necessary: *I remember as a kid I was trying to get my horse to go through some trail obstacles and I couldn't get him to do it,* recalls Mary Fenton. *I got madder and madder and I finally got off and jumped up and down on the ground screaming in frustration, flailing my hands until I was calm again. I got back on and he went right through the obstacles. It was important for me to get the anger out, but not to hit my horse, so I expressed it in another way.* Although seemingly out of control by screaming, jumping, and flailing, Mary had enough control to direct her rage away from her horse. Once her anger was released, she was able to cue her horse calmly and successfully through the obstacles.

Persuasive Manipulation

Fighting anger with anger usually creates more anger. Dr. Robert Miller discovered he could defuse a situation by refusing to fuel an already blazing emotional bonfire: *I am by nature an impatient person, and yet I know the worst thing you can do with a horse is lose your temper—that's absolutely the worst. By working with* horses, I have learned to enjoy manipulating their behavior—to bring them around to what I want them to do. So I started doing the same thing in my business.

When I had an angry client, instead of responding with anger, I'd say, "Tell me what the problem is," and I'd listen to their complaint. Then, even if they're completely wrong, I'd say, "I don't blame you for being upset," and I'd repeat everything they'd said about why they were angry. "You spent three hundred dollars trying to get this horse well, and he hasn't responded. You were hoping that after spending that kind of money you'd see your horse well, and he's actually worse...." Most of the time when I'd take this attitude instead of saying, "Well, just go somewhere else if you're not happy!" people would say, "Hey, I know it's not your fault...I know you tried." Then suddenly you've got them on your side instead of opposed to you. I learned this technique from horses—not to respond to another's fear or anger with the same emotion.

Later on I realized I could handle employees the same way. Unfortunately, it wasn't until after my kids were grown and away that I thought, "Why didn't I do this with my kids?" The thing that means the most to you is the last place you learn, because your emotions interfere with the thinking process.

I could work with strangers' horses and never lose my cool—never get upset, never get angry. Since I was forty years of age, there was no horse that could make me upset or angry—except my own. That's because with mine, I'd get emotional. As soon as you're emotional, you lose your capacity to reason. I have a saying, "Reason flies out the window when emotion steps in." It's hard not to be emotional about your own horse, your own dog, your own kids.... And because of the emotions involved, this is the last place we can apply this philosophy. But that's what horses taught me—to use persuasion rather than coercion. Horses have definitely shaped my life and made me a better human being...no question about it.

Recognizing that it doesn't pay to escalate an argument with a horse, Dr. Miller applied that conciliatory stance throughout his life with tremendous success. For even when we know we're right, combating emotional upset with emotional righteousness only fuels the flames of anger. Regardless of who is at fault in an escalating argument, it takes at least two parties to create a dispute, so conciliation may be the most effective route to resolution.

Personal Accountability

Being accountable for the consequences of our own actions—judging what works and what doesn't and then adjusting appropriately—develops a valuable personal assessment process. When we are able to monitor, assess, and modify our own actions responsibly, we increase reliability and may earn greater autonomy and respect: *If you want a horse to believe you're just, never, ever say, "You must!"* recites Monty Roberts. *If we could all stop demanding and allow people to be responsible for their own actions, we'd go a lot further.* Being personally accountable relieves those around us of having to assign demands or monitor our actions, and lays a foundation for dependability, mutual respect, and trust.

When things don't go as planned, people have a tendency to say, "It couldn't have been me. It's the stupid horse!" notes Larry Mahan. *People can come up with every excuse in the world, but the horse doesn't have to make an excuse—he's always right. Whatever he does or whatever he presents to us is an honest thought. The horse really feels this is what he has to do in this situation. So it's up to us to change the request—and it's nothing more than a thinking game—we ask again, a different way, until we're both right.*

Acknowledging our own culpability in a problem or dispute is difficult, yet it is the first step to success: *A couple of the players at my polo club were desperately trying to get their horses to do things right and make goals,* relates polo director and coach Susan Stovall (p.86). *They were blaming every mistake on their horses and everything else. But as time went on, and they became better riders, they accomplished the goals and it was like they saw the light! They finally realized what they'd had to do was to become better riders. When they could control themselves, they could control their horses, and then they were in control of the situation. It wasn't the horses that were at fault—* it was them. Only by focusing on the actual cause of a problem are we able to improve a situation. By deflecting blame, creating scapegoats, or refusing to accept responsibility, we hinder effective resolution.

Punishment

Misplaced blame most often leads to misplaced punishment: *I've been teaching a long time,* remarks Jane Savoie. *I've done a lot of clinics, and I've only once walked out on a lesson—in Connecticut, many years ago. I was working with a woman who had a tense, hot mare off the track. The woman was so frustrated, she kept punishing the horse hitting her in the teeth with the bit and hitting her with the stick until the horse was wild! I tried to appeal to the woman's logic and said, "Listen, I know you're frustrated and upset, but just think about it.... The more you punish your horse the more tense she gets, so it's counterproductive. It's not helping you, and it's not helping the horse." She looked at me and said, "But it makes me feel better." I realized then that she was beyond my help and told her, "Well, I can't help you," and I was outta there!*

When you take lack of self-control, emotions, and frustrations and abuse an animal, and that makes you feel good.... I just don't get it. Take a set of dishes and throw them against the wall if you want to vent, but don't vent on an animal! Rather than blaming the horse, you have to look to yourself and develop body and mind control in order to become a better rider and a better trainer. If you cannot control your body and your emotions, you have no business expecting that you can control a horse.

There are times when I do use power, but it's always short and sweet. If I do use strength, it's never to punish; it's always to educate. To get a point across...then it's gone. I'm not a bleeding heart; I do use a strong aid occasionally—but not in anger and not to dominate, only to educate.

We have a part and an effect in every relationship in our lives; thus we have a part and an effect in every reaction within those relationships. If we accept that we are personally accountable for a portion of each problem or argument that comes our way, we can start with ourselves in assessing the problem. That is the most productive starting point toward resolution—how can *I* begin to effect a change? If we are going to be fair to our horses, we must look in the mirror first. In doing so, we acquire a powerful tool in temper control and conflict resolution—personal accountability.

Retaliation

Revenge—delayed punishment—does not work with horses since they cannot relate a past action with a current retaliation. However, horses need to be justly reprimanded at the time of an error, or misbehavior, as a part of their training: *You should never work a horse when you're mad, but there are times when you have to work through a disagreement with a horse,* says Mary Deringer Phelps. *Horses have taught me to pick and choose my fights. I've learned to pick my fights just like I pick and choose my horses—I only pick the ones I can ride.*

Forgiveness

Forgiving a wrong is often the best gift we can give ourselves. Simply releasing the hurts, resentments, and demeaning feelings of revenge liberates us to a new beginning without the stress of harbored animosity. *Working with horses has taught me to always forgive my horse,* says Susan Stovall. *And people deserve that same courtesy. Everybody makes mistakes—everybody. Most people wouldn't have a job if mistakes weren't allowed. Learning this lesson of forgiveness has certainly helped me work with people.*

Skills for Success

I always refer to the horses at The Thacher School as members of the faculty, says Jack Huyler. *Our oldest son went from Thacher to Princeton, then on to the JFK school [John F. Kennedy School of Government at Harvard University] and was a Navy pilot for a while…and I'd bet he learned more value from his horse than from any other member of those faculties. Horses are teachers, and what they teach for boys, probably more than girls, is temper control. If you blow your stack, you reduce yourself to the animal's level and take him on brute force—155 lbs. against brute force of 1000 lbs? 1000 lbs. will win every time, so you've got to learn to use your noggin!*

Beyond the values of responsibility and personal commitment, we've seen that horses can help us develop the skills of an open, flexible mind that diverts frustration, lessening the frequency of angry outbursts. We can learn methods to control or deflect anger by accepting authority, turning away, changing the subject, or venting responsibly. We can change another's mind through persuasion rather than coercion—a powerful tool for negotiation and mediation. We learn to view problems from a position of constructive accountability, by first looking at our own part in it, then at other contributing factors which could lead to resolution. We use discipline as a tool to educate, not retaliate. And we learned that forgiveness can be a wonderful gift to ourselves.

So next time you're losing control and you're told to "Hold your horses!" pour yourself a tall iced tea and—starting with your own behavior—reflect on the situation, then transform your frustrations, resentments, and anger into constructive *HorsePower!*

MONTY ROBERTS, b. 1925, is a renowned trainer with world champion western and race horses to his credit, as well as a horse psychologist specializing in equine communication. His best-selling book, THE MAN WHO LISTENS TO HORSES, espouses humane training techniques. In 1997 he was awarded the Equitarian Award for contributing to the welfare of horses, and was named Man of the Year by the American Society of Prevention of Cruelty to Animals in 1998. Monty and his Quarter Horse, Dually, slide to a stop in competition.

MARY DERINGER PHELPS, b. 1940, is a hunter/jumper and equitation instructor who has trained a number of champion horses and riders in Texas and in Maryland. Named Trainer of the Year by the Delaware Horse Show Association in 1998, Mary is shown taking a fence at the Worton Park Equestrian Center on Dragonette, a Thoroughbred gelding.

HOLLY PETERSON MONDAVI, b. 1959, is an accomplished chef who began riding as a child and enjoys many aspects of equestrian life: jumping, trail, cross-country, hunting and competing. Most important to her are the friendships, laughter and wonder horses and riding have provided. Holly and her Thoroughbred gelding, Bacchus clear a water jump in fine form—an obstacle Bacchus consistently refused before teaming up with Holly.

Zaven Ayanian, b. 1934, real estate broker and land developer, is shown on Haji, the Anglo-Arab gelding that later became the author's daughter's horse. Zaven enjoys riding along the vineyards and byways of Napa Valley during casual weekend outings on one of his mounts. These quiet equine adventures provide Zaven with a respite from the fast-paced life of business and city living.

Charlotte Dicke, b. 1972, is a publishing assistant who began riding at five years of age and rode English until the spirited Peruvian Pasos won her heart at age sixteen. At nineteen, she began showing Peruvians and has won a number of championships and national titles. Charlotte is shown on La Mejia Negra RCR, aka Magic, after winning the National Champion of Champions Pleasure Mare title at the 1995 U.S. National Show in Santa Barbara, Calfiornia. Magic was a rescue case Charlotte's mother purchased as a weanling and who blossomed under the training of Julio Soto, Jr.

CHRIS HAWKINS, b. 1931, is a passionate horsewoman of Comanche heritage who was instrumental in winning the fight for the Wild Horse and Burro Protection Act of 1971 that legislated the preservation and control of America's feral horse herds. Still a dedicated equine advocate, Chris breeds and trains registered Quarter Horses at her Washington state ranch. She is seen here riding her Appaloosa, Khans Silver Tipper.

SUSAN STOVALL, b. 1945, is Director of Polo at the El Dorado Polo Club in Indio, California. She has won the United States Polo Association Governor's Cup twice—in 1984 and 1989, when her team won over 26 competing teams. She was on the winning team for the Women's International Polo Event in England in 1997. On her Thoroughbred mare Lea, Susan closes in for a shot during the Women's Challenge at El Dorado Polo Club in 1994.

CHAPTER FOUR

HEALTHY AS A HORSE

Therapeutic Riding and Fitness

The road to recovery is faster on horseback.

"Mom, I love you, but I can't go on. There's too much pain...and if I'm not able to walk...I'd rather die now."

Jene Kugler stared down at the gauze mummy in the hospital bed that was twenty-eight-year-old daughter, Carole Fletcher (p. 112). The formerly vibrant teacher had given up; this test was just too much for her—for anyone. For months, Carole had battled to survive after a pilot light ignited gasoline fumes in her garage, touching off a fiery explosion that turned her into a human torch.

The burns were excruciating...but the treatments were a prescription from hell. To combat fatal infections, every day the oozing, open wounds covering sixty-five percent of Carole's body had to be "debrided": while submerged in a stinging disinfection solution, old dressings were peeled off and wounds scrubbed to remove contaminants; then new dressings were applied. Even through a Demerol fog, the pain was agonizing.

Always petite, Carole's normal weight of 105, fell to a life-threatening 68 pounds. Now, upon hearing the doctors' concern that severe ligament damage and the taut rigidity of grafted skin on her legs would probably make it impossible for her to walk, Carole had lost hope. The image of life as a scarred, disfigured cripple was too much to bear...and too little to fight for.

Jene understood her daughter's decision, but she could not give up....

The next morning, upon wakening, Carole saw that her mother had hung a new picture beside the bed—a poster-sized photo of Carole's Palomino, Bailey, with a banner that read, "He will carry you."

Carole smiled, suddenly realizing that even if she couldn't walk, she could still ride. At that thought—with tears in her eyes and new hope in her heart—she steered her life back onto the road to recovery.

After seven months in the hospital, thirty-six surgeries, and three grueling years of physical therapy, Carole was able to coax her body into functioning on its own. As soon as she could, Carole returned to the barn, where she found security since the horses didn't stare at her red scars like people did.

One day, a Pinto horse with glassy-blue eyes and a pale pink nose was boarded at the barn. "Well, you're a different looking guy, aren't you?" Carole chuckled as she stroked his spotted neck—then a thought struck her, "I'm different looking, too; maybe we should get together...." Carole bought Dial and rode him daily—stretching, suppling, and strengthening her legs until she could walk unaided.

She also trained him to perform tricks. A quick study and to-tal ham, Dial learned a repertoire that inspired Carole to show him for entertainment. Pride in her horse and her own training abilities prompted Carole to overcome the stigma of looking different. Thus, one horse inspired Carole to get well, while another got her on stage—front and center!

The communication between Carole and Dial was so special

that people began asking her for help with their own horses. Today, Carole is a busy trainer and trick-rider with a video out and a book in the works. Although the accident left indelible marks—patchwork scarring on her arms, legs, face, and torso, and limited use of her distorted left hand—what is most evident in Carole's smiling face is the determined, grateful spirit that gave her the strength to heal physically and emotionally. Her beloved Dial is gone now, but his legacy lives on in Carole as she performs with Night Train, her current "different looking" partner.

Riding Therapy

Science has yet to measure the strength of human willpower, but as Carole's story illustrates, when therapy is combined with hope and willpower, medical wonders do take place; add to that equation a good dose of *HorsePower!* and the results can be miraculous.

National Center for Therapeutic Riding founder, Bob Douglas (p. 113), understands the preceding formula intimately: *At the time I bought the stable, I had never seen a therapeutic riding program. An organization had started in Michigan, around 1970, but it wasn't national. I came up with our program really on my own. I knew with the stable I could do two things: teach normal riders the basic skills in riding, and begin work on strengthening my legs, stomach, and back muscles [weakened by multiple sclerosis]. I also became mobile: I could ride through the park if I wanted to. On a horse, I did not feel like I was handicapped at all.*

Recognizing the many benefits of riding as therapy, I found some money on my own and did a pilot program. I wanted to study established classes of learning disabled to show a correlation in their academic improvement. I fought to get the schools to try the program for about a year and a half, but they just could not conceive of a learning relationship between horse and man, and certainly not between horse and a disabled individual. Because of my scientific background, I real-

ized that what I needed to do was to measure the improvement. We worked with three different types of disabilities: twelve young people who were disabled from having muscular dystrophy and cerebral palsy, twelve young people who were emotionally disturbed, and twelve children from ages six to twelve who were learning disabled. All came from a special education setting.

The program had the teachers using the horse as a vehicle for language skills, vocabulary, math, as well as physical skills. We did pre- and post-testing on all students: academic skills, perceptual skills, ability to make judgments, muscle tone, muscle strength, and balance; to see specifically if the act of horseback riding was the vehicle for their improvement or not. We found that self-esteem and confidence improved right away, and their academic progress was so incredible that most of them could mainstream back into regular classrooms. When I went back to the school district with actual test results and teacher reports I asked, "Look. This is what I have here, what are you going to do?" They were so impressed, they said, "We have five hundred students you can start with...." When it rains, it pours!

We developed a curriculum with a basic goal to improve the students' academic standards, self-confidence, and self-esteem so that they all can become productive citizens. It's not just a matter of putting a student on horseback—all of our instructors are certified therapeutic riding instructors—horseback riding really is their second therapeutic training.

When I first became ill and started regular physical therapy, I never wanted to do it because I felt handicapped, and felt like I was being forced to do things I didn't enjoy, Bob recalls. *Now I ride every morning, seven days a week, even though I'm in pain—severe pain—I still ride everyday. It's something I want to do. It hurts, but I know it helps, and I enjoy doing it. So now my therapy is my daily recreation. I can see that same feeling reflected in the young people in our program...their eagerness to change is there. Especially students who are emotionally disturbed—their whole attitude changes when they are here. When you have enough positive attitude changes, soon it becomes permanent because you begin to like yourself more.*

Another interesting aspect of our program is that we get the actual classroom teachers involved in the program. Most of these teachers have never been on a horse either, but are mounted with their class. They go through the same fears and anxieties that a student goes through. As a result, the relationship between the teacher and students begins to balance out. With that shared experience, the communication gap closes. Those students now have something to speak to the teacher about in a positive manner, knowing that the teacher will understand. So there are a lot of positive things that go on.... And here we are today with probably the largest program in the United States.

Bob Douglas continues, *One young lady in our program is blind as a result of childhood diabetes, and has adapted by counting off strides so she knows roughly where she is in the ring. She's now jumping between two-and-a-half and three feet with total confidence. Total confidence. Whatever takes place, whatever communication is going on between her and her horse feeds that confidence...I swear that the horse knows that she's blind! I really believe that's true.* The literal leap of faith that jumping blind represents requires courage and partnership that is hard to imagine!

At a benefit for a handicap riding program, relates trainer and clinician Richard Shrake (p.114), *I watched children who were like rag dolls—they couldn't move until they were put on the back of a horse. Then, all of a sudden as they were led around the ring, boy, the smiles and the relaxation on those kids' faces! At the end of the day, the therapists asked if anybody else wanted to ride...and one father brought his daughter over. She was about eight years old, could not raise her hands any higher than her shoulder, and had never said a word in her life that anyone could understand. She would make noises, but she couldn't make words. The father brought his little girl over to the mounting platform where an old rawboned horse stood waiting. This horse was a renegade from a bucking string originally, but now, with many years of training on him, his special qualities fit this handicapped riding program. That day, this old horse was magic.*

Her dad was helping to put her on, but when they just about had her on this horse, all of a sudden, he plucked her off, put her back in the wheel chair, and said, "No! I can't do this" and wheeled her away. Everybody looked around wondering, "Whoa! What went wrong?" It was kind of embarrassing, really, because he was real quick about it. He was so protective of his little girl that he wasn't going to trust this horse, or what was going on.... I watched the mother follow them down to the car, and I saw her talk him into it, and they came back. He said, "Okay, I'll try this."

So the old horse went back in, they got the girl down in the saddle, and away they went.... He made one round, and just the rhythm of his walk, and absolute total patience and quietness, you could see this little girl start to smile. On the second round, this little girl threw her hands up in the air in excitement—something she'd never done in her eight years. Now here's the one that raised a tear in every eye in the place—the little girl looked right over to her dad and said, "Horse" and then "Dad"—the first two words she ever spoke. True story.... Now how could a go-cart or a bicycle do that?

A number of interviewees who had first-hand experience with therapeutic riding programs reported moving accounts, (similar to Richard's experience above, and Bob Douglas's related in LIVING WITH *HORSEPOWER!*) of autistic youngsters uttering their first word or first independent sentence while riding. These stories were so numerous that I could not include all of them. The very numbers intrigued me, and when I attended a lecture by, Temple Grandin, a remarkable woman who has written two books about her life as a high-functioning autistic, I asked for her thoughts on why so many verbal breakthroughs seem to occur on the back of a horse.

Dr. Grandin explained that autism is related to immature brain development that causes bouts of sensory scrambling or overload, resulting in a fairly constant state of flight-or-fight response, depending on the severity of autism. She noted that many autistics respond well to rhythmic activities such as swinging, swaying, stroking, and singing. She believes that the even rhythm of the equine walk soothes those over-stimulated sensory systems enough to effect a sensory calming that allows the individual an opportunity for connecting. Then, rather than rejecting the world around them, which is normally too chaotic or frightening to cope with, that connection, coupled with the special thrill of riding on the back of a horse, sets the stage for expression.

One beneficiary and advocate of therapeutic riding who has no trouble expressing himself is former Presidential Press Secretary, James Brady (p. 113). In spite of everything he's been through since being shot and suffering brain damage during an assassination attempt on President Reagan, Jim has managed to keep his sharp wit and Irish bluster: *There's nothing I hate more than an English saddle, says Jim emphatically. There's nothing to grab on to to keep your butt in those saddles. Bob Douglas is a real tough trainer, he hollers, "Your legs! You don't need to hold on to the saddle—use your legs!" Bob's tough because he's been there; he rode himself right out of his wheel chair, so he knows it's all for the better. I think if Bob had treated me like a cripple, I probably would have ended up riding like a cripple.* Thankfully, Bob Douglas knows how to bring out the best in his students: he sets the example of working hard to get results, so they do the same.

In 1984, two years after Jim Brady was shot, relates Bob, I went down and talked to his neurologist to convince him—not that it would work, but that hippotherapy would be safe for Jim to do. The neurologist was concerned because Jim had an open-head injury and if anything happened to him, he could be right back where he was before, or worse. I had to convince him, so I convinced him. In fact, the neurologist came and checked out the program.

When we started working with Jim, it took five people to get him mounted and to work with him; that went on for a couple of years. We are at the point now that normally just the two of us go riding together. It's incredible!

When you love an activity, even if it hurts, its rewarding. "No pain, no gain" is a truth Bob Douglas has lived with for more than twenty-five years now, but he and his many handicapped riders still appreciate the healing fun of horses.

Keeping Fit

The dude ranch guests hobbled around the dining hall after their first day on the range—so stiff they could barely walk, and so sore that they "...prefer to eat standing up today, thank you...." Riding is a full body workout that introduces you to muscles, joints, and parts of your body that you never knew you had: *I always read that horseback riding is second only to swimming for overall exercise because you move every muscle in your body,* notes Richard Shrake. *I don't know why the horse industry doesn't come out and really tout that.* Perhaps because it sounds painful. Luckily, the pain normally subsides with each successive ride....

I hated horses from the time I was three until I was six because I had a wretched Shetland pony that threw me off every few minutes, declares Jack Huyler. *Then, when I was six I got a nice old horse—an escapee from the plow—and I've been a convert ever since. My whole family rode, so I rode.*

When I was playing football in college, we'd do rather vigorous calisthenics, but I never got stiff and sore like the other guys. I hadn't built up big muscles, like the boys who'd worked in icehouses in those days, but the jig, jig, jig, jig, of riding all summer kept my muscles toned and in good condition.

Unlike many activities that offer full-body involvement, riding is considered a low-impact type of exercise (as long as you remain in the saddle). Riding regularly strengthens and stretches muscles, bones, and joints without undue stress: *I can no longer ski or play tennis because of my arthritis and double knee surgeries, so I went back to riding,* equine sculptor Phyllis Eifert (p.115) reports. *Now I ride two horses a day and hunt twice a week. I'm riding more than ever before and I'm very happy.*

For years I was plagued with lower back muscle spasms that laid me up for weeks at a time, and even landed me in the hospital, in traction. Since I've taken up riding I haven't had a single episode. Now, I'm not claiming riding is a cure for back problems—many riders develop back problems—but for me, the actions of the walk, rising trot, and canter have suppled my lower back and strengthened my abdomen, which, along with reducing stress (which riding also does for me), were the recommended therapies for counteracting my back spasm.

When you think about it, there's really very little that normally takes place on the back of a horse that would hurt a person's back—provided you ride well—there should be minimal jarring, stress, or pulling. However, if you ride stiffly, are always out of sync with the rhythm, get thrown, fall off, or do extreme sports such as endurance and cutting when not in trained condition, all bets are off. I've yet to be hurt *on* a horse—only when I've gone *off!* Additionally, the work that accompanies horses—bucking hay, shoveling loads of manure, shoeing, hauling tack trunks—if not done properly, may cause back problems.

At any rate, you don't need the physique of Adonis and the power of Hercules to be a good rider—all you need is the interest: *I love sports and competition, but I did not get a great set of genes for athletics,* claims Stagg Newman. *I grew up loving sandlot football, but five feet, seven inches does not make a very good football player. I became a cross-country runner because I was too slow for anything else. One thing with riding, particularly endurance riding, is that you can perform at a high level and be very competitive even if God didn't give you a great body, because results really depend on the athletic ability of the horse and the brains of the rider. (My Arab, Drubin, would disagree with that!) Riding allows for a healthy mind and body, plus it puts me in touch with the non-analytic, non-logical side of myself, which makes me more of a whole person.*

A whole person: one who attends their physical, mental, emotional, spiritual and material needs, achieving a healthy balance in life. Riding is a part of that balance for many people: *Everyone needs something that they enjoy as recreation or a hobby,* says accountant Mary Mansi (p.115). *If you're all work and nothing outside of work, that's not physically or emotionally good; you need diversity. I know because I have been stressed out in my own business and it affected my health adversely, and I don't want to ever be there again. Riding has been an excellent investment for my overall health: it's changed the shape of my body as well as the state of my mind.*

As a recreation, you're guaranteed a playmate: *Riding gives me something that I love to do that's **active**,* notes Mary Fenton. *Riding is always with someone—even if there's not another person there—it's a relationship. It's also cerebral—it peaks my interest. Riding encompasses the physical, the mental, and the spiritual and they all mesh in balance. I love to do artwork too, but I find that very isolating. Riding is companionable and I have someone else's attention—a soulmate at times.*

Once you're hooked, riding can be a great motivator to stay active, agile, and fit: *To me, horses are grounding and rejuvenating; they provide me with refuge and joy,* explains Macella O'Neill. *I have gone through periods of my life without being involved with horses and riding, and my life was a shambles; just really not the way that I would want to live. It's good for me to be involved with horses on a daily basis because horses, riding, and competing are my incentive to keep myself physically and mentally well.*

I try to get all my students to not only do the stretching exercises of tai chi, but to pay attention to the philosophy behind it. It's incredibly helpful for anybody who rides well to get into a selfless, clear, kind of Zen state to really connect with the horse. I find riding as an art and a

*sport to be much more comparable to what I call an oriental orienta-
tion, instead of occidental thinking. There's a lot more give and take,
flow, cycles, interdependence, relationship, the whole yin-yang thing; as
opposed to the more rigid, structured, linear, adversarial orientations,
which are completely useless in riding. What separates great riders from
good riders is the ability to convey to their horses what they want, and
have their horses want to do it for them; such accomplishments are least
of all physical.*

Obviously riding provides exercise for both horse and rider,
and a healthy horse is a wonderful thing to see: *Our endurance
horses are happy because they're fit,* claims Stagg Newman. *Watching
these horses going down the trail—provided they haven't been over-
ridden—you see horses that are really enjoying being out there. A properly used working horse is a happier, healthier horse. A lot of our endurance horses live to very healthy ripe old ages.*

Conversely, just as with humans, an unfit horse is prone to
more ailments: *A horse that is not worked and has gone barn sour is
more in jeopardy for colic, muscles tying up, and neurotic habits,* notes
Pat Lawson. *A lot of horses begin to crib due to lack of exercise and
work. When a horse is worked regularly, and is fit, the horse is less
likely to be bored, and is going to feel better. So, it is best for the horse
to be exercised and worked regularly.*

Since the major role of horses in America shifted from the
transportation and work horses of the last century to the recreation horses of today, horse "work" has largely become human
sport: *I've had animal rightists challenge me and say, "Why do you do
this to your horses? Competitive driving is not natural for a horse,"*
reports world champion driver Jimmy Fairclough (p.116). *But I
can tell you my horses love their work; they wouldn't reach the level
they're at unless they loved what they're doing. On the other side, you
have the people who pamper their horses until they're nothing but fat,
lazy things in the back yard—nothing but couch potatoes, and that's
not right either.*

Being in condition and warmed up is as important for equine athletes as it is for human: *Cutting is really fun and it's incredibly athletic,* says veterinarian Dr. Patty Latham (p. 117). *However, horses, if they're not in just excellent shape and warmed up, can do damage to themselves, just like a runner. A cutting horse can snap a bone or pull a tendon from pushing off too hard. Horses have such incredible heart, it's sometimes too much for their bodies.*

It's up to their human caretakers to monitor the horse in order not to over-work, over-ride, or over-compete a fit and willing animal. With the growing empathy among horse trainers—the move from "breaking" to "making" horses—people are getting more and more tuned in to the animal itself for guidance: *My grandfather was the leading race-horse trainer in Moscow in 1905, with eighty-seven winners in Russia,* Linda Tellington-Jones relates. *He attributed his success to two things: 1) Every horse in the stable was rubbed after grooming with firm, short strokes all over the body to improve their physical fitness. 2) He never raced a horse unless it told **him** that it was fit enough to win. So I grew up with the concept of hands on horses and listening to them.*

The long-distance runners of the equine set are the endurance mounts. Like their human marathon counterparts, many of these animals develop a determined attitude along with their physical fitness: *Endurance riders have to stay pretty fit for distance riding,* notes equine photo-journalist and endurance rider Genie Stewart-Spears (p. 117). *So, in addition to riding, a lot of us run or bicycle because you actually ride a lot on balance rather than muscle. The major factors are being strong in mind and having perseverance. Perseverance is what gets the endurance team to the finish; the will-power to continue even though you're hurting or exhausted. I've been hurting on rides—excruciating knee pain—but I've learned to overcome it. And it's the same with the horse. Like my mare—at ninety miles on this one ride, it's one in the morning, and my Lord, we'd been going since six a.m.! You can't tell me that mare wasn't tired and sore* and wanted to quit; but because of her mental attitude, she never quit. There are horses that would just stop in the trail and refuse to go on.

I really love five-day rides where we're out in nowhere—only me and my horse—and we have to be able to deal with whatever comes. It's rejuvenating for the soul to go through this. People go off to meditate for days or weeks, and this is the same kind of thing. The importance of the bare essentials of life and how unimportant material things are. It comes down to your life and your horse's life.

Another aspect of equestrian exercise that surprises many newcomers is the amount of energy it takes. Although it may look like the rider is just sitting in a rocking chair, riding is not a passive activity. Depending on the horse and the discipline, it can be a major workout. Directing a fit thousand-pound horse through its paces, or controlling it over a course of jumps, requires balance, suppleness, strength, and lots of energy. A rider soon discovers that a healthy regimen is as important for himself as for his horse: *If you listen, horses are always teaching in the sense of taking care,* notes Anne Kursinski. *I think a lot of people don't take enough care of themselves; that's a problem today, lack of self-care. I know that I've learned a lot by taking care of the horses: their diets and their nutrition. By watching and paying attention to how they're eating, how much water they drink; watching their legs and their eyes; we take their temperatures every day. It carries over to my own life. I'm certainly smarter about what I eat than I used to be. Most of the horses that I know are taken such good care of; they're not only given carrots and apples, but bandaged and turned out in beautiful paddocks, groomed to death, given regular veterinary and blacksmith care—they're really pampered. That's why I love this sport for children; because you're always dealing with yourself as well as another living being, you learn a lot about caring and taking care.*

Longevity

Riding has many older enthusiasts. There is something about

the equine world that has the same effect as a cool draft from the fountain of youth: *I'm soon going to be forty-seven years old; and I have friends my age or a year older, who I have watched go from being young women to old women,* Pat Lawson observes. *Not only did they physically break down faster than me, but their mentality is older than mine.*

One friend who was riding with the Ebony Horsewomen got fearful of her horse and gave it up. I've watched that girl age from the moment she gave that horse up until today. Everything hurts on her now. She's got bursitis in her shoulders; her knees swell up; her feet swell. I look at that and think, "Even if I can't mount, I'm gonna get up there somehow; I'm going to ride," because I've noticed that riding has retarded the aging process in me mentally and physically. I tell you that's the honest-to-God truth. Without the zest of a passion in life, one can succumb to old age very quickly. We all need a reason for being, and a reason for doing, in order to keep going strong.

A fellow endurance rider, Maggie Price, calls endurance "the sport of the forty-year-old housewife": the woman who's looking for a sport and rediscovers her love of horses when her kids move out, Stagg Newman relates. *Our team to Holland in 1994 was the "Forty-Somethings." The youngest member turned forty just three days after the competition, so we were all in our forties.*

Maggie Price was sixty-one when she won her team silver and individual bronze medals at Barcelona in '92. The last hundred-mile ride I won in California, the woman who finished fifth (out of thirty-some riders) was seventy-one, and her seventy-six-year-old husband was eleventh out of fifty riders in the fifty-mile ride. So you can see, this sport invites longevity.

Riding is a lifetime activity open to enthusiasts of both sexes and all ages: *I've been riding seventy-two years, and still am riding—some competitively—mostly pro-horse competitions and gymkhana events,* reports Jack Huyler. *Riding and sailing, (and driving trotters, but I've never had the opportunity) are the only competitive things I can think of where an old geezer like me doesn't have to step aside for the young fellah; where increased know-how offsets your loss of alacrity. I can compete without concessions to younger people—golf, tennis, or anything like that, they have to give you handicaps. I can still ride as fast as the horse can run! That's why it's such a wonderful sport— you can participate almost all your life—and that's what means the most to me now. When I get on a horse, I'm still active. I'm still young when I'm on a horse—I think I am. I feel young when I'm on a horse. And that's more than half the battle; feeling young, capable, useful…however you want to describe it, it surely beats the alternative of surrendering to Father Time.*

So frequently I see people who are old, yet ride regularly and retain their youth and agility, observes Dr. Robert Miller. *I was at a farm bureau meeting recently with a professional horse trainer who's eighty-six years old, and still rides five to six horses a day—mostly colts in training—he's wonderfully agile, with a spring in his step. General Wayne Kester, who was chief of the US Army veterinary corps for many years, lived until his late eighties and rode three-hundred-sixty-five days a year. He stayed remarkably youthful! Ronald Reagan is another example that comes to mind. I don't understand it, but it's very, very common to see people who ride, and are in their advanced years, remaining youthful.*

One impressive story is of a horseman who not only rode into his sunset years, but trained at the highest level of equestrian competition until he was "called home": *My father, Ted Williams, was a professional horse trainer,* relates retired Olympic trainer and sculptor René Williams (p. 118). *When I was a little boy, back in the twenties, he had a bad fall on a high jumper and was unconscious for almost a week. When he recovered, the doctor told him "Ted, don't ride jumpers anymore; your heart isn't the best." Well, my father went right back riding. Dad did what he loved all his life, and never gave up. At a hundred years of age he was still training the driving part of the U.S. Olympic team! The Olympic driver, Jimmy Fairclough, was a student of dad's at a hundred. Dad was a marvel. He passed away just a couple of years ago at one hundred and five!* Ted not only outlived that doctor, but the doctor's children, and probably his grandchildren as well!

Perhaps no one will ever solve the equestrian conundrum: does riding foster good health, or does good health foster riding? Who can say for sure? Riding can promote physical, mental, and emotional fitness; yet there seem to be other intangible benefits that reward devotees with a vitality and sense of well-being that supports a long, active life.

Medical Practice

A critical part of horse care is veterinary savvy: implementing preventive medicine routines such as deworming and vaccinations, regularly checking your horse's condition, acquiring a sound knowledge of equine first-aid, knowing when to summon the vet, and diligently following directions for prescribed care. Much of this equine veterinary knowledge can be applied to human medical needs, and vice versa: *Because we're all mammals, horses can have almost everything you and I can have,* reports Rex Peterson. *I've seen a horse have a heart attack; I've seen a horse with hives; I've seen a horse with cataracts. Several years ago, I was brought a horse because the owners constantly had problems with him: this horse was thin, would not put on weight, and colicked at least every other day. From the moment you got him saddled, he was wringing wet. I messed with him for a month, and ended up buying him, because I had to figure him out. One day the vet and I were talking about this horse, and he said, "That horse has ulcers."*

I said, "What do you mean he's got ulcers?"

"You have them, don't you?" he replied.

"Yeah." I started listing symptoms I have, and this horse had all of them; so we went to grinding up Maalox. We fed him about twelve tablets a day, every day for a month. Once on the road to recovery, this

horse became fat and slick, got over the nerves, and became as good a riding horse as I ever owned. About six years after I sold him, I saw his owners and asked, "That horse ever colic?"

"Not since we've owned him." I couldn't believe it—ulcers!

From similar ailments to comparative anatomy, horses present many opportunities for learning about physiology, anatomy, kinesiology, and medicine: *I teach a lot of basic—not fancy—physiology; because if you don't know how the skeleton works, the joints articulate, and the quality of muscle, you can't understand how your body works,* states Sally Swift (p.114). *Any portion of your body that's locked, the horse will lock there too. If you have tight hips, your horse is not going to move his hips right; if you have tight knees, he isn't going to move his stifle right.... The rider has to learn first in order for the horse to move properly. I have people say, "Well, my horse did this, my horse won't do that...." And I say, "What about you?" Then I pull it out of them, we correct their problem, and they learn....*

Many advances in breeding, feeding, and conditioning; as well as preventing, treating, and rehabilitating injuries have developed through research by the Thoroughbred racing industry. There are a number of research projects studying endurance horses as well. Obviously, such research benefits the entire horse industry: *Endurance riding has probably contributed more to the body of knowledge about how horses and the equine metabolism function in competition than any other sport, due to all the vet checks that monitor the horses' conditions,* notes Becky Hart. *And I have learned a great deal about alternative treatments like massage therapy, cranial/sacral osteopathy, as well as the importance of exercising, stretching, and body awareness.*

Years of experience tending her horses has provided world champion barrel racer Martha Josey (p.119) with a more proactive attitude toward her own health: *Learning about my horses has been a wonderful education that's made me more aware of my own body. Now when I have something wrong with me, I'm often able to tell the doctor what it is.*

Martha has also learned to seek additional opinions, so as not to give up hope too soon: *I had one really great horse that had something wrong with his throat. I kept taking him to different vets over and over and over; finally at Texas A & M they found that he had something lodged in his throat. They got it out and he was fine. That showed me that if there's something wrong with a horse or a person, get several different opinions—don't give up. Keep asking, keep looking for the answer.*

Wild horse management specialist Ron Harding (p. 118) had a fascination with all things equine that inspired him to go on to college. It also instilled in him a lifelong habit of reading to gain knowledge that has served him and his horses well: *When I got out of high school, I swore I was never going to school anymore. But what got me to college? The bloomin' horses; because I wanted to be an equine veterinarian. As it turned out, I got my degree in wildlife, but I've probably doctored more horses than most vets due to the nature of my job with the wild horses. For me, horses are more than a career; my whole life revolves around horses, and that's caused me to read and study doctoring,* Ron explains. *That study has helped a lot; for instance with Dani Jo…a filly out of a mare of mine called Flash. It was just luck that I was there when Flash's baby started to come…. One foot came out like it's supposed to; I knew the other one should have been right there, but it wasn't. Flash had another contraction and that other foot came out through her rectum. It had gone through the ceiling of the uterus and the floor of the colon…and here I am, by myself! My wife had just left, and I couldn't raise anybody to help. I thought, "Jees, I gotta do something, or I'm gonna lose this baby." I tried to push the baby's foot back into momma, but it wouldn't go. Then I remembered reading: to right a colt in a bad position, wait until the mare lets off on the contraction. So I kept pressure on that leg and the minute she went off contraction, I shoved it back in, then with the other hand, went into the uterus and got it righted. The foot started out the track right, but with the next contraction, the foal's little ol' nose gets caught in the hole that was torn. Its head is being bent back and I'm trying to get it, and finally out of futility, I just grabbed the top of her vagina and pulled up. I had my finger over the foal's nose and out it popped. She starts wrinkling her little ol' nose and then I went ahead and delivered her. That was great—that was a good one! We got Flash sewn up and she healed completely.*

That story's been told so many times...not only did I learn from it, but it's taught a lot of other people to be prepared. That situation gave me a confidence, and it also made me study harder; because if you study harder, then you get more knowledge, and you're even more prepared. There's been a lot of veterinary science that I can relate to, so I'm able to deal with my health better, too.

I am not advocating that anyone act as their own doctor or veterinarian; obviously a trained professional is paramount for proper medical treatment. The point is that the experience gained through doctoring horses provides a better understanding of things medical, allowing an individual to address their horse's, and even their own health in a more responsible manner.

Healing

A true passion supplies a great deal of joy and energy to one's life, and can serve as a tremendous motivator: *I gave my brother a kidney in April and I wasn't supposed to ride until the next year,* reports Pat Lawson. *But that was absolutely impossible. I just couldn't stay away from riding that long. I started again in August.*

Another example of the healing powers of positive attitude and incentive is recounted by Martha Josey: *In June of 1982, I was thrown by a horse. My pelvis was broken in four places, and I had a badly broken right arm. At first the doctors said I'd never walk again— surely never ride again—but I won my first [post-accident] barrel race in September '82! I've had people call me and ask, "I've got the same kind of injury that you had, now what did you do?" My first thing is I learned how to enjoy what I was doing. When I was in that bed and couldn't get up, that's when I started writing horse articles, and think-ing about different things that I wanted to do as soon as I could get up.*

By providing herself with positive incentives to get well, Martha actually inspired herself out of bed. *The worst part was when I first started walking, because this was a very serious injury...and the first time I got on a horse it was pretty painful...but from then on it got better every day,* Martha recalls. *I think the exercise on that horse was good...we see that in so many of the special schools out there...they feel that horse moving under them, and it does so much good.*

But three month's recuperation was not a timetable that her doctors had envisioned: *No, it was unbelievable,* admits Martha. *The doctors were amazed. But I knew I was ready.....And I wouldn't have done it too early either, because I use quite a bit of common sense on that too. But I think that horse people can come back faster because riding does keep the body physically fit.*

Yet another word of caution: the above cases are not meant to promote the countermanding of doctors' orders. Both Martha and Pat were under the care of doctors who adjusted the timetables in light of their patients' remarkable rates of recovery. Are these medical marvels, or more examples of *HorsePower!?* I'd say, both.

I've had a lot of horses who've torn ligaments and suspensories, and I've done a lot of the slow work to bring them back physically: everything from icing, to handwalking, to swimming therapy, relates Jimmy Fairclough. *So I'm very aware of all the rehabilitation that has taught me caring, nurturing, dedication, and sticking to the pro-gram. I had a young horse tear my shoulder out twice and then I tore it a third time, wrestling. It had to be rebuilt, but now I have full range of motion in my shoulder. I did exactly what the doctor said. It was the same dedication to sticking with the program every day—not one day off—every day; just as with the horses. You'd be amazed how many times that dedication pays off.*

One of the most powerful weapons in the medical arsenal can-not be purchased or prescribed: it is the indomitable spirit of one who has the invincible will to recover. Add to that a passionate incentive, plus dedicated therapy, and medical mountains do get moved.

Preventive Education

Even if recuperation can be foreshortened by a healing desire to get back in the saddle, the best medicine is still preventative: a suitable mount, quality equipment, and a sane attitude. Whether it's a helmet, a saddle, breeches, or reins, every piece of tack and clothing should be appropriate, well-fitted, and in strong, serviceable condition to promote safe performance and prevent accidents caused by failure or hang-ups. While a high price doesn't necessarily guarantee quality, cheap equipment is never worth the price of the risk, so it pays to buy the best you can afford.

A novice rider also should avoid a cheap horse—the $150 range-bred mustang, or the $500 racetrack Thoroughbred are tempting only to the uneducated: *We get letters to the Journal [MICHAEL PLUMB'S HORSE JOURNAL] from people wanting to know how to space trotting poles for a three-year-old off the track,* reports veteran Olympic eventing champion Michael Plumb (p.120). *It amazes me how many people think they're stealing something by getting a young Thoroughbred off the track for $500 or $600. I just throw up my hands—where do you start talking to people like this—without being rude?*

Beware! *Horseflesh gets marked down for a reason:* untrained, unsound, or problem horses come cheap, while dependable, well-schooled horses are worth their weight in rubies. Unless you are a talented trainer, ignore the "bargains" and invest in a horse that can help you learn the ropes. You won't be sorry, for you'll progress faster, and when you're ready to move on, you won't have trouble selling a sound school horse.

As evidenced in a number of earlier accounts, one can get hurt on the gentlest of horses. With that in mind, protective headgear is now recommended—though not required—across the horse industry; there's even a helmet designed to accommodate a western hat. *A rider needs to learn to take care of himself, and the first thing is: wear a helmet,"* states Becky Hart. Such an ubiquitous safeguard reinforces the concept of safety equipment as a part of everyday life, indirectly supporting the use of seat belts, bike helmets, and other protective gear.

Proper Use of Equipment

Of course having quality equipment, proper tack, fitted habit, and a perfectly turned out horse are no good if you don't know how to use them. Proper technique is as important as proper tack: *Many, many people ask me what kind of bit or bridle to use for one problem or another,* says Monty Roberts. *I tell them the most important part of any bit and bridle are the hands that hold it. A perfect bit for overcoming a specific problem, in the hands of a fool, will not solve the problem; while the worst bit in the hands of a genius can still probably solve the problem.*

With all the various equestrian equipment and procedures, I am constantly reminded that know-how is critical, since guesswork can create real problems—just wrapping a horse's leg improperly may damage a tendon, and a seemingly harmless halter can prove deadly: *Believe me, when used correctly, a twitch is not a bad tool,* remarks Rex Peterson. *And used correctly, a halter is not a bad tool; but used incorrectly, I've seen horses die from them—caught on a tree or post and strangled when the halter won't give way. You name the tool and I can list its bad points as well as its good.*

Once again there is no substitute for experience and education.

Equipment Failures

Equipment failures on horseback can be costly and dangerous, so it's important that all gear be in *proper* working order before swinging into the saddle: *We were in the Pennsylvania mountains for Drubin's third fifty-mile race,* recounts Stagg Newman. *He had some heat bumps so I decided to change how I saddled. I added an extra foam pad and made the mistake of using a string girth that had been washed just before the ride and had shrunk. Drubin is a very round Arab, almost like a barrel, and I just couldn't get that girth tight on him. I kept trying, but the ride was starting, and it still wasn't tight enough. I knew we wouldn't be galloping until after the first checkpoint, and I thought I could cope with a little bit of a loose saddle until then. But a couple miles into the ride, we started up the first hill, and the saddle slipped back to Drubin's flank—the bucking strap position. He starts bucking like crazy and I go flying off looking for a soft rock to land on. Then the saddle rotated under him, and he goes berserk and takes off. (I discovered later, from his previous owner, that the same thing happened the first time he'd ever had a saddle put on him.) I go running after him thinking, "I've had this horse for less than a year, and he's a really good endurance prospect; now where is he?" Since it had rained, I was able to track him. More than three hours later, I found him standing in a stream, with the saddle still hanging beneath him— minus pads and stirrups. Drubin was afraid to move with his strange "saddle anchor" and was very happy to see me. I waded into the stream, got the saddle off, and saw that he was okay. I led him back to the starting point, which happened to be close to the midpoint of the ride. I borrowed a saddle pad and stirrups, rode out to the midpoint, waited for my wife to ride by, and rejoined the ride for the last twenty-five miles. But we didn't get our completion on that ride due to some minor technicality about missing miles three through twenty-five!*

Michael Plumb has a story about technique winning over tack: I was trying to get by without using a breastplate on my horse, so I put an overgirth over the saddle. *We set out fine, but had a bad jump about the sixth fence, and the saddle slipped. I thought we could make it, so we kept going. Then, at the third-to-last fence, the saddle slid under the horse's belly and I was riding bareback. We finished the course with the saddle between his hind legs and won the event!*

Once again we're reminded there are no guarantees in life or riding, and even the best quality equipment can fail: *I've never had a horse hurt me, but I've had equipment break and nearly kill me, reports Helen Crabtree. I was riding a very talented and very tough mare called Alla Magee, when I heard a pop like a pistol shot and part of the girth let go. I was thrown out to the side, hit a projection on the wall in the aisleway, and was dragged under the horse. She panicked, headed for the end of the barn, and I thought, "Well, I'm dead," figuring this crazy mare would trample me to death. Just then she stepped on my sternum with her hind foot and that held me to the ground enough that it tore the rest of the girth and released the saddle and me. I had five crushed ribs right up next to my spine, I was just a quarter of an inch away from breaking my spine when the girth broke through. It was a new girth, but it had faulty leather in it.*

This happened in the deep wintertime, which actually saved me, because I was bundled in heavy layers of clothes. I had on my brand-new, beautiful down jacket, and when I got to the hospital, the nurse said, "I'm going to have to cut this off of you." I told her, "Don't you dare! Take it off—I can stand the pain—but don't you dare cut up my new jacket." About the time we were arguing about the coat, the nurse at the other end of the gurney said, "I can't get her socks off." And I explained, "That's because they're pinned to my long underwear." With that we all started laughing. Now one thing in life you do not want to do is laugh with five broken ribs! But I got to laughing, then crying with the pain, and then laughing again with tears streaming down my face. At that point, my neighbor who'd followed the ambulance from my house, arrived to check on me. She walked into the emergency room just as this all erupted and got very upset. She thought everyone was hysterical because I was in the last throes of dying—but we were just laughing! That was years ago, and to this day we still laugh about it. Another thing I learned from that experience is where the sternum is; I'd always thought you sat on it, but you don't; it's in the front of your chest!

Skills for Success

Through the many moving tales of improved health and happiness, we've seen that riding offers therapeutic, fitness, longevity, and healing benefits to anyone who cares to sit a horse. Working with horses presents opportunities for "medical practice" through exposure to veterinary care, often motivating individuals to pursue careers in the fields of science or health. It also promotes a mindset for preemptive safety measures to avert illness and accidents. And finally, riders learn the value of quality equipment for enhancing performance, and develop a pride in its maintenance, as well as their personal turn out. All these valuable health and safety benefits promote personal strength and welfare—through *HorsePower!*

CAROLE FLETCHER, b. 1947, is a former teacher with a masters in education who suffered burns over 65 percent of her body as a result of a devastating accident in 1976. Driven by a desire to return to riding, Carole survived her ordeal and became a well-known trick-rider and trainer. She is shown with her Pinto gelding, Dial, in 1988.

BOB DOUGLAS (right), b. 1933, was a successful research biologist
who helped develop a vital screening process for rubella in women at
the National Institutes of Health. In his thirties, he contracted multiple
sclerosis and was forced to make a career change. He founded
the National Center for Therapeutic Riding in 1972 and serves as
executive director, providing therapeutic riding to hundreds.

JAMES BRADY (left), b. 1940, former Presidential Press Secretary,
received a debilitating head injury when shot by John Hinckley during
an assasination attempt on President Reagan in 1981. Since then Jim
and his wife, Sarah, have successfuly lobbied for handgun control.
Recipient of the Lincoln Award for being a National Hero, Jim
attributes a good part of his remarkably successful rehabilitation to his
equine partners such as Birney, shown here with Jim, Bob Douglas
and Blue enjoying a truly therapeutic walk in the park.

RICHARD SHRAKE, b. 1944, is a professional trainer, instructor and judge whose resistance-free training methods have produced national and world championship horses and riders.

SALLY SWIFT, b. 1912, master riding instructor, developed the innovative and highly effective Centered Riding techniques by combining clear visualization techniques with her knowledge of anatomy and kinesiology that resulted from her lifelong education to counteract the physical effects of scoliosis. Centered Riding makes riders aware of their bodies' actions in relation to those of their horse, thus promoting more relaxed and integrated interactions.

MARY MANSI, b. 1954, pictured on her Thoroughbred gelding, Magic, after a relaxing hack, is a certified public accountant who took up riding at the age of 37 and was hooked. She soon became a horse owner, then a multiple horse owner, and learned to jump. Mary credits horses with enlivening her life and teaching her many wonderful lessons.

PHYLLIS EIFERT, b. 1929, is a painter, sculptor and avid rider since the age of six. She has raised ponies, was a horse-show mother for nine years, and currently rides with the Tryon Hounds in North Carolina. Here, Phyllis and her gelding, Mountain Man, are ready for the 1997 Thanksgiving Day Hunt.

Jimmy Fairclough, b. 1958, as President of Fairclough Fuel Co., a World Champion competitive driver, and involved family man, Jimmy enjoys success in many arenas. At the 1991 World Pair Driving Championship in Austria he claimed an individual fourth and the USET Team Gold Medal. Jimmy is shown navigating a course with Jane F. Clark's handsome foursome of Cordon, Taro, Jeffry, and Mambo at the 1996 World Four-In-Hand Championships in Belgium.

PATTY LATHAM DVM, b. 1947, runs a successful veterinary hospital with her veterinarian husband in California. Patty's equine experience predates her veterinary exams—she's been raising, showing, barrel racing and cutting with Quarter Horses since she was eight. Here Patty, 13, naps with her yearling, Lillie Too, a gift horse from the rancher Patty had worked with in Missouri. Lillie and Patty shared an active 23-year partnership during which Lillie accompanied Patty to vet school and later became her children's beloved school horse.

GENIE STEWART-SPEARS, b. 1950, is an equine journalist, photographer and endurance rider who has covered many of the highlights of endurance competition. She is shown with Heatzon, an Arabian she bred, trained, and competes in 50-mile endurance rides. Genie's other competition horse, Commanders Lory, is a Saddlebred/Foxtrotter cross that carried her to 13th place in the 1994 National Championship Series and captured first place in the lightweight division of the rugged 5-day, 285-mile New Mexico Renegade Endurance Ride in 1994.

RENÉ WILLIAMS, b. 1916, grew up in a famous horse-training family and has seen tremendous success throughout his career in a variety of disciplines: jumping, hunting, showing, racing and breeding. He was a trainer for the U.S. Olympic teams for many years at Gladstone, N.J. and after his retirement became a self-taught equine sculptor of international acclaim. René is shown in 1975 working on a scale model for a life-size sculpture of the racing champion, Kelso.

RON HARDING, b. 1938, is a horse trainer, breeder and wild horse management specialist. He started with the Bureau of Land Management in 1974 and became Wild Horse Coordinator and Specialist for Oregon and Washington from 1982 until his retirement in 1996. In 1977 he gathered the Kiger Mustang herd and helped establish the Kiger Mesteño Association. Ron and his Registered Quarter Horse filly, Dani Jo, prepare for the stock horse halter class at the 1994 Harney County Fair.

MARTHA JOSEY, is a world champion barrel racer, renowned clinician and V.P. of Josey Enterprises who exudes success. Career highlights include being a National Finals Rodeo contestant in four consecutive decades on eight different horses, winning both the American Quarter Horse Assocation (AQHA) and Women's Professional Rodeo Association (WPRA) World Championships in the same year, capturing an Olympic medal and the National Barrel Horse Association (NBHA) World Champion. Here Martha rides Orange Smash at Augusta Georgia where they won the 1997 NBHA World Championship, Senior Division and Reserve Championship in the Open Division.

MICHAEL PLUMB, b. 1940, is a trainer and three-day eventing champion who holds the U.S. record for selection to the most Olympic teams: 1960 in Rome with his horse Markham, 1964 in Tokyo on Bold Minstrel, 1968 in Mexico City on Plain Sailing, 1972 in Munich with Free & Easy, 1976 in Montreal, where he won an individual silver medal and a team gold on Better and Better, 1980 Fontainbleau alternate games on Laurenson, 1984 in Los Angeles with Blue Stone, and 1992 with Adonis in Barcelona. Michael and Count Trey make a splash as they clear the timber.

CHAPTER FIVE

BRINGING UP BABY

Parenting Skills and Discipline

Hittin' a horse makes him smart, not smarter.
— *©L.D. Burke III*

"As I turned the corner I saw him standing there. His dark complexion glowed and his long ebony hair blew in the cool breeze. Although I was only in sixth grade, when his eyes met mine, I knew we were destined to be together. During that first encounter, emotion and warmth filled my heart, and I knew something special would develop. Over time we came to know and trust each other, and accept our obvious differences. He became a vital part of my adolescent life; a large part of my maturation and preparation for life was a direct result of my relationship with Bruce.

Our partnership evoked new and exciting feelings, emotions, and values. I soon developed a strong sense of honesty, self-confidence, and accountability—all invaluable life-long skills. Then, as with any relationship, priorities had to be established and personal sacrifices made so that our relationship would work. On many occasions, my friends would go off on carefree adventures and I had to decline in order to be with Bruce, but I learned that not all life is carefree and immediately rewarding. I discovered that in real life there is the "down and dirty" and realized no job was too small or too distasteful to do when needed. Finally, my relationship with Bruce helped me manage my schedule so that I could optimize both my schooling and extracurricular activities.

I wanted to be a good friend and partner to Bruce, but the process was slow and often arduous. Learning to deal with our different personalities was extremely difficult, yet those situations resulted in my paying more attention to my inner voice and changing thoughts, and gave me a chance to acquire conflict resolution skills, building the background for good decision making. Perhaps the toughest challenge for me was when, and when not, to compromise my ideas and ideals. Eventually, Bruce became my "best friend."

Bruce and I constantly faced new and risky challenges and obstacles—both mental and physical—like the time Bruce and I had worked long and hard on a project, but the day of the event Bruce did not come close to fulfilling my expectations of him. Despite such disappointments, we did experience some glorious triumphs that far surpassed my expectations. Over all, "challenge" was probably the most common word to define my life with Bruce.

I became aware that life and relationships cannot remain constant…. Both Bruce and I were changing. By the end of my freshman year in high school, it became obvious that it was time to terminate our relationship. Suddenly, I had to say good-bye to a part of my life, and had to face losing my best friend. Even now, three years later, I visit Bruce. Obviously, our relationship is not the same, but I owe a great deal of happiness—now and in years to come—to the time we spent together. Bruce was my first horse."

This remarkable example of insightful adolescent maturing was excerpted from the college application essay of sixteen-year-old California student and rider, Dede Marx (p. 146). It's a valuable dividend paid to Dede's parents for their investment in *Horse-Power!* by the name of Bruce. The admissions committee also saw merit in that mutual investment, for Dede was admitted to her first choice school—the University of San Diego.

Forming the Mold

There is much to learn about raising a child from the process of working with horses. The first salient point is that each—horse and child—are separate and distinct beings, not possessions or clones to be bent to a guardian's will: *Because horses obviously have a different perspective than I do, I have learned to compromise to accommodate both our needs,* remarks vintner and show jumper Sarah Hafner (p. 146). *Through that training, I have learned to listen to the needs of those around me—in business and in the family—because we each have our own viewpoints. Now with my children I say, "I understand where you're coming from, and it makes sense, and this is how we could compromise to make things go better." Learning that art of listening and compromise has been a definite life lesson for me.*

The greatest success in training and parenting is achieved by those who can recognize innate talents, then assist in developing that unique potential: *Getting reinvolved with horses has reaffirmed for me that the best way to live is to find what you love and do it,* states pleasure rider and psychologist, Jenny Butah (p. 147). *That conviction also supports one of my major goals as a parent: to encourage my kids to follow their own path.*

Determining that personal path is critical, for when any being, human or animal, is forced into a discipline for which it has no heart, it cannot shine. Likewise, if pushed along the training path too soon or too hard, burnout or stress can kill youthful enthusiasm: *One of the biggest problems in horse training occurs when young horses are still growing mentally and physically, and we put too much pressure on them,* remarks Dr. Patty Latham. *Many of them develop a kind of "tension factor." Those are the ones that don't make it on the track or in the big futurities because they were pushed too young.* This same phenomenon is evident on playing fields across America when overzealous parents push their children into stressfully competitive situations. The real trick in training and parenting is to assist in determining the individual's aptitudes, then supportively allow each to develop to his best ability.

Retiree Bobby Christian (p.147) has no children of his own, yet his spotted hackney ponies attract eager young helpers to his barn where he generously passes on his knowledge of driving and horse care: *I don't push work down their throat, I make them want to do the work,* says Bobby. *Kids'll play ball 'til they're bloody and don't get paid a dime! When they're doing what they enjoy, their reward is in "Look what I can do!" Finding what your child loves to do—even the child within you—that's the answer. Don't be reluctant. Don't think you're doing the wrong thing. If it's a passion within, go forward—some good will come out of it. It's amazing the different things that people like to do.*

As noted earlier, there are no "universal horse training tactics," since what works for one horse doesn't necessarily work for another. Recognizing that same individualism holds true in children; a parent benefits by adopting the creative mind of a trainer: *We never had any problems with our children in terms of going to bed and staying in bed because my husband and I decided that we were not going to fight the traditional battle,* Octavia Brown explains. *Our daughter, who's borderline hyperactive, was allowed to run around the dining room table—lots of people raised their eyebrows. She was perfectly happy, but she needed to work off energy. She would be in constant motion and then all of a sudden, there would be silence and she would be asleep in the corner of the room. Whereupon, one of us would pick her up and take her to bed, give her a kiss and a hug, and she'd be in bed until eight in the morning. Now you know, if we had fought the battle at 7:30 to say, "You must go to bed now and stay in bed." She'd have been up half the night. So we threw out all those rules that say you must have a set bedtime in favor of common sense, which said let this child get the energy out.* Rather than imposing a universal bed-time rule, Octavia acknowledged her daughter's need to release excess energy and employed a technique known to many riders— allowing her daughter to "free-longe" around the dining room until her energy "high" dissipated.

Parents should identify and honor each child's unique nature and abilities, and children must get to know their parents' true character: *When you're training a horse, you must be yourself to get the horse to feel who you are; and you must listen to the horse, to feel what the horse is,* observes Rege Ludwig. *If you can do that, you stand a much greater chance of developing a good unity. The most im-portant thing a parent can do is to live the example he would like for his kids to follow, which is essentially saying to be yourself. You can only respond well when you are yourself—you can't respond well when you are trying to contrive because there is too much control involved. When you are yourself, you relax, you flow, you're free and you move naturally with the situation. Therefore, when you are rearing your chil-dren, be yourself, and allow them to be themselves.* With such examples of individual authenticity, a child can become his or her own per-son.

In the course of developing their own talents, children may rely on teachers, coaches, and mentors outside the family. Some parents find it difficult to allow others into their children's lives without feeling resentful or jealous: *One thing that getting back with horses has shown me is my possessiveness,* notes Jenny Butah. *"That is MY horse. Do not touch MY horse without MY permission and what do you mean talking about MY horse that way?" All this stuff that I didn't know was lurking in my soul. I just realized a few weeks ago that all these people who wanted to help with MY horse were not trying to take my horse away from me, but were trying to support me with this horse. I can translate that with my kids now too. I can say, okay, MY kids can get help from other adults, other people—I don't have to be the sole model in their life. I've realized my children come through me, but they are not of me....* By recognizing her own possessiveness about her horse, Jenny came to understand that others can contribute to her horse's—or her children's—well-being without threatening her connection to them.

Finally, as children mature into their adult identity, parents have the ultimate (and often the hardest) parenting lessons to learn: they must step back, hand over the reins, and let each child go his own way: *When I moved to California to work with Glenn Randall, my dad was very upset,* admits Rex Peterson. *Because Glenn and I were so close, Dad and I didn't speak for almost seven years. It was a very, very hard situation, but we were a family that never really talked out problems between us. When Glenn passed away, Dad and I finally had a long talk and I told him, "I'm not mad at you...I love you dearly for everything you've done for me and all the things you taught me. I just have to live my own life." Then, when articles came out about me in major horse magazines, I told him, "This is for you, Dad. You put me back on that horse years ago, and made me get on horses I didn't want to get on—you made me the horse trainer. Glenn meant a lot to me, but Glenn was never my dad and never will be." I think that helped—sitting down and talking to him about things like that...it helped me. It's made me see that no matter how bad you think it will be, if you get it out in the open and get it over with, you can then forget it. It's been good for both of us.* Rex Peterson took the lessons of his youth and built an independent, professionally successful life that he loves—what more could a parent hope for?

Nurturing

The experience of caring for horses is valuable preparation for the responsibilities of parenting: *I know I'm a much better mother and grandmother because I took care of horses,* declares Mary Fenton. *When I was a kid I did competitive trail riding, and when I was done riding fifty miles, I was tired and would like to just plop down and relax, but my horse had to be taken care of first. The discipline of caring for the horse really carried over for me in a good way.*

One grows beyond the selfish focus of a child to the selfless concerns of a caring guardian: *I guess it's the feminine motherly thing in me, that makes me like to take care,* reflects nineteen-year-old student Tina Schuler (p. 148). *To know that this horse depends on me and I'm there helping it: I'm feeding, grooming it, and taking care of it. I went to a horseback riding camp for six years. We lived in tents and got up early every morning, got our horses from the pasture, took them down to the barn, groomed and fed them—then we could go to breakfast. We rode during the day, made sure the horses got lunch, and then at night, we gave them dinner, groomed them, cleaned the barn, and put them out to pasture. That was such a great feeling—taking care of these horses—that definitely gave me a sense of responsibility, like I can't be selfish because I have responsibilities for other people, and animals....*

The long hours and conscientious care required of the horse owner relate directly to the intense schedule of a new parent: *When my first child was born, a friend told me, "Oh, your life is going to change now—you can't go away and you can't do this, you can't do that—you've got to worry about home,"* laughs Jimmy Fairclough. *I assured him, "I've been doing that a long time now." With all the horses in the barn, I can't leave—I've got to be there for them, so I was already prepared for that lifestyle. The all hours of taking care of the animals—children are the same way—both are a never-ending-twenty-four-hour-a-day job.*

Within that never-ending-twenty-four-hour-a-day-job is found a payback of symbiotic relationship that sustains the devoted caregiver as well as the dependent: *My babies are all four legged,* states Chris Hawkins. *But caretaking and nurturing come as much from them as it does from me. We do it for it each other.*

It is that personal payback that creates the mixed emotions

when, for whatever reason, our job as caregiver is over: *When I no longer had horses, I had an extraordinary feeling of sadness as well as a feeling of relief,* recalls Diana Cooper. *When you're going out there at six in the morning and bashing the ice out of the buckets at ten below zero—everybody would rather not do that—but you do it because you're responsible for that animal. That notion of being responsible for somebody else's life may be foreign to many people…but a child who's really been responsible for a horse day in, day out, knows something about what is required of a person who is responsible for another crit-ter—regardless of species—and it's really, really hard. When it's done right, horsemanship demands a clarity of intention that is good in deal-ing with anybody—I've just brought up my children to be good dogs and good horses—I don't know anything different about children.*

Parenting

Successful partnership with horses teaches a great deal about family relations: *I know I'm a better parent because I was around horses,* says Mary Fenton. *I understand that things have to go step by step. I was divorced, not very rich, and scared by the responsibility of suddenly being a single parent. I remember saying to my kids, "Now it's just me and you…we have to tell each other the truth, we have to depend on each other and be a team. If we don't, we won't be able to stay together. In order to be strong as a family, we need truth and trust." I relate that understanding directly to my life with horses. You need to trust your horse, and you must be just and truthful with him in order to gain his trust—then you can become a strong team. It's a personal responsibility and a mutual accountability relationship.*

Sarah Hafner concurs: *The patience, flexibility, and compromise I've learned through being with horses have made me easier to work with in our family business, and more understanding as a mother.*

Just witnessing the special relationship of mare and foal can produce valuable parenting lessons: *When my mare, Easter Bonnet, foaled, my children were four and six years old,* notes veterinarian, anthropologist and author Dr. Elizabeth Lawrence (p. 148). *She was just a marvelous mother; her colt was a little bit impish, and tended to bite, nip, and do things that she never did. Now I was a patient mother, but seeing her being so patient with her foal—patience with a capital "P"—I was very, very inspired.*

Horses can be a full family involvement, allowing parents and children to share hard work and special times: *As a result of learning gentleness, compassion, and responsibility from the horses, and then sharing that experience with my children, I'm a better parent,* claims Mary Deringer Phelps. *There are so many sports that parents and kids can't do together, but horses the whole family can do. Our horses were babysitters for my youngest, Devon; while I was mucking stalls, she was sitting on a horse in that stall, so I knew where she was. Devon and I grew up together with the horses...now she's all grown up, but I'm not....*

Occasionally a horse arrives complete with babysitting credentials that attract children like a four-legged Mary Poppins: *Some of the best babysitters in the world are horses,* says cattle rancher, Allan Jamison (p. 149). *We had one old horse here when my daughter, Lila, was just a little kid. Lila'd go down to the barn with just a string, that old horse would hold her head down, and get the string around it. Lila would lead her over and climb on the gate there in front of the barn to get on her and ride her around—sometimes with nothing on her even. That horse was a mare, and they can be ornery, but I believe she knew it was just a kid on her.... Now, I've also seen some horses that you put a kid on its back and they just panic, so I'm always really careful about taking a small child and just sticking it on a horse's back—you need to know the horse.*

Again, there are no hard and fast rules around horses, but many have witnessed a remarkable equine gentleness around young ones: *My children all grew up with our pony, Yankee Doodle,* recalls Phyllis Eifert. *He pulled a little antique trap cart and we had the best time on picnics and treks; the children all learned to drive the cart. It was the most wonderful way to raise children. Yankee Doodle was gentle—didn't bite, didn't kick—but he had a will of his own, and he could open any door. He hated to be penned up; he'd slip rails on the fence, get out and let the other horses out. Occasionally he'd let himself into the house when the children were having breakfast, so they'd pour him some cereal and he'd eat in the kitchen with them. He was a marvelous babysitter and one of the best experiences of our lives. The children learned a lot of lessons from that pony, and so did I: we learned about feeding, harnessing, cleaning tack, organization; in addition, that pony taught all of us about patience, tolerance, freedom, self-determination, kindness and love—quite a lot from just one little pony. When he died I remember thinking, "He's probably very happy because there are no fences in heaven." I've planted lots of flowers on his grave.*

Child Training

Horse training and parenting skills go exactly together, notes William Steinkraus. *When Sonny Jim Fitzsimmons, renowned trainer of five Derby winners, was asked, "What do you do with young horses?" He answered, "You bring them up the same way you do young children: give them a lot of love and don't let them get away with anything." That's a pretty good prescription for parenting and training.*

Many such training tenets are as effective at home as they are in the arena: *I've taken the positive feedback practice from my riding lessons home to my kids,* says Jenny Butah. *You can really see a horse respond to a verbal reward rather than to criticism. Kids are the same way—it's important to praise and reward rather than criticize—always end on that positive note.* Such a simple idea, yet so rewarding for parent and child. Imagine if parents took the attitude that all interactions with their children must end on a positive note—what a different world this would be!

Working with horses offers practice recognizing that bad *behavior* does not mean bad *character*. Many parents would benefit from such a balanced perspective on discipline—learning to address bad behaviors while still loving the child: *I've raised three generations of kids and I used exactly the same skills in parenting as I do training a horse or rider,* says dressage coach and author Jill Keiser Hassler (p.149). *I ended up getting divorced, but even my ex-husband says I was really good at raising children, and that's directly because of my work with horses. There are a lot of correlations with child rearing. If you can learn to communicate with a horse, you can communicate with your children, with patience and tough love. To me a strong half-halt with a horse is tough love; you let the horse know what you want done, expect him to do it, and when he does, immediately love him regardless that he bucked through the first corner. You correct the bucking and say "No" very firmly and then as soon as you finish the rest of your pattern successfully, you say, "Aren't you wonderful!" I deal with teenagers right and left and I know it's very hard for a parent who is mad at a child just caught stealing in the local store to reprimand that child and then love him equally as much as they were angry with him. But that ability—that tough-love factor—is one of the most significant parenting skills horses have taught me.*

As noted previously, a confused horse becomes agitated and cannot perform correctly; in order to obtain proper results, simple, clear requests are essential. This is also crucial when dealing with our own children: *One of the beautiful lessons for people who tend to be nebulous or unsure is that in order to get a horse to do things you have to be clear in what you ask them to do,* notes Linda Tellington-Jones. *And the same holds true with children—they are much more apt to perform successfully when shown the process or given a set of specific instructions, rather than a general request to, "Clean your room." That's like telling a horse, "Go!"—you get action, but it may not be exactly what you wanted.*

Along with that essential clarity, consistency and self control are prerequisites to successful discipline: *Just as with training horses, you have to break things down in small enough pieces for kids to learn from,* remarks Dennis Marine. *You don't just throw them an encyclo-*

pedia and say, "Memorize this, I'll ask you questions tomorrow." You teach it a paragraph at a time. And you have to be consistent. If there's a time when the kid's doing something wrong, but you're too busy to deal with it, so you ignore it; then the next day, you get all upset and whip his butt for it, there's no consistency.…You're gonna scramble his mind…just the same as with horses. You need to take the time every day to do it right, and do it consistently.

You can avoid battles with your horses (or your children) by setting up the situation so that the desired response is one the horse (or the child) would choose voluntarily. *Choice is real important,* agrees Maxine Freitas, therapeutic riding instructor and founder of the EquiEd riding program (p.153). *Whenever I'm working with adolescent kids, I give them the power to make a choice between two appropriate alternatives: do you want to muck the stall, or do you want to clean the tack? They will choose one of those things because it's part of what is expected, and they're more willing because the choice was their's.* A request through choice is more apt to elicit cooperation, while demands may cause resentful resistance.

Another master horseman who has made effective use of horse psychology at home is Larry Mahan: *The parallel between developing young horses and raising children is so closely related that it constantly amazes me. When my seven-year-old, Eliza, is trying to pull something off on me, I just think back to how I deal with a horse. Instead of raising my voice and demanding, I'll come up with an approach to make her stop and change her way of thinking.*

In January of 1994, Eliza and I were out riding in Arizona. I was leading her on a gentle old horse and she starts begging, "Daddy, I can do it by myself. I can do all this. I can do it!" She talked me into letting her go. Well, her horse starts to trot and then goes into a canter—that kind of scared her—Eliza grabs the saddle horn and starts screaming and this old horse takes off with her.… Eliza fell off and hurt her arm. Scared me to death! When I got to her, she's laying flat on her back gasping for air, about half out. She finally comes around and gets up, screaming at the top of her voice. Thank God she wasn't hurt badly. I knew she was all right when the first thing out of her mouth was, "I hate horses!"

*That was a traumatic experience for both of us, yet I knew I wanted to change her mind about horses—from her side. So, I scooped her up and said, "Okay, honey, you'll never, ever have to get on a horse again unless you want to. When we get home, we'll sell Jock, and Frosty, and Buck." Suddenly from a screaming, "I hate horses!" came a kind of a thoughtful sob, "No, Daddy...I want to ride again, but not right now." All of a sudden, because she loves **her** horses, she realized that, "Whoa! Maybe I shouldn't have been so rash in making that decision." Now that new decision was hers as well—I didn't tell her, "You have to get back on and keep riding." I just agreed with her and planted a thought for something she wanted—by understanding the nature of the other, then making the right thing easy.*

Guided choice is a valuable process for training a young mind to consider factors beyond immediate gratification: *I owe a lot to my mother allowing me to find my own way. As a teenager, when I'd start going off on a tangent—more interested in partying—she would say, "Okay, if this is something you want to do, you need to make some choices,"* then *I would,* explains saddle seat champion, Camille Whitfield Vincent (p.150). *That was a lesson in maturity for me—to consider what I want in the long term, not just immediately. At times I didn't make the right choices, but even with that I learned "Okay, that wasn't a great choice, but what are you going to do...move on." I was really fortunate to have that unconditional support of my mother.* In this way, a child matures into that process, parents can gradually withdraw, confident that a viable decision-making mechanism is in place.

Chores

A common point of irritation between parent and child centers around chores—specifically keeping living spaces neat. This is another dividend of riding, for organization is essential in a barn for safety and sanity's sake. Horses, tools, and tack are cleaned and put away after each ride—a habit that is often brought home: *My two daughters were into riding and horses,* says René Williams. *At the barn, they felt free, happy, occupied, and understood. They also learned discipline without even knowing it: the grooming, the care, and orderliness eventually showed up in their taking better care of their rooms at home. It was wonderful.* Getting a job done is only one advantage of chores. Developing employable skills, learning accountability, focusing attention, expending energy, and productivity are valuable benefits as well.

One trainer has elevated the routine of mucking out stalls to a spiritual ritual, inspiring her students to habits of tidiness: *Another practical aspect of daily stall cleaning is that I do a lot of thinking while I'm doing that repetitive work—I call it "stall meditations,"* relates Mary Fenton. *I've found it's the day-to-day work that tends your soul. It gives me a sense of physical and mental order that my young students pick up on and amazingly learn to keep their own space in order. For many, keeping their rooms clean is a direct lesson from the barn.* Youngsters who work in the down-and-dirty-horse-world of mucking stalls and stacking hay, develop a tolerance for hard work that stands them in good stead in all areas of employment.

Keep Them Busy, Wear Them Out

With today's computers and labor-saving technologies, kid-power is greatly underutilized. Manual chores are fewer and considerably less strenuous than in generations past. Free time, excess energy, and an idle mind can lead to youthful trouble with a capital "T". But, plug a horse into that equation and suddenly a youngster's time and energy get used up, while his mind gets focused on a new purpose: *The mother of one of our students, Shane Hatch, said to me, "Horse kids don't have time to drag Main Street,"* remarks Martha Josey. *What with all the practicing, traveling, competing, then tending your horse, your equipment, and yourself, a horse-kid doesn't have much time left over for being bored or getting into trouble. After winning the Josey Junior Barrel Race here in 1988, Shane went on to win many high school roping titles, then won the College National Finals, and on to his first year of professional rodeo. He came by and spent the night with us recently and I've never seen a better twenty-year-old.*

When healthy but idle youngsters begin to stray, an effective tactic is to give them useful work until they're happily exhausted: *I've had some horses that would test your temper a lot,* notes retired harness driver Irving Pettit (p. 153). *The best thing is to keep them going up a hill or on soft ground until they get tired; then they're much easier to handle. Some harness horses get what they call "speed crazy"—they want to go too fast all the time. You have to teach them that they are supposed to go how you want to and not how they want to. I've jogged horses ten, twelve miles, before they'd slow down and get to understand that, but once you get through to them, you've got it done.* The same goes for the two-legged youngsters.

Most horses are trained one-on-one, and like the colt that tests your temper, youngsters may need individual attention in order to get focused: *Working with horses gives me an advantage of understanding people,* says Ron Harding. *I do a lot of public speaking before high school students, who sometimes tend not to want to listen. Say I've got forty young people and thirty-eight of them are paying attention with two of them sitting there asleep. Some people say, "Forget about the two." Well, being a horse trainer, I'm not going to forget about them—those two are my challenge. So I've learned some tricks. First I try to make eye contact and talk straight to them; but still, some will kind of smirk at you, you know, "You're an old fogey with white hair; you don't know nuthin'...." So I walk over and get in front of them and talk right to them—like it's them and me alone in the round pen.... I guarantee you they're not sleeping very long, and probably they're going to be the ones that learn the most. So there are little training tricks that help you through.*

Discipline

Our son Brooks broke a school rule in his sophomore year at boarding school and was placed on general probation for six months. Brooks accepted his punishment, but then worked hard to earn his way back to good standing. Yet at each review, the disciplinary committee kept extending probation, explaining that since a second infraction meant expulsion, they felt it was a good control measure. They held Brooks in check with that threat and never gave an inch. After two years, Brooks' sincerely contrite attitude had turned to angry resentment. He'd lost respect for the disciplinary system and hated the school: *That's a perfect example of authority without feeling, notes Richard Shrake. Pretty soon he'd have taken the bit in his mouth and you've got a runaway.... That kind of blind authority causes rebellion in horses and children. You've got to be caring in setting the rules, for there's a fine line between discipline and punishment.*

In order to be effective, the authority must be respected: *Horses in a pen, in a corral, or in a pasture, establish a pecking order of respect that remains undisturbed until a new horse enters the group, and then it's readjusted, notes Jack Huyler. You, the rider must fit into that pecking order and it darned well better be at the top of the hierarchy. That respect is important. Love isn't enough with horses or children—love's important, but respect sets the boundaries.*

Such boundaries of respect also supply a measure of security: *For your own safety, you need to be the horse's herd boss: I feed you, I take care of you, and I am the herd boss, says world champion endurance rider Valerie Kanavy (p.152). I can be a benevolent dictator, but if you cross the line I can be your worst nightmare. Now, if you truly don't understand, or it's a very frightening situation, then patience has to come into play. So, first I have to evaluate the action or reaction to make the decision how to handle it. But number one is I must establish that I am in charge. Horses, like children, feel safe when they know who's the boss.*

When respect is firmly established, control can follow: *Some people can control their children and never raise their voice,* observes Sally Swift. *And it's the same sort of thing with a horse; you don't have to raise your voice, but the horse has to know you mean it. Once in a while, you may have to scold them, but mostly they like to please, just as most children like to please.*

Occasionally authority is tested and must be reinforced: According to Western screen star, Roy Rogers (p. 151), *Kids and horses are a lot alike in some ways. They both need correcting and guiding. And if they're doing something bad and won't quit it, you may have to give them a spanking. Trigger and I used to do an act where we'd be on the road for up to four weeks, and every show he'd have to go through the same routine. Well, one day, he just got tired of it. I gave him the cue to bow and he just stood there, looking at the audience. I give him another cue and he gave me a look that said, "Nuts to you, sucker." Finally I had to step to the microphone and explain, "Ladies and Gentlemen, as you've noticed, I've been asking Trigger to do something and he's not wanting to do it. You may have the same problem occasionally with your kids at home." And I said, "Here's what I do to fix 'em, cure 'em, change 'em, and get them back on track." I reached up and took the little quirt off my saddle. Suddenly Trigger went through about five different tricks at once. I put the quirt back and said, "That's what we have to do—and sometimes we even have to use it."*

Whether disciplining a horse or a child, you need clear boundaries, an open mind, respected authority, and a guiding hand.

Punishment

Since many parents dislike disciplining their children, they spend little time considering effective punishment. Thus, penalties are often ill-thought-out emotional reactions sparked by anger, frustration, or fear: *I think every parent should have to train a young animal of some kind, a dog or a horse, because the principles of conditioning have a great deal of merit,* states Octavia Brown. *I be-*

lieve we need to put less emotion into bringing up our children, and more thought. Parents get suckered into getting very emotional and indulging too much temper. If you do that with an animal, the animal shuts down. The lessons from training any animal are very, very fundamental. In dealing with our son, who had quite alarming temper tantrums, my husband and I went through a range of responses quite consciously. We sat down and said, "Okay, under certain circumstances, when his will is crossed, he has a temper tantrum. We don't like that. We would like to help him learn to control his temper and we don't want to lose ours in the process." Then we went through several strategies. We tried physical contact—a smack on the thigh to try and break his concentration. That was absolutely no good. We tried talking to him, forget it. We tried holding him, that didn't work. Finally we tried isolating him. He was to stay in his room until he was feeling better and then he could come downstairs. When he did come down, we asked, "Are you feeling better?" He'd say, "Yes," and we'd give him a hug and a kiss and go on. By that method, we found we could detach from the screaming and concentrate on the behavior. I learned that from training animals through conditioned response.

The adage, "make the punishment fit the crime" indicates that there should be a variety of penalties for different infractions, the result of which is correction, not simply castigation. By foregoing our emotions and utilizing the thoughtful trial-and-error training process described above, parents have a greater chance for effective education through appropriate retribution.

The reprimands of spanking a child and hitting a horse are as ancient as mankind, yet only recently have such actions drawn controversy. Some would like all corporal punishment banned, while others consider it an important disciplinary tool. I believe it's a matter of degree and the best answer is found in a just balance: *You can be too harsh on a horse and you can be too soft,* claims Rex Peterson. *There has to be a middle ground and you must strive to find it all the time. There is a lot to be learned from that because you can be too harsh or too soft on children, too. Nowadays people are against spanking. Well, my dad spanked me for several different things when I was growing up; but you know, I can't remember one spanking I got that I really didn't deserve. The one I remember most was about crossing the highway by our house. Three kids had been killed on that highway in eight years. Dad told us, "Don't you ever, ever cross that road without your mom, me, or your older brother taking you across." Well, I got to crossing on my own. I did it a bunch, then got caught. The first time Dad said, "Never, ever do that again." But I did it three or four more times and didn't get caught, and got back in the habit. One night he caught me and spanked me severely. It's been over thirty-five years and I still remember that very, very vividly. But you know something? Three days later another kid was killed on that highway. Dad hadn't done that because he hated me, he did it because he loved me.*

Now it's hard for me to spank my own children. It is so, so hard for me to do, but I finally have to sit down and say, "I don't want to do this. It hurts me as bad as it does you." Suddenly, I remember somebody else saying that many, many years ago. It's sometimes so hard to do, but I do it for a good reason.

Punishments should be reserved for correcting wrong actions. Hence, whipping a racehorse makes little sense, for the animal is doing what it's supposed to do—running hard. After a point, it won't go faster—flogged or not: *I'd like to see this country go to whipless racing,* Monty Roberts states. *In Germany, two-year-olds are raced with a little noodle whip which can't cause any pain. I think that's wonderful. But in the United States, we're so driven by the bettor—when he puts his two dollars down, he wants the bastard whipped to win. He doesn't care, he wants that horse hit. I was watching the Belmont Stakes yesterday, and the horse that won ran untouched, while the horse that was second was head and head with the winner a hundred yards from the wire, then had the hell whipped out of him in the last hundred yards, and ended up a full length behind. There are stud-*

ies which prove a whipped horse eventually runs slower than an unwhipped horse. You can scare him a few times to run faster, but then he gets used to it, comes to resent it, and actually goes slower when he's whipped. So, the more you punish, the less effect it has. Punishment must be just.

Appropriate punishment serves a number of purposes: correction, control, education, and penance. An unjust punishment, served up by rage, domination, or ignorance can create very different results: fear and resentment, followed by rebellion or resignation.

Generational Ties

From parent to child to grandparent, a mutual interest in horses is a common thread that strengthens the fabric of family: *I see families absolutely brought together through horses,* states Richard Shrake. *Someone once said, "A teenager's like a terrorist, except that you can reason with the terrorist." But yet, everyday, I see fathers who come to our seminars with their teenagers and they have a relationship that is unbelievable because of the horse. I've seen husbands and wives communicate who maybe would never communicate as well if it wasn't for something in common with a horse. And I've never seen anything more wonderful than an old rancher whose face has so many miles on it—more wrinkles than a Shar-Pei dog—but boy that smile when he sees his grandkid ride in the horse show. That's worth ten million dollars.*

Supportively working together allows the parent-child relationship to take on new dimension: *I'm so grateful for all the sacrifices my mother made for me to be able to ride and compete—not just financially, but time—a lot of time,* exclaims Camille Whitfield Vincent. *Raising three girls and going through five years of my father slowly dying after a succession of strokes.... I will never know how she did all she did. Once she saw that riding was a true love of mine she gave me unconditional support. The experiences we had traveling to all those horse shows, laughing and crying together…how grateful I am for those. Money couldn't buy those times and they could never be replaced. When saddleseat equitation became my forté, I needed a better horse and a specialized trainer in Houston. That was another sacrifice my mother made. I'd fly from El Paso to Houston one weekend every month. I had an aunt there who drove me around to horse shows when mother couldn't. My riding has been a real family affair and I just can't express my gratitude for all the selfless support of so many.*

What evolved out of all that is a real friendship with my mother. We went through some hard times when I was a crazy teenager— typical things—but even my husband comments on what a good friendship Mom and I have and how unusual that is. It's because we had all that bonding together through my riding career.

Since riding can be enjoyed equally by both sexes, it's a wonderful project for a father to share with his girls: *My sister and I rode ponies and horses at my grandpa's farm. We'd just cling on like little rats more than ride, but we stayed on well,* recalls Diana Thompson. *The Christmas that my sister was eight and I was six, we got a two-year-old unbroken palomino pinto horse of our dreams—golden with white spots and white mane and tail. Her name was Trixie. Our dad helped us train her. We did it all ourselves. After school, we'd take the bus to my dad's office; he'd rented a barn and pasture nearby. We kept the horse there so he could supervise us and help us with her whenever he could break free. A year or so later, we moved to a neighborhood with riding trails and we kept Trixie in the backyard. Dad got a big gelding and rode with us—we rode as a family…very much a family.*

Horses are natural vehicles for exploring life lessons with your child: *Being around horses has taught me a lot about life, and I pass that on to my son,* says Lt. Carl Clipper. *I've had him riding since he was six. He'll be ten in August, and he enjoys riding with me. I don't think there's a better thing out there for kids. I know for a fact that horses kept me out of a lot of trouble. Having horses teaches a child respect and responsibility, keeps them busy doing shows, teaches the competition aspect of life—and it's clean fun—something that's miss-ing for a lot of kids today.*

Sharing the experience of a father's recreation is a treasured education for any child: *Now that my two boys are getting older, they go out with me almost every day,* Jimmy Fairclough reports. *I drive roughly five hours a day in the carriage, and they usually go with me for an hour or two. If there's not a lot of training involved on a drive, I like to take the boys so that I can pay attention to them. My older son, who's eight, rides quite well and drives a bit; when the team is being good, he can drive them home. This gets them involved and helps them enjoy the horses.*

When the avocation of horses becomes a vocation, business and pleasure can mix into a formula that enhances family ties: *My mom used to ride a lot; she was put on a horse when she was three and rode in a drill team until she went to college,* relates Charlotte Dicke. *But she had spinal meningitis and has a lot of back problems, so riding is difficult for her now. My mom supports my riding immensely. It's probably the biggest thing in mine and my mom's relationship—our horses. It gave our relationship a basis. It's a business for us also, which is hard, but we talk it all out: buying, selling, showing, what the horses did, and what to name the babies. We've had the normal problems of a teenager and a parent, but our relationship has improved a lot because of the horses.*

Working as well as living together gives children an opportu-nity to share a wider scope of life with their parents: *My older daughter started riding when she was four, and rode the whole time she was in grade school, high school, and college,* notes Bob Douglas. *She has always worked with me at the stables, weekends or evenings. The most important thing about our whole horse family is that she has seen me in every mood that a father can be in. Normally your children only see you between the hours of five in the evening and bedtime, so we experience each other in almost the same role every night. But my daughter and I have seen each other in the whole spectrum of life. It's been very interesting for her, seeing that her parents go through the same things she does.*

From the youngest to the eldest, an entire family can enjoy a joint venture in horses: *Don't just buy the kids a horse, get involved with them,* says Martha Josey. *That's one thing about barrel racing, the whole family can do it. I've had three generations of a family attending my clinics at one time!*

Raising Winners

The hard work, the tempering, and the discipline of a life with horses build a foundation for taking on many of life's challenges: *Six or seven years ago, about two hundred Crabtree riders came to Louisville for a reunion,* Helen Crabtree recounts. *It was such fun to see how these riders' lives had developed, and there were some surprises. One of the girls had been a bit of a featherbrain when she came to us as a student—she couldn't stop giggling long enough to cluck! But she was so engaging, we all loved her. I knew if she was able to just get up and ride off, she'd keep giggling through life, so I decided to challenge her with kind of a tough mare. Well, that girl buckled down—she learned discipline, focus, and to work with her mare. She had to in order to keep up with that ride. And now she's an engineer designing offshore drilling rigs.*

Then there was another girl whose father had a prominent brass foundry in Cincinnati. She was a flighty little kid—a good little rider—just a nickel's worth spoiled...not mean with it at all, but a touch self-centered. She had trouble with discipline and the fact that when I said to be at the barn at ten o'clock, I meant ten o'clock. Now this gal has taken over the brass foundry and developed some process for brass that was absolutely revolutionary.

Those were two kids that were just off in the wild blue yonder, but I know the horses helped them get their lives together—they said it did—and I'd watched it. And the countless others, the horses touched their lives too, maybe not so profoundly—not everybody can be a mechanical engineer or develop a brass process—but an amazing num-ber of our riders are just so successful as human beings...it's really wonderful.

Helen's students are not the only ones with solid track records: *I joke that I don't have any children, but my husband, R.E., and me—we've got thirty thousand kids! That's how many students have been through the ranch in thirty years,* explains Martha Josey. *We love the teaching, and we love to see our kids go on and fulfill their dreams. Some call us every day telling us how they've done, what they've won...and that's pretty rewarding to R.E. and me. We've seen so many of them go on and do so well. Actually, we don't know of any that went bad.*

There were times when we saw kids change in front of our eyes with the horses. We had one mother bring over her teen-age boy who wasn't really interested in anything. He spent two weeks with us at our roping school, went home, sold his motorcycle, bought a roping horse and he's still out there winning.

Another one of our students who's done real well in rodeoing is Ty Mitchell. He started here as a student and he's now helping at our clinics and helping us to train horses. R.E. and I are real proud of our students. We have really enjoyed seeing them win—when they win, we win. Not only winning in calf roping or barrel racing, but in what they accomplish in life. The doctor I've got now was my barrel-racing student, and our dentist was R.E.'s calf-roping student. I think in-volvement with horses definitely helps kids to learn. The responsibility and commitment of having to take care of a horse is not easy, but these kids learn that if they do commit, they can do good—and win!

Skills for Success

No set formula exists for properly raising children or training horses. Success in either case is an elusive, custom mix of loving concern, perpetual work, creative education and playtime, effec-tive discipline, trial and error, and providential luck.

Working with horses teaches us to nurture the unique character and talent of each child; to condemn the behavior, not the child; to end each lesson with praise; to make the right choice easy; to set clear boundaries and make simple requests; to guide with a firm hand, a sensitive heart, and a just mind.

Being responsible for a beloved horse can transform a selfish child into a selfless caregiver, and on to a productive adult.

As Buck Brannaman observes: *There sure are parallels between raising kids and horses: with both by the time you're all done, you have a good idea how to do it—but at that point the information is totally useless.*

There are no guarantees in this work of raising kids or training horses, but Martha Josey's thirty thousand winners and just plain good kids indicate there is something positive at work here—raising our children with *HorsePower!*

SARAH HAFNER, b. 1957, is a graphic designer living on a family vineyard in the California wine country, where she and her two young daughters are active riders. Sarah is shown clearing an oxer on her Appendix-Quarter Horse mare, Clementine, in an adult jumper class at the Brookside Equestrian Center show in Sacramento, California.

DEDE MARX, b. 1976, is an enterprising student who learned many important lessons from her equine partner, Bruce. They enjoyed a number of successful shows in California: becoming the 1990 Children's Hunter Champion at the Menlo Circus Club; Reserve Champion, Children's Hunters at the 1990 Monterey show; and 1991 Reserve Champion Children's Hunters in Murietta. Bruce was instrumental in helping Dede get into her first-choice college. They are shown together in 1989 at Spring Down Equestrian Center in Portola Valley, California.

JENNY BUTAH, b. 1945, is pictured on her uncle's buckskin in 1950 at the very start of her riding career at San Luis Obispo, California. Jenny rode until age 18, when she turned her attention to other pursuits for some thirty years, returning to riding in her late forties. Today Jenny is a wife, mother, and licensed psychotherapist with a retired Thoroughbred gelding, Dusty, and an Arabian, Cajun, a former endurance horse with whom she enjoys trail-riding and dressage.

BOBBY CHRISTIAN, b. 1917, has trained, worked and enjoyed farm horses since he was a child. In retirement, Bobby devotes his energies to his hobbies: restoring carriages, training ponies and teaching neighborhood children values such as responsibility and honesty through horsemanship. He's shown here in 1994 with Hackney ponies Candy and Muffin, plus four of his happy students.

TINA SCHULER, b. 1976, has been a devoted rider since the age of seven, when she discovered riding lifts her spirits, helps her rebalance from hectic schedules, and gives her an arena for success beyond school. She is shown with Heron, her riding partner while attending college in Maine.

DR. ELIZABETH LAWRENCE, b. 1929, Professor of Environmental and Population Health at Tufts University School of Veterinary Medicine, is both a veterinarian and an anthropologist. This combined vocation, coupled with a deep affection for horses, has inspired Dr. Lawrence to research, write, teach, lecture and author three books on the subject of the human-horse relationship. Dr. Lawrence is shown on her lovely Morgan mare, Easter Bonnet, ready for a ride through the woods near her home in southern Massachusetts.

ALLAN JAMISON, b. 1925, enjoys success as an accomplished horseman, pragmatic administrator and highly respected rancher in the tough terrain of northern California's Coastal mountains. Allan is pictured in 1994 performing some of his duties as the Marshal of the Round Valley Rodeo aboard V-Hill, a Quarter Horse/Morgan gelding.

JILL KEISER HASSLER, b. 1944, is an instructor and manager of Maryland's Hilltop Farm, a comprehensive sporthorse and educational facility. Jill has served on the board and committees of the U.S. Pony Club and loves helping pony clubbers prepare and achieve ratings. For almost twenty years Jill offered an Easter Seals Handicapped Riding Program. The author of two popular training books, IN SEARCH OF YOUR IMAGE and BEYOND THE MIRROR, Jill has shared the pride of training dressage and eventing riders to national titles. Jill shows early winning form as she and Demi Tasse fly over a jump at the Long Island National Pony Club Rally in 1960.

CAMILLE WHITFIELD VINCENT, b. 1959, has retired from the show ring and settled in California where she happily cares for her growing family and takes Steve, her Saddlebred gelding, on leisurely trail rides. Camille and Elation, her Saddlebred mare, show their winning style at the 1979 Pin Oak Charity Horse Show in Houston, Texas, after clinching the Ladies Three-Gaited World Champion title.

ROY ROGERS, King of the Cowboys, 1911-1998, and DALE EVANS, Queen of the West, b.1912, are two of America's most beloved stars of television, rodeo and the silver screen. Partners on screen before becoming partners for life in 1947, they shared a number of personal trials along with their many "Happy Trails." Roy on Trigger and Dale on another golden palomino are pictured saluting fans at one of their many personal performances in the 1950s.

VALERIE KANAVY, b. 1946, enjoyed her most successful year of competition in 1994, claiming six major wins, including a gold medal at the World Equestrian Games in Holland. At the subsequent 1996 World Games, Valerie placed second—crossing the line an instant behind the victor—her 25-year-old daughter, Danielle. In 1998 in Dubai, United Arab Emirates, she became World Champion riding High Winds Jedi. Valerie and her champion Arabian, Pieraz, aka "Cash," are pictured traversing a pine forest in Arizona during the North American Endurance Riding Championships.

IRVING PETTIT, b. 1907, is a retired mortician whose avocation was harness racing. He bred, trained, raised and raced Standardbreds for forty years until retiring from racing at the age of 80. Irving and his wife are pictured with their driver and one of their homebred colts, Undertaker, following a win at Brandywine Raceway in 1957.

MAXINE FREITAS, b. 1953, is a youth counselor and founding director of EquiEd Therapeutic Riding. She is shown coaching her client, nine-year-old Lauren Anderson (whose incomplete limb development resulted from a congenital birth defect) prior to the trail class at the CALNET (California Network for Equestrian Therapy) Horse Show at the Los Angeles Equestrian Center. Lauren and her partner Goldie, a Quarter Horse mare, took fourth place in trail and two firsts in equitation classes.

CHAPTER SIX

PARTNERS

Relationship and Partnership

*The dog may be mankind's best friend, but the horse is
mankind's best partner.*

When I was growing up there were many legendary Hollywood partnerships featured in the movies and on TV: Fred Astaire
and Ginger Rogers, Spencer Tracy and Katherine Hepburn, Grace
Kelly and Cary Grant...but the pairing that won my heart and
filled my head with thrilling fantasies was Roy Rogers and Trigger! What perfection those two were! The gorgeous, talented,
smart Palomino, and his sweet, virtuous, handsome cowboy were
my idea of heaven. How I yearned to be the cowgirl to steal Roy's
heart and be swept into the saddle by him to ride off on Trigger's
golden back into the warm western sunset...Becky Ferran...
Queen of the West!

Unfortunately, seven-year-old Becky Ferran was stuck in the
East and Dale Evans (p.151) seemed pretty well entrenched as
Roy's Queen. The closest I could get to Roy and Trigger was to
crowd up to the television screen, risking eye strain and radiation
exposure. That was until "The Day of Miracles, 1954," when
Daddy took my sister and me for a surprise drive, refusing to say

where we were going. Debby and I hadn't a clue until we turned the corner to the Boston Garden and saw the huge poster of Trigger rearing up with Roy confidently fanning the sky with his hat. I could not believe it: Roy Rogers and Trigger had come to Boston—to see me!

That show thrilled me more than any other spectacle I have ever witnessed. Sawdust and horse perfumed the air, while starry reflections shot off Trigger's silver-studded tack and danced about our seats. We were up too high to reach Roy as he and Trigger circled during the finale, shaking hands with the lucky buckaroos down front, but I had *seen* them. I had been there—with Roy and Trigger—*in the flesh* and I had sung along lustily with them as they wished us all "Happy Trails."

Little did I realize that forty years later, November 30, 1994, I would actually visit with Roy Rogers and Dale Evans (p. 151) and once again sing "Happy Trails" with them after our interview on *HorsePower!* What a lucky buckaroo!

Dale and Roy were just as I knew they would be: kind and funny and generous with both their time and memories as we sat discussing their unique partnership with Trigger: *For my first starring role in the movie,* UNDER WESTERN STARS, *Republic Studios sent over a number of really fine horses and told me to select a movie mount,* Roy began. *I chose a palomino stallion named "Golden Cloud." During that shoot, I renamed him "Trigger" because he was as fast as a hair trigger in a quick draw. The picture turned out pretty good—critics and audiences both seemed to like it—so I was sent out on a bunch of promotional tours. It was then that I realized a cowboy really needs his horse; it seemed Trigger had made as much of an impression with the moviegoers as I had...probably more. People kept asking, "Hey, cowboy, where's your horse?"*

In 1938, as a contract actor at Republic Studios, I was making $75 a week and barely making ends meet, what with having to pay for my own costumes and responding to my own fan mail...but I knew I

*wanted Trigger to be mine. So, three months after that first movie suc-
cess I went over to the Hudkins Stable and bought Trigger for the impossible sum of $2,500. In those depression days, that was a pile of
cash. I made arrangements to pay the note off over time, and Trigger
and I became permanent working partners.*

*Shortly after, the studio wanted me to do a picture called FRONT
PAGE, in which I was to play a reporter that got drunk. Well, I turned
it down.*

*The head of the studio steamed, "You've got to do it; you're under
contract."*

*"Maybe I was under contract," I said, "But I'm not going to play
that kind of a shady character."*

*He fumed, "Well, if you don't, I'll just buy Trigger and put an-
other cowboy on him."*

"No, you won't."

"What do you mean, 'No, you won't?'"

*That's when I told him, "I just bought Trigger." And I had, just a
week or so before.*

*Trigger was out of a cold-blooded Palomino mare and Thorough-
bred stallion. He took the good parts from both: good-natured, good-
looking, and fast. He was always sound and ready to go. He was a
stallion, but he didn't have a mean hair on him—I've got pictures of
seven of our kids on him from his ears back to his tail.*

Once, when we were in a hotel in Edinburgh, adds Dale, *they
brought Trigger into the lobby, and he never even switched his tail. He
never bit at anybody or kicked, no matter what they did. He was the
most wonderful horse....*

And he was a ham, Roy chuckled. *He loved to do new things.
I'd even take him into hospitals, and he'd ride right in the elevator just
like a person.... We had a pair of little leather boots made for him; I'd
buckle them on his hooves, and he'd walk right up the stairs just like
he'd been trained on a Stair-Master. Old Trigger was extra smart to
start with, and well educated to cues, so I never was worried that Trig-*

ger wouldn't do things I asked him. I could trust him, and he could trust me, because I knew what he could do and what he couldn't do. If I wanted him to jump across that walk out there, [Roy points to the concrete walkway outside the window], I could come at it wide open, and he'd jump it, because he knew I wouldn't be asking if it was too wide. All those years of association, I only asked him to do things I knew he could do.

In the winter of 1954, we did a tour in the British Isles. We'd con-tracted with several theaters, and they'd arranged for us to do a great big press interview—a big deal—with Trigger and the whole crew. Well, Dale and I came down with that European flu and about died. We were hospitalized with fevers of 103. We were laid out in bed with steam going and a private nurse on the sixth floor of the hospital, try-ing to get well because our contract only allowed us two days off.

When we had to cancel that big press conference, everyone thought we were just tired and kinda doggin' it. So a group of them convinced Glenn Randall, our horse trainer, that we needed visitors. Glenn put those special leather boots on Trigger, and they all hiked up the six flights of stairs with Trigger carrying a bunch of jonquils in his mouth for us. When they got in our room and saw how sick we really were, they didn't want to hang around much, so Trigger left the flowers, and they all sneaked back out.

After eighty-eight movies, more than one hundred television shows and thousands of personal appearances at rodeos, horse shows, benefits, orphanages, and hospitals, Trigger was retired in 1957, and died in 1965, at the august age of thirty-three.

There was a terrific bond between Trigger and Roy—a real connec-tion, remarks Dale. Even though I usually had third billing—Roy Rogers and Trigger with Dale Evans—I was never jealous of Trigger. I always told Roy, "If I had that horse, I'd look good, too!" I did get to ride Trigger in one picture, MY PAL TRIGGER, and I loved it—I thor-oughly enjoyed being on him.

People experience the world of horses as they do life: through dialogue, cooperation, relationship, and partnership. As L.D. Burke notes, *"Any fool knows it's faster to travel alone...maybe that's why they do it."* Traveling alone may be faster over the short haul, but ultimately, the soul, the psyche, and the body wither in isolation. No being thrives in the vacuum of self. Riding, like living, is not about traveling alone, or about traveling the fastest; it's about traveling the best way together, and for millennia people have realized the value of traveling in partnership with the horse.

Matchmaking

The process of finding the right equine or human partner is really quite similar. It takes a number of blind dates, matching chemistries, and a good bit of providence before the right mix results.

One time my trainer, Macella, gave me a new horse to try. He was big and athletic, and I simply could not get in sync with this animal. After about ten minutes Macella called over, "Well, I can see this is not a match made in heaven. Tomorrow we'll put you on a different horse." I thought, that's so simple and straightforward, why can't people be that way with human matches? No guilt, no recriminations, no "I'll call you next week..."; just move on to the next prospect when it doesn't work out.

Eventually suitable pairings find one another: *As the saying goes, "There's a horse for every rider and a rider for every horse,"* quotes Susan Stovall. *That is so true. I think my horse is great, but when I give him to somebody else, they can hardly ride him because they're used to a different kind of horse. It takes awhile to find the horse for you; most of the time, you have to adapt to the horse; the horse isn't going to change its nature for you. People have to realize that.*

Some very effective pairings may be based on compensation— one partner counteracting the other's deficiency: *I remember a student of [renowned hunter/jumper trainer] Gordon Wright's named Elsa, who was so uncoordinated...*Sam Savitt recounts. *I watched her* *on the mounting block, ready to mount up, then her horse moved, and she nearly killed herself. Gordon found her sort of a half-Appaloosa horse called "The Ugly Duckling." This horse would do a course despite her. Gordon would tell her, "As you're approaching the fence, put your hands up on his neck, and leave him alone." The horse went on and jumped well. Judges looked at that duo and thought, "Look how well that horse took the course, and his rider never helped him a bit." Elsa and Ugly Duckling won again and again, which built confidence in the rider and the horse. Matching horses to people takes a lot of know-how, and Gordon understood as much about people as he did about horses...maybe more.*

The maxim, "opposites attract" applies to riding as well as romantic partners, with some qualifications: *In riding, opposites should complement each other,* notes Richard Shrake. *If you've got a real sensitive horse and a very aggressive rider, you have an over-ride, which will be a wreck in a minute. And if you have a very passive rider on a very insensitive horse, nothing will ever get done.*

Complement is the critical word here, as it takes that magical mix of chemistry for opposites to complement rather than clash; the alchemy of matchmaking makes success both elusive and rewarding: *For a while I had a small horse business, so I had to match horses with riders,* recalls art historian Carol Stratton (p.178). *There are a lot of nice horses out there, and there are some real lunkheads. It was difficult, but fun, because it's like arranging a marriage; chemistry was terribly important. When I did find just the right horse for just the right kid or person, it was great. I could see why marriage brokers feel terribly proud of themselves. It's a marvelous thing to arrange a good match. All that matchmaking experience worked for me—I didn't get a lunkhead; I've got a good horse in Brother and a very, very good husband!*

Criteria of Choice

Effective partnering takes consistent and honest evaluation of yourself, your abilities, and your horse. If you're not honest about the various evaluation factors, you will come up against those factors time and again, until you are forced to come clean and deal with them realistically: *I'd like everyone to be a realistic horseman,* states Rex Peterson. *Nowadays horses have to be a pleasure for people to own, since most horses don't earn a living anymore. We own them for the enjoyment we get out of them and the pleasure they give us. When you don't enjoy one, either put him with a trainer and have the problem rectified, or get a different one—if you aren't enjoying him, what's the point?*

In horse hunting, it's easy to be swayed by equine beauty and buy an animal simply because you fall in love with its looks. To avoid that, determine your criteria, and evaluate the prospect's talents and potential carefully before you commit: *The most important thing in matching people and horses is for people to decide what they want to be doing with the horse and what their goals are; then write that down, and go find the horse that fits,* notes John Lyons. *If they want to drop the reins and ride down the trail, or if they want to train a young horse, then they need to get a horse to fill that need. That's important when looking for a horse and even more important when looking for a mate.*

We'd better decide what type of person we want to be married to before we go pick one out. If we just kind of do it by happenstance without stopping and thinking of the characteristics that would make us happy...whether the person is strong spiritually, or is a hard worker...we might find a real pretty girl, or a good looking guy, who is absolutely worthless as far as moral character, work ethics, or the things that we know are going to be very important to us down the road. Picking horses can teach us how to pick mates real well.

The process of buying a horse would be simple if it were just a matter of honestly matching desired criteria of the buyer, such as size, age, sex, temperament, use, and ability with a corresponding animal. Not a problem—until human emotion, imagination, and ego enter the equation. When a good-looking, snappy won-der-horse is brought before you, suddenly your careful criteria evaporate. I had been searching for a really calm, trusty, experienced horse that could help me learn to jump and regain the confidence I'd lost jumping my lovely, erratic mare. I found a prospect, Tico, that was everything I was looking for: an older, experienced gelding, he carried himself beautifully, moved like a dream, took every jump he was aimed at rhythmically and round, was push-button responsive to aids, and thousands of dollars less than anything I'd seen. He had only one flaw, which I discovered during my trial ride, when, out of the blue, he blasted from zero to sixty in two seconds flat. I managed to stay on, even though I'd never before gone that fast on anything without a seat belt and an airbag!

Tico was a bolter—and a bolter was NOT what I needed to restore my confidence! However, since I loved everything else about Tico, I suddenly found myself thinking: "I could get used to bolting...I could train it out of him.... Once he gets to know me, he won't want to bolt...." I became my very own worst horse trader, rationalizing a fatal mismatch by *lying to myself!* Ultimately, I regained my sanity about what I needed, and what I am capable of, and what I am not capable of. Only then did I give up my crazy delusion of reforming that handsome, life-long bolter on a wish and a prayer.

In the end you must look beyond pretty packaging; an elegant ring box offers no evidence on whether you're getting a real gem or just a worthless chip of glass. It's only prudent to discover what's on the inside before saying "Til death do us part" to anyone—horse or human; occasionally, the most valuable gifts arrive in a brown paper bag: *A winning partnership takes a great horse, and there's where I've been so lucky,* claims Richard Shrake. *I look at myself and my own talents and realistically, I'm a very lucky guy with average talents, but I've had some great horses. You've heard it a million* times: *good horses make good trainers. I am testimony to that. Those great ones—there might only be one in a lifetime—but when they come along, you need to embrace them and keep them as long as you can.*

One such horse is The Highwayman. He was so common to look at that he was stabled next to my horse at a show, and I walked by him for ten days and never noticed him. Then I saw him move, and all of a sudden, boy, the hair just stood up on my arms. I had to buy him! I bought him for a client who showed and did real well nationally in the pleasure division—just a great horse. Another horse that was not impressive in the stall was Windjammer. Luckily, when I walked by, something said, "Hey, better get him out and look at him." Well, we bought him. But when I was trying to qualify him for the World, in the first three shows, I was disqualified on him. Now that was pretty embarrassing, because we'd paid a lot of money for this horse. But the next seven we won. Then he won the All-Around at The All American Quarter Horse Congress and was placed in the top ten in western pleasure at the World Show.

These winning gems, though hidden in common wrappings, revealed their brilliance when put to the test.

Getting to Know You

Many riders have witnessed a horse who is considered troublesome that moves on to a new owner who creates a formidable team with him. Such was the case with Jane Savoie and her Olympic reserve mount, Zapatero: *When I first got Zapatero, few of my colleagues saw him as a champion,* recalls Jane. *One top rider told me, "He's a bull, and he's pushy." and I'm thinking, "I don't see him that way." Another top rider, who had tried him in Holland a month before I bought him, said, "He's a naughty, disobedient piece of doo-doo." Now these are top riders that I really respect. One says the horse is a bull and the other says the horse is a piece of naughty doo-doo. And I'm looking at the horse and seeing that he is sensitive and gets worried, but tries his heart out.*

I have a mutual friend with the other two riders, so I went to her and related the various evaluations, and she said a very astute thing, "People tend to put their own personalities into their animals. The person that called your horse a bull is a little bit of a bull. And the person that perceives your horse as naughty is a bit of a fighter like that, and you're sensitive, and you try your heart out all the time. Think about it. You're all projecting your own personality onto the same horse."

I got Zapatero when he was seven years old and from day one I saw him as a champion Olympic horse. I believed in him so much that he grew into that self-fulfilling prophecy. In hindsight, I think maybe he wasn't as great a horse as I thought he was, because now I have Eastwood, who is twice as good as Zapatero, movement-wise. But because I saw Zapatero as a champion, I believed; he believed, and we did it. That's the power of psycho-cybernetics.

Jane's positive view of Zapatero paid off—she saw a champion, trained a champion and got a champion while others viewed Zapatero quite differently. Jane projected success onto Zapatero and he delivered. Of course, an inherent danger of projection lies in making an erroneous appraisal at the outset. Projecting a desired result only goes so far by itself—there must be a foundation of possibility to support it.

As powerful a tool as positive projection is, my friend and trainer, Macella O'Neill, also believes in "revelation." She views each new horse as a bag of jigsaw puzzle pieces with no finished picture to refer to. Some horses are simple and straightforward: a few large pieces that seem to fall into place easily; while the more challenging mounts are the tiny, thousand-piece variety. There are a few traditional tricks of the trade—start with the outside, then work in toward the more complex center—but no stringent ways of going. Mostly you have to just "mess with it": throw all the pieces on the table and use different tactics to puzzle, try, and sort the pieces out until you discover how they all fit together.

Once you complete the puzzle (if you ever do), then the portrait of that individual horse is revealed to you. Rigidly forcing the pieces to fit a wished-for preconception simply does not work: since no photo comes with this jigsaw puzzle, you must first solve the puzzle to find the finished picture of each horse. Some puzzles are a snap, some are a challenge, and some are a folly that eludes you forever. For Macella, the fun is in "messing around" with the puzzle. She does not get anxious when a horse doesn't react the way she expects, she just continues messing with it until it reveals who it is and how to deal with it most effectively. The intrigue is in the mystery of what the end result looks like, the fun is in the messing, the challenge is in getting it to work, and the satisfaction is in the ultimate revelation—all in all a great game of "Getting to Know You."

Choosing the Rider

There are times when the partnership choice is ultimately made by the horse: *In the 1972 Tokyo Olympics we had a little sixteen-year-old horse called Grasshopper,* recalls René Williams. *He was by a Thoroughbred horse out of a Connemara pony, and at only 15.1, he was the smallest horse we had. But you could always count on Grasshopper to finish a course due to his strong second wind. He had been to three Olympics and won a lot of medals.*

He had a lot of bad habits, and most riders could not handle him. In a sense, Grasshopper chose his rider. Mike Page got along with him great and rode him in two Olympics and two Pan American Games. In Tokyo, Mike and little Grasshopper finished the grueling cross-country course in deep mud and won a bronze medal. Sixteen years old, 15.1! Hard to believe, but he was extraordinary!

As Olympic team manager, I'd hold the horse as each United States entry finished while the rider went to weigh out (they all carry 165 lbs). After they're weighed and checked out, I take the horse to the groom, waiting outside. While I was holding little Grasshopper, he was looking all around searching the crowd. After that terrific 8-mile cross-

country course and a mile-and-a-half steeplechase, he saw his groom, Peggy Grant, through the rain, the mobs, and everything, and whinnies to her. She came and led him out, and he was happy. Isn't that a match? Grasshopper obviously had his list of partnership criteria, and when he found the rider and groom that suited him, they became a wonderfully successful team.

Yet another example of equine selection is related by Holly Peterson Mondavi: *I was wanting to get a horse, but wasn't quite ready to buy. The first time I tried Bacchus was a lot of fun, but we were not together at all. He was a lot for me—he's strong—a real handful. The next time we were better, and I kept wanting to ride him. Then his owner, Tacie, went to Europe and asked if I'd mind riding him for her. I was overjoyed at the thought of being able to ride Bacchus for a month and just loved him—everything clicked. I told Tacie, "If you ever want to sell him...not that I'd be able to afford him, but let me know." She suggested I half-lease him for a couple of months, so she and I alternated riding him every other day.*

Bacchus and Tacie were not doing very well together. At one show, Bacchus stopped at a water jump, and Tacie went flying over his head, landed in the mud, and was furious. Her hat came off and all her glorious long black hair was covered in muck. She had her crop in hand when she came out of that bog and Bacchus was standing there looking at her like, "It's Godzilla, the monster from the black lagoon!" Well, Tacie comes stalking up to him, and she's mad, and she's muddy, and the horse cannot even move he's so scared.... She climbs on him filthy as can be, whips him, and gets him through that water jump.... To this day I have trouble with him at water jumps. You can imagine why—he's expecting Tacie to pop up.

So, Tacie and Bacchus weren't getting along, but Bacchus and I were! Then Bacchus started getting welts all over his body: all over his eyes, his cheeks, his neck...big hives. His eyes were swollen shut; he had them everywhere when Tacie rode him. When I would ride him the welts went away. Tacie came out to ride, the welts appeared.... I'd never seen anything like it....This went on for two months; it was not just a one-week thing; it was consistent. There were times when she would ride him for three days, and he had hives every single day. Then I would ride him for a week and not a hive anywhere. Finally Tacie asked, "You still want to buy this horse? Hives and all? He's going on sale—cheap!"

I was ecstatic, thinking, "I can't believe how lucky I am—she wants to sell him to me." And she's thinking, "Oh God, how lucky, I've found someone who wants this bag of welts."

So I always say, Bacchus picked me. I liked him, but he picked me. That was really one of the more interesting things I've ever seen a horse electively do. He was doing some type of communication—or he was just nervous—and that's how it was expressed. But I thought that was pretty weird. It seems fairly evident that Bacchus was screaming, "Hey! Blondie! I want you! Not the black-haired witch from the mud swamp. I want you, and I'm gonna make sure you know." Thankfully, Holly heard him. They've been having fun together for years now.

Chemistry

Horses and people recognize a certain chemistry that allows rapport, one to another, and appreciate it as a critical factor in a successful partnership: *I got to go to Russia with Linda Tellington-Jones to work with their Olympic jumping team,* reports Diana Thompson. *That's where I first learned about matching the horse and rider. When I went in 1985, the Communist regime was still in control; they owned all the horses. Mounts were assigned to a rider depending on how they got along. It wasn't about who owned the horse and tried to control it; it was about who matched up the best.*

I remember watching a horse and rider go by in this big beautiful arena, and they were fighting with each other. The Russian trainers were talking, and I asked the translator, "What are they saying?" He stumbled around for the words and then said, "Well, it is how you say, their energy doesn't mix." To them, that was plenty of reason for those two not to be together. They were looking for the match of a good horse and a good rider and recognized the importance of mutual affinity.

When chemistries between man and beast clash, things can get very tense: *In the movie,* THE BLACK STALLION, *the young actor, Kelly Reno, rode that stallion, but there were always people behind the camera keeping that stud in tow,* declares Rex Peterson. *That horse got to the point where he hated Kelly Reno; wanted to tear his head off because Kelly agitated and irritated him all the time. We had to constantly keep that stud in line. You have to be a realist to deal with horses, and Kelly and that black stallion did not mix well together.*

However, when the mix produces harmony, the results can be fantastic: *When you're riding your horse, whether it's in the show ring, or punching cows on the ranch, it should be like two people dancing together,* Buck Brannaman observes. *You've probably seen a couple dancing, and you'd swear that they don't notice anyone else on the dance floor, 'cause they're so in tune. If you ride with your horse like that consistently, you can't help but be successful—no matter how you happen to define success.*

Marriage

When you find just the right equine partner, the alliance becomes much like marriage, for it requires mutual respect, discovering each other's assets, acknowledging differences, accepting idiosyncrasies, communicating openly, working together, caring, bonding, forgiveness, compassion, and integrity.

I treat my horses like a partner and work toward mutual cooperation; I don't necessarily have to be in control, says Chris Hawkins. *As a result, my horses probably are better than most, simply because we are partners. I don't own them; they don't own me; we're partners in this together. That may sound crazy, but it works for me. I just wish my husband would learn that. He keeps thinking he's in control of me...but I've got news for that boy!*

A partnership built on respect, understanding, and love has a solid base that allows for the fluent give and take that's as vital in riding as it is in marriage. Police Officer Laura Bianchi's horse showed her that relinquishing a little control can improve a relationship—at work and at home: *When my husband, Dennis, was promoted out of the mounted patrol, I started riding his horse, Big Al, who has a really sensitive mouth,* explains Laura. *One evening at home, I was on Dennis's case about something. I can't even remember what, but I was just hammering—you know how sometimes you just can't help yourself for nagging? Dennis is really patient, but I'd almost sent him over the edge.*

Somehow or another, into this nasty, nagging tirade, I started to talk about how I had noticed that if I just let the reins go, Big Al is happy. And when I tie him up, if I give him a really long lead line—almost longer than is safe—Al's happy because he can look around and relax....

Then Dennis says, "Well, why don't you do the same for me?" That's when I realized I had to cut him some slack, too.

Skills acquired through her years with horses proved valuable when Camille Whitfield Vincent became a newlywed: *One thing the horses were instrumental in teaching me is to influence control by psychology more than power. Since I can't possibly control a horse physically, I had to learn to do it through understanding, ingenuity, patience, and compassion. I'm now applying that ability to my marriage, as my new husband and I are learning to adjust to each other. Before getting married at age 35, I'd always lived on my own; now my husband's office is in the house to boot, so I'm really going through an adjustment—from total independence to mutual interdependence. That's meant learning what I can and cannot control, and how to influence that, which is how it is with the horse.*

Helen Crabtree agrees: *Riding is a complete partnership, and if it isn't, it just doesn't work; the horse will tell you right quick whether it's working or not. If you're going to make it with horses, you have to see the entire picture, appreciate the other's view, and consider both sides. The ability to see attitudes other than your own, to understand and adjust to them—there isn't a better training ground in the world than the back of a horse for that.* That training of consideration, acceptance, and adjustment works to strengthen many other relationships in life: with friends, colleagues, spouses, children, and others.

Open Acceptance

Being open to accepting and appreciating another for who they are is a valuable gift we can give to any and every one we meet: *The thing I love most about my therapy horse, Freckles, is that she accepts me without reservation,* says Tracy Cole. *She doesn't care that I can't walk straight. She doesn't care that my legs are at different levels on her, or that they're extremely tight. It may bother her a little, but she deals with it, and she deals with it really well.*

Most people, when they first meet me, all they see is someone who walks kind of funny, so they think I can't do too much. If they get to know me, they realize that I am a whole person. But it's the people that see that right away who become important to me, like my high school teacher, Mr. McNabb, and my riding instructor, Octavia Brown...and Freckles.

The beauty of appreciative acceptance is that once given, that gift is often reciprocated. As Linda Tellington-Jones elaborates: *People often ask me, "Linda, how can you walk up to a horse you've never seen before and suddenly the horse acts like he's known you for years?"*

It's because I don't see a separation between the animal and my being. By experiencing animals at the cellular level as being the same as we are, I experience our sameness at the nucleus of the cell. It's an acknowledgement of their being and our oneness.

I think God put horses on earth to work with us in partnership. However, like any partner, we must work with horses with respect for them as individuals. I'm convinced that recognizing each individual partnership is what made me such a successful catch rider in my teens. You can get on a horse and come from an ego point of view and say, "I'm going to win." Or what I was able to do, thanks to the influence of my grandfather, which was to get on a horse and wonder, "How can we do the best that we can together? And if we win, great." By accepting and appreciating each individual horse's attributes and abilities, Linda played up the best in each and success followed.

Working Partnership

According to most competitors, the best rides occur when they become a virtual silent partner and their horse performs with them as if at liberty: *My trainer, Jimmy Williams, used to say, "The sign of a great rider is a happy horse." That's really true,* agrees Anne Kursinski. *When it looks effortlessly simple, that's a winning effort. That unity—the feeling that the horse is going as if he was a loose horse. You're galloping to the jumps and not getting in his way—you're letting him do what God gave him to do naturally.* Communication becomes so subtle, so electric between horse and rider as to be indistinguishable from the motion. Both partners are implicitly aware and receptive to the other's actions and intentions. This is when riding becomes that dance of joyful unity that is magnificent to watch and a euphoric thrill to perform.

When ability and enthusiasm are shared by both partners, the results can be exceptional: *"This chestnut horse I have, I may never have another one like him,* claims Rex Peterson. *I probably won't, because when the goin' gets tough, this horse gets better. He's proved to me thousands of times he knows more than I do. He out-reads me. I've seen him do things that other trainers have stood right there and said, "You can't do that; it will not work." With any other horse, probably not. But I'm gonna try it with this horse...and he's proved them wrong time and again.*

I call him "High Tower." Most anybody in the movie business knows him. [High Tower portrayed Pilgrim in the movie of THE HORSE

WHISPERER]. He started out as a ranch horse, a catch colt out of a really expensive mare. I've been offered $50,000 for a half interest in him. He's thirteen now, and I wouldn't take half a million dollars for him.

Years ago, I got a call for a movie job where we had to drag a guy throughout the film; the guy's being dragged to death. I started three horses on that film, him being one of them because I'd roped cattle on him. When we finished the job, High Tower was the only horse still working. I ride him; I drive him; I jumped a wagon four-and-a-half feet with him—people couldn't believe it. I've had him upside down in some terrible predicaments, and he's always let me get him out of them—never panicked. I don't think there is another one like him in the world.

His reputation's why I got this job in Hawaii. They called and asked, "Who owns High Tower?" They didn't call for Rex Peterson; they called for High Tower. I think it's hilarious.

Whether horse or human, it only makes sense that successful partners must have confidence in each other working as a team. John Lyons explains: *If people want their horse to be partners, then they have to treat them like a partner and stop acting like they're against them. When people say: "The horse is trying to get away with it." "The horse just won't do it." "The horse is being ornery." Those aren't things you say about your partner; those are things you say about somebody who is against you.*

Suppose you and I are partners on the same two-man basketball team, and the winning team gets ten thousand dollars. Now, as my partner, are you ever going to shoot the ball and miss the basket? Odds are, yes. Even if Michael Jordan were my partner, he's going to shoot and miss the basket some of the time. Now, when you shoot and miss, are you doing that on purpose? Trying to make us lose? No. And are you ever going to throw the ball away, have it intercepted by the other team? The odds are yes. But are you trying to do that? Again, the answer is no. Because you're my partner, and we're working towards the same goal.

So, as long as he's physically able, the only reason that my horse *doesn't do something that I want him to do, or does something that I don't want him to do, is because I haven't explained well enough to him what it is I want from him. The onus is on me, not on him. He's my partner, so he's never against me, and I have to treat him that way. So words like, "He's being ornery," or "He's just trying to get out of it," or "He doesn't want to do it," just don't fit in how I work with my horses or think about my horses. You see, **it's my attitude that affects my horse's attitude; not my horse's attitude that affects mine.***

If you and I are going to develop a friendship or a partnership, I can't say, "Well, I'm going to wait for you to be good to me first." We have to treat a partner like a partner first, not like an adversary. You treat him like a partner first and foremost.

When Partnerships Falter

Life is always going to get tough, notes John Lyons. *You have all these aspirations, then you run into frustrations, and you want to quit and give up. That happens in horse training, in business, in marriages; it happens in most all endeavors. It's easy to quit when you're down; that's the time when most do quit. But if you quit then, you don't know if you're quitting because you don't like it, or just because you're down. No one likes being on the bottom, but we have to learn to work through that down period until we can teach the horse to do exactly what we want him to do and then say, "Okay, I don't want to train anymore; it's too much work." That applies not only to horse training, but to our marriages or businesses: **if we're going to quit, we have to make it perfect first and then quit**—on the upswing not on the downslide. Then we know we're quitting for the right reasons. Learning that sense of commitment with horses has helped me throughout all of my life.*

Of course there are some relationships that are not worth saving, and the only healthy choice is to get out and move on: *One gal I teach wants to ride on the A circuit, but her horse is a nut case because somebody beat it,* reports Anne Kursinski. *She says, "I just*

can't afford a better horse," Well, I'm sorry, no matter how much training you give it, or how much money you pour into it, that horse is not
going to get her where she wants to go. She deserves to ride better horses,
but she also has to believe that she is worth it.

She was married to an alcoholic and always made excuses, excuses,
excuses for his behavior—"He's better now; really, he's better now...."
Now it's the same with her horse; she makes all these excuses—today
he's better. But last week he threw her into a hedge, and the week before he bucked her off in the pasture.

There's a very big life lesson in learning that you deserve better—
but you really have to believe that you're worth it—like being married
to an alcoholic and getting out of that relationship to protect yourself.
In order not to fall back into the same trap in the next relationship, you
need to raise your standards and believe that you deserve better. I find
that you can tell a lot about people by the kinds of horses they ride; the
horse is a reflection of what they feel they deserve on a deeper level. I
really believe that.

Reconnecting

After divorce, or the failure of a relationship, some individuals
seek a respite from human companionship for a time, preferring
the simple attachment of a pet or equine partner. Mary Fenton
observes: *At a lot of my clinics, during introductions, there are women
who say, "I just got a divorce and got a horse," or "I got a horse and
then a divorce."*

Some find that the horse allows them to connect or reconnect on a non-sexual, yet still intimate level, with another partner:
*When I was separated from my husband for two months, having my
horse in my life satisfied my need for intimacy on some level,* claims
Jenny Butah. *It filled an empty space in a way that I can't explain,
but which I know is real.*

Occasionally, a person may project a role of surrogacy onto
their horse as a substitute for the lost relationship during their time

of healing: *For a while there, Star was my surrogate husband—not sexually—but he was the male I spent my free time with while I got my psyche back together,* Pat Lawson concedes. *I knew he wasn't going to cheat on me. I knew he wasn't going to leave. I knew he wasn't going to do a lot of things that humans do, so he became my closest companion.*

For others, equine connections happily fulfill their companionship needs: *After my divorce I dated mostly horsemen,* remarks Mary Deringer Phelps. *But I never felt the need to be married again. I didn't need that. If I hadn't been so horse crazy, I'd probably have met a lot more men and had a lot more boyfriends, but I don't think I'd have liked them as much as I enjoyed the times I've had with horses. Horses are so much a part of my life.... I do know horses took away a lot of nighttime entertainment for me. Hey, I could have been a barhopper or a wanton woman, but I was out feeding horses! No...seriously, if I have lost anything due to the horses, it's nothing compared to what they've given to me. If I had my life to do over again, I'd probably add a few more horses.*

Amity

The word "amity" with its root, "amor"—love—perhaps best describes what many horse people discover in their favorite steeds: a comfortable relationship of friendship, goodwill, camaraderie, harmony, peace, unity, fraternity, and rapport. Such relationships can be moving and memorable to witness: *Years ago a Thacher student, Brooks Crawford, had a horse named Mosquito,* recalls Jack Huyler. *One of the great shows we used to do for the parents was to gather on the hill overlooking the stables. Brooks would lead Mosquito down to the stable shop and have a friend hold Mosquito while he ran about the barns. We'd watch Brooks go in and out of various doorways of one barn and then another. Finally he'd hide in a manger or some place, put his fingers in his mouth, and give a shrill whistle. Mosquito would jump to attention; the cohort would let him loose, and that horse would take off, looking for Brooks. He'd retrace Brooks' trail exactly—in and out of all those places—like a bloodhound! And when he'd find Brooks, he'd squeal and kinda kick with delight. It was one of the greatest sights I ever saw!*

Another Thacher boy, Kenny Scott, had a little Arab named Ali Pasha, but everyone called him "The Little Dog" because he just was. When we would go camping, at night we tied the horses to trees—except for Ali Pasha. Sometimes when we'd go to bed, that horse would be clear out of sight.

Kenny always took his sleeping bag out about a hundred feet from the rest of us, because in the morning, we'd wake up, and Ali Pasha would be lying next to him. It gets me emotional even now.... It was wonderful....

Here's a report of one husband who thinks he's better off because of his wife's equine attachment: *I have a rider whose husband says he wishes she loved him as much as her horse, but since she got the horse, it's improved their marriage relationship ten-fold,* claims Jill Keiser Hassler. *He's very happy with her loving this horse.* Well, it's pretty hard to argue with a ten-fold improvement.

Women may express affection more openly than men, but the male contingent is no less taken with their equine partners. However, they may consider it as more of a profound friendship and be less apt to express it physically: *All humans need companionship, and it doesn't need to be other humans necessarily,* says Stagg Newman. *Horses give us a way of getting in touch with our emotional side and fill a need for companionship. Next to my wife, Drubin is probably my closest friend.*

Counting your horse as your second closest, or perhaps only, friend in the world is another fairly remarkable endorsement: *I had a pretty tough situation with my dad that ended with the state taking my brother and me away from him and putting us in a foster home,* relates Buck Brannaman. *During all that time in foster care, I felt like the horse was not only my best friend in the whole world, but maybe my only friend in the whole world.*

Horses offer many such lessons in the value and art of stead-fast friendship, genuine amity, and real love: *I've been accused of thinking more of these horses than I do of my family,* admits Rex Peterson. *I love them truly. There's one horse I've been through thick and thin with; he was with me before my family was: my big Paint horse, Hell On Wheels. It's hard to explain.... I've been through so much with that horse. He pulled me through a time that I believe I wouldn't be here today if it hadn't been for him. I'd get on him, ride on top of a hill, and sit up there for hours by myself—but I wasn't by myself—I was with him. I could sit and tell him all the problems, and he didn't argue with me; he didn't condemn me. He didn't criticize me, and he didn't lie to me. He was there. He is by far a very true friend to me for that because no matter what was wrong, he took it in stride. He didn't have any back talk, "You should have done this; you should do this, or you gotta do that." He's probably one of the truest friends I have. That horse is probably worth $2,500–$3,000 at most, but I spent $13,000 saving his life here a few years ago when he'd twisted a gut. People go, "How can you spend that much on that horse?" I tell them, "If your child was sick, what would you spend to save his life?"*

Love may command a big price, yet has no price tag. That's why true horse people don't fret much about the cost of keeping their horses. Money's simply not the issue—love is: *I've done the whole thing, from being a trainer to an instructor, to a judge and now doing these seminars,* says Richard Shrake. *And there's one thing that I can really tell you: 99.9% of the horse people really love their horses. They do.*

Skills for Success

At a time when contemporary American society is moving away from physical connection on many fronts—families fractured by divorce, children raised in day care, generations scattered far from ancestral roots, seniors sequestered in gated communities where pets and youngsters are only allowed to visit, and elderly parents relegated to nursing homes—a connection with an animal offers a nurturing, reassuring bond.

At a time when we no longer gather for meals—we drive through; we don't converse on the phone—we use voice mail; we don't know our bankers—we program a machine that spits out currency; we don't send letters—we "email," a feeling of oneness with another being is a personal gift of intimacy.

Even when personal relationships disconnect, partnership with a horse can offer solace, companionship, fun, and love. Such relationships offer lessons of acceptance, alliance, allegiance, respect, friendship...many aspects of everyday life that are becoming harder to find in the human arena. This is why staying linked with animals is vital to our humanity.

Mankind has used horses to vanquish armies, conquer new frontiers, transport cargo, and cultivate the earth. Now that horses are no longer needed for those functions, let us ally with them in recreation, amity, and pleasure—as partners—to expand our humanity, stir our souls, and sow the seeds of personal growth with *HorsePower!*

CAROL STRATTON, b. 1929, is an art historian and avid rider who, in 1949, was Vermont State Champion in Senior Equitation. Carol and her 1996 New England Field Hunter Champion, Brother, are seen enjoying the course at Green Mountain Horse Association in South Woodstock, Vermont during the three-day educational horse trials.

CHAPTER SEVEN

SHOWTIME!

Goals and Competition

*You lose some you don't deserve, and you win some
you don't deserve. —Macella O'Neill*

The two sweating beings fought to regain control and complete their dance in a cadence that would climax in a high that
only soulmates experience. The agile woman breathed deeply as
her long legs gripped the powerfully muscled torso of her anxious partner. Through an unspoken language that had grown out
of their long alliance, they became one in an exhilarating exhibition of physical prowess and conquest. With a final driving rhythm
they realized their shared goal—the two had jumped the course
clean and won their first Grand Prix!

The preceding tongue-in-cheek, purple-prose scenario is
meant to call attention to a very real, yet rarely discussed aspect of
riding—the sensational physical, emotional, and spiritual rush that
occurs when human and horse experience perfect harmony in the
throes of competition. The romance of riding as dance, the phenomenon of equine partnership filling emotional needs, the profound connection felt when man and beast are in sync, have all
been discussed as important factors in the human value of horses.

Such alliances, however, are innocent romps when compared to the heart-stopping heat of competition. The thrill of the action, risk and that "perfect ride" achieved in competition are emotional highs that seduce contestants to return again and again in search of equestrian euphoria.

The Rush

About seven years ago, I had a guy (I'll call Pete) in my polo clinic at the University of Virginia who had never played before, relates Rege Ludwig. *After the first day it was evident that he was going to need extra help.*

*Through the week Pete's riding came along well, but in playing polo he was much, much slower than everyone else. At one point, a player controlling the ball had another guy trying to ride him off it, so he hit the ball hard, and it sailed up past Peter. Those two tore after the ball, looked up, and here's Pete in front of them going **very slow**— so they split—one whips around Pete's left side, and the other flashes by on his right; they meet in front and resume their ride off.*

Pete was taken completely by surprise, hearing the pounding of hooves behind him only seconds before being engulfed by the action, then left with his senses reeling. The ensuing adrenaline rush was something Pete had never experienced before, and he cried out, "Hot Damn! This is better than sex!" He wasn't trying to be funny—he wasn't even aware of what he'd said—but everybody on the field almost died laughing. As Pete discovered, you don't necessarily need to win to get your juices flowing—you just have to get in the game.

I enjoy what I consider the more dangerous horse activities, notes Valerie Kanavy. *In endurance riding, there's an element of danger— some of the speeds, some of the country, and the way you travel at times. I used to fox hunt, and I got a thrill out of surviving that fantasy—a rush from surviving something that was really difficult or threatening.*

Thankfully, the rush of equestrian euphoria is available to those who enjoy less dangerous horse activities as well. Since equestrian sport and competition run the gamut from in-hand classes to polo, pleasure riding to timber racing, there is a niche for almost every conceivable skill, risk, and financial level—a contest for everyone with an interest in horses. *I can remember shows where it seemed like the ride was almost in slow motion,* recalls Richard Shrake. *Everything kind of stops—I don't hear the crowd—the horse just becomes part of me, and all of a sudden, it's like somebody opens up a window in a real stuffy room, and you feel that little breeze of perfection for about ninety seconds....* Ninety seconds of perfection. Richard doesn't mention a *win*—just the rush of becoming one with his horse for ninety seconds of perfection. That is the prize.

Competitive Challenges

As with many activities, when done well, riding appears effortless, so the uninitiated may have little appreciation for the ability, discipline, courage, and athletic talent required. It can be disheartening to hear, "What's so tough about riding? The horse does all the work!" Or, as overheard at an exhibition of the Royal Lippizaners when the dazzling stallions were performing a complex dressage movement requiring lead changes with every step, "Oh look, honey, they're skipping—how cute." Or the spectator at the Napa Valley Classic Grand Prix jumping benefit complaining, "Five feet? That's not a very tall jump!"

Before I started to ride, like may nonriders I didn't have a clue what it takes, says Mary Mansi. *Recently, my husband, Steve, asked to ride my horse, Magic. He got on, and I led him around at the walk. Instantly Steve's feeling really insecure with nothing to hang on to—suddenly he was scared. He asked, "How do you stay on at the trot, at the canter, let alone over a fence?" He'd never realized what it was like to have to work with the horse's motion. You really don't know until you do it yourself.* With that short walk about, Steve discovered it's a good mental and physical exercise to not only walk in another's shoes, but to ride in their stirrups in order to have a true appreciation for what they do.

A "simple" game of polo is a complex event that challenges players to strategize fast-paced action at breakneck speeds and requires skills from across the equestrian spectrum: *If you want to be good at polo, you have to be able to figure how to get along with each pony and get everything out of it in order to perform at your maximum,* declares Rege Ludwig. *Now that's the same challenge of any other equestrian sport, but in polo you also need to be able to work with three other people on your team, plus you have the challenge of hitting that little white ball, which at speed becomes quite difficult. Finally, you're trying to do all those things while the other team is trying to prevent you from doing any of it. Putting all that together is a big task, but that's the neat thing about polo—that complex challenge.*

In polo you have to be able to: ride forward like a jockey over the horse's center of balance as it's running; ride like a cutter to stay centered when the horse makes very quick lateral movements; ride like a dressage rider, able to collect the horse for brief moments until you need an extension or a turn; ride like a roper to stay in the saddle as you quickly speed up, quickly slow down, or make a fast turn; and occasionally ride like a trick rider hanging off the side to reach the ball…. So, in a polo game you're adjusting in and out of a lot of different seats—hopefully with the dexterity of a ballet dancer so you don't interfere with the balance of your horse.

From the chaotic battleground of polo to the manicured arena of the show ring, successful competitive teams never cease to impress and inspire those in the know: *My background is horse show competition,* says Richard Shrake. *I just can't imagine when you watch somebody win a cutting futurity or a jumping grand prix, or a world championship reining routine, and see that team compete and say that that's not an absolute piece of poetry. The dedication and the lifetime of total commitment that it takes to reach those levels of competition…. Have you ever watched Susie Hutchinson win a grand prix—jump-*

ing with just a thong through her horse's mouth? Now if that doesn't put goosebumps on ya', nothin' will. I have a very healthy respect for the people at the top.

The easier it looks, usually the harder it is to achieve—that's the dichotomy of success.

Competitive Goals

Though we can't predict the final outcome when we pursue a goal, we do know that competitive goals are reached first and foremost through the mastery of basic skills. In the equestrian arena, where progress depends on the training and temperament of two disparate beings, headway may be slow and at times frustrating, yet it cannot be rushed or compressed. In the horse world, especially, as Mary Deringer Phelps quotes, "There is no elevator to the top—you have to take the stairs."

An individual blessed with innate talent may start off on stairs with higher risers, while a plodder is relegated to mount many more shallow steps; still, as the two perfect their crafts and approach the top floor, their climbs even out. The stairway to equestrian heights, however, is not conventionally engineered or precisely architectural. It's more like a fragile staging one might find in a fun house: fraught with uneven risers, unforeseen drops, surprise twists, and at times, disconcerting gloom—all destined to trip us up. The daring soul who persists in navigating this bizarre passageway successfully survives a memorable adventure that challenges and strengthens abilities, while building resolve.

Through the process of competing one learns how to work toward a goal, to be patient, to be progressive, and not to be greedy, notes William Steinkraus. *My goals have been progressive; my first goal, I suppose, was to learn how to do a posting trot. I remember with my old teacher in Wilton, Connecticut, my second goal was to be able to canter without losing the dollar bill that she put underneath my seat. Then to be able to jump, then to be able to jump 3' 6", then to jump 4' and so on to the Olympics....*

I do think goals have to have some relationship to where you're starting from. If you have very, very lofty goals and you don't have any understanding of the mechanism that helps get you there (which you cannot have at the very beginning), you're going to be frustrated so much of the time that you may give up. But, if you have realistic goals that are progressive steps forward, you realize that, yes, maybe there is a pot of gold at the end of this rainbow. Then you also realize that you have to pay your dues.

A strong goal is perhaps most important in the face of setbacks and defeats, for at those times, we have only the gossamer promise of success rather than tangible, measurable victories to rely on for incentive: *In 1989, when my back gave out due to a degenerating disk, the first doctor I went to said, "Oh, you'll never ride again,"* reports Becky Hart. *But I found a sports medicine doctor who said, "Well, we'll get you on a horse, but I don't know about hundred-mile rides." I knew if he could get me on a horse, I could do endurance. As it turned out, I was off for about nine months. During that recuperation, I'd be at the gym on the Stair-Master, going up and down thinking, "Oh, God, this is so boring." But I had a goal that motivated me to work: the 1990 World Championships at the first World Equestrian Games in Stockholm.* Becky and Rio found a gold medal at the end of their rainbow in Stockholm, when persistence, patience, and promise paid off in winning that World Championship.

I started off with a goal of completing a single hundred-mile race, says Stagg Newman. *I never dreamed that I would have a horse like Drubin that's completed over twenty [hundred-mile races] and won the 1992 National Championship. Now my goal is to be doing hundreds for ten years with Drubin. To me that's really the mark of excellence: to keep the horse going as well at sixteen as he was at six—actually better because he's got all the conditioning and training—that's when you know you've done your best. Yeah, I have fantasies of my horse being one of the all-time great horses.... Goals often cross into fantasies.*

Fantasies produce goals that in turn can generate new fantasies, so that competitors are always resetting the bar: *I've dreamt about marathons, I've dreamt about competing, and they turned into goals,* remarks Jimmy Fairclough. *The closer I've gotten, the harder I want to work for those goals, and I still dream. One day I thought I'd be happy with a team gold medal, and we achieved that. But then I was fourth individually, and now that is not good enough. I'm looking to the individual gold.*

Thus, the process of setting goals is not static—it's as dynamic as the tides: the surge and ebb of desires and accomplishments, the peaks and troughs of expectations and disappointments, the distraction of undercurrents, the splash of achievement, with the ensuing ripples of new dreams born.

In addition to being dynamic, goals are unique to each person, for even though many may be vying to win the same contest, each is competing for various personal reasons: *I think one life lesson is to figure out why we compete and what our personal ambition is,* observes Linda Tellington-Jones. *Is it simply to feed our ego? Is it to develop a relationship with another animal? Is it to amass blue ribbons? Or is it to test the best that we can be? That's very individual and useful for each person to look at.*

For me, winning was never the primary goal—it was to see how good a partnership I could develop with the horse. Competition is a way of challenging myself; it's a way of judging progress and finding a scale by which I can judge myself without necessarily judging myself against others.

When I did the Jim Shoulders Hundred-Mile Endurance Race in 1961, I made cards describing every mile of the trail. I had in my mind where and how I was going to ride for a hundred miles ahead, and I put my horse there with me so that she knew what was going on. We finished that race in thirteen and a half-hours—six and a half hours ahead of the next horse—a record time that stood for seven years.

Now a hundred-mile race is a real challenge, and what I learned from it is that when you just chunk down life—piece by piece—some-thing that seems like an impossible task becomes very simple.

Obviously, a goal remains intangible until realized, and the route to fruition may be subtle and painfully indirect, as Mary Fenton explains: *If you work and ask in small increments, suddenly the result you want will fall into your hand like a ripe plum falling off a tree. You're not striving for the plum to get ripe—you can't make it get ripe—you can only support it and know that it will get ripe with time and the proper steps taken to support its own process. I used to wonder what that meant—after all my years training, teaching, and competing with horses—now I get it.* As with most procedures in life, transforming the seed of aspiration into a ripened result re-quires a process of sequential growth achieved through nurturing and tending.

Being Judged

In many equestrian contests the victor is determined objec-tively: the fastest time in a race, the most goals in a polo game, the least number of faults over a jump course.... Such impartial mea-surements generate relatively incontrovertible results. However, a great deal of horse showing is determined subjectively—based on the opinion of one or more judges. Hence, it is in this arena where sportsmanship is most often tested. As Buck Brannaman reports, *Anyone who's been to a horse show and lost has disagreed with the judge. With shows being a subjective kind of a thing, you're going to get that. There have been times when I thought I really did well and the judges never even noticed me, and then there were other days when I thought I should have been given the gate and I won the show. So things even out over all.*

But actually, showing is a nice thing to do with your horse. It's fun to take him to town and see what he looks like compared to everyone else's. You might never have much for goals if you weren't shooting for something like that, so I think it's a good thing.

With all the thousands of students, horses, and shows Helen Crabtree has experienced over the years, she still laments one judging incident even decades later: *Years ago I had a student, Eddie Lumio, who had a very uncooperative mare,* relates Helen. *She was nice-looking, and Eddie was a handsome young man, so they were a pleasing picture, but that mare was difficult to ride and truly didn't think right. But she was all he had, so Eddie worked, and worked, and worked with that mare.*

Now this was back in the days of saddleseat equitation when boys were a total rarity, and many judges would look up, see Eddie coming, and just eye-skip over him to the next girl. They just wouldn't consider a boy.

At the world championships in Louisville one year, I could see Eddie was winning his class. Eddie had his mare set up right and doing all she could do splendidly. It was not an obvious effort, but you could tell that she was good **because** *he was good. Unfortunately, the man judging Eddie's class was not an equitation judge and tied Eddie out of the money. My heart just bled for this boy because he was winning that class with his expertise and ability.*

I told him, "Eddie, I believe that's the best ride you've ever made!" He came out of the ring as sincere as he could be and said, "Miss Crabtree, that's the best I've ever been able to get that mare's head." And that's all he said. And here he was out of the money and should have won the class. Now I don't often say anything—I leave the judging up to the judges. But that class just irked me because the judge really wasn't judging a class he understood.

With our students we never stress winning or where you place; we never have. It's always "Make every step that horse takes a little better than the last one he took." By just doing that, you create your own reward. Then you understand that it's your ability that's important, not "the win." You don't have to have somebody else reward you for doing your best. The thrill of competition is great, and winning the class is wonderful, but it's not the most important, so we never stressed winning.

Within the philosophy of the Crabtree school, Eddie's performance actually reflects two points of pride: first, the success of the ride itself, and secondly, Eddie's sincere sportsmanship in the face of frustration that his best performance was not acknowledged by the judge.

When competing, you have to learn to accept another person's opinion of you, your horse, and your abilities: *In being judged, you have to learn how to accept what somebody else thinks about you,* notes Becky Hart. *You just have to say, "Okay, that's what they think..." whether you agree with it or not.*

I remember one time when I showed an Arab in western pleasure and everybody else was showing Quarter Horses. My horse had done really well, and it was a schooling show, so I asked the judge what could I do to improve. She said, "Nothing really; your horse did everything right. I just would never place a horse like that." I was devastated, but I learned not to show with her again. Most competitors would agree that over the long haul of subjective competition, undeserved losses usually balance out with undeserved wins.

Although most professional horse show judges are trained to be neutral and make decisions based on criteria of the class or breed, they are still human and as such, may consciously or unconsciously slant decisions according to personal preferences or bias: *Because of my color I am judged the minute I enter the ring,* says Pat Lawson. *Since black women generally don't do what I do, I get judged on things that aren't even in the mix—like whether or not I should be there—which has both helped and hindered me. I've had judges who admire my individuality, and I've had judges who were unhappy that I was competing and felt that I had entered an area that was not for me. I've learned not to let any of that bother me because if I did, that would be letting someone else define me, and I don't allow that. If I've made the assessment that my horse and I have done our best, given all the elements, I'm happy regardless of what the judges say.*

Before reaching such a level of mature security, young competitors may take judging decisions very personally: *I had some really nice kids who could win and lose, but then I had others who would come back from the ring and say, "That judge hates me."* reports Mary Deringer Phelps. *I'd tell them, "That judge doesn't even know you. Do you think that judge walked in the ring and said, 'I'm taking this girl out because I don't like her?' Quit blaming it on somebody—you win, you lose—it's life. Accept it; learn from it, and do things a little better the next time."*

Even the most professional and impartial judges cannot possibly see everything going on in a class, an event, or a game. Thus, it is crucial to realize that judges and umpires are not appointed because they are always correct or just, but for the sake of order—someone has to make determinations during the course of competition, and contestants must then defer to their decisions: *Polo has umpires, and just as in football, hockey, or basketball, whatever the umpire calls is what you go with—period,* states Susan Stovall. *That's taught me respect for authority—I may disagree with the umpire, but he is the judge; he is the jury; he is the tournament committee, and he is doing the best he can.*

An interesting aspect of polo is that the umpire position rotates, so the Golden Rule—you know, do unto others—helps keep things balanced. In polo, sportsmanship is important and part of sportsmanship is respect of authority and giving umpires the benefit of good judgment. In running the polo club, I'll often get people coming up to me saying, "That guy didn't do a very good job of umpiring." But ninety-nine percent of the time it's the losers complaining.

Although at times they may seem like adversaries, judges and umpires are vital partners in competition, for without them a contest could quickly become a war of abuses.

In endurance, winning is based on time, but veterinarians at checkpoints throughout the ride decide whether a horse is fit to continue, explains Stagg Newman. *One lesson I have learned is to respect the veterinarians—they're making the judgment and even though it's not totally objective, in the heat of competition, their judgment is probably better than the rider's. The rider may have a different set of data from the judge—there are some things you know about your horse because you know the horse—but when you're competing, your adrenaline gets going, and sometimes your desire to win takes the edge. In an endurance ride, you get out there seventy, eighty miles, and you're tired and not functioning at a hundred percent. Most of us try to remember that in endurance the judges are really our partners. They're trying to help us get through the ride consistent with the safety and protection of the horse, which is paramount.*

When a competitor's goal is the blue ribbon or the trophy itself, subjective judging may block that goal; but when the competitor's goal is his personal best, then a judge's decision becomes irrelevant: *I'm actually my own worst critic and judge,* declares Valerie Kanavy. *But it's my opinion of myself that's really important. You need to trust yourself, trust your own experience, and your knowledge—take other people's input—but don't live on their input. Trust yourself, believe in yourself.* That ability for personal assessment is the bottom line in competition. Surely, winning the trophy may add an element of excitement, but when you know you've performed your finest ever, the absence of a ribbon or any external acknowledgement should not diminish that personal pride.

Winning and Losing

Since equestrian competition has sprung from a desire to learn how to improve stock or riding and training skills, there is an inherent educational motive in most events. The mounted patrol has a challenging competition for the special duties of their officers and mounts: *I'd only had Big John about a year when he went through the National Police Competition for the first time,* says Lt. Carl Clipper. *Between 85 and 120 police horses from departments all over the United States and Canada compete in the three phases of the competition: uniform horse appearance, the hack class, and the obstacle course. The obstacle course is made up of monsters from a horse nightmare. It's everything that you do on duty and then some: shooting your gun from the saddle; placing a ticket on a windshield; going over grates; passing through a demonstration line; dismounting, handcuffing a subject, and remounting; throwing tree limbs into wood shredders; going up to five standing fans with streamers blowing; jumps—from one-and-a-half to three-foot—depending on the point value you go for.... You lose points if you refuse or pass up any obstacle.*

There was one test where we had to go through a tunnel with sprinkler heads laced through and water shooting out. The worst was the jack hammer on the steel plate—that put a lot of horses away. When your horse takes these obstacles at your request, you're very proud of that animal. Big John did everything I asked him to do. He didn't come out in the top ten, but he hung right in there. It's tough, but it's really good training, and we pick up a lot of new techniques.

It truly is amazing what tests we humans conjure up for horses in the name of competition. But by competing, both horse and rider face new trials, gain new skills, test aptitude, and expand confidence as they progress from good, to better, to best.

Those who truly enjoy competing can focus on learning and improving rather than winning: *No matter how hard I practice or train, I lose many more competitions than I win,* admits Anne Kursinski. *And that's okay, because a competition is really a test on the homework I've been doing to see how far I've come, what I need to work on to be a little better, to go a little faster, jump a little higher, or use my eyes a little differently. Every competition is filled with life lessons; it's always a test, and, oh God, it's another lesson.*

This attitude toward competition is difficult for many to grasp, since much of professional sports today is summed up in a win-loss statement on the news. Shots of the victors joyfully pouring champagne on their coach while the losers glumly slink off to the locker room supports the message that winning is everything.

We had a headmaster at Thacher at a time when there used to be a big state show—one year there were 1,040 entries, remarks Jack Huyler. *When I was doing shows like that, the headmaster would ask me, "Well, how'd the show go yesterday?" And I'd say, "I was very pleased." Then he'd exclaim, "Oh, you won!" and I'd say, "No, I didn't win, but my horse and I worked well together; I was pleased." Occasionally I'd report, "Well, I cleaned up, but I wasn't pleased." He never did understand these exchanges because winning was it to him. But any horseman knows, it's the teamwork of horse and rider—how you do against your own standard. That should be true in life.*

Certainly any competitor would love to win, but that is not necessarily the only reason to enter: *For me, competition is more to exhibit skill rather than to win,* claims Pat Lawson. *When I go into competition, it is not to beat anybody but myself. It's not for the ribbon; it's not for the acclaim; it's not for the applause. It's to perform my skills, to show, to exhibit, to beat myself. If I fall short, I don't feel like a loser, I just realize that something was missed and there is more training to be done to get it.*

Even when I barrel race, I know I'm running against the clock, but it's my clock. I'm not running against the arena clock; I run against the clock in my head that my horse and I have already set for ourselves. That's much more enjoyable to me. If other competitors come out ahead of me because of someone else's timing, so be it. If I beat my time, I'm happy. If I happen to beat my time and theirs too, I'm really happy.

Having only yourself to beat can take a lot of pressure out of the competition: *Competing in tennis, one-on-one against another person, is extremely intense for anyone, but especially for a young person,* says Diana Thompson. *I was doing this when I was ten to fifteen years of age; I won the sectionals five years in a row, was ranked third in the Pacific Northwest Division of the United States Lawn Tennis Association, and was second in the Washington State Championships in AAA. The pressure of being good, winning a lot, and then being in center court for finals at that age by myself made me nervous.*

In contrast, competing with a horse was so much easier than being out there by myself. That remains to this day. I can do a demonstration in front of five hundred people with a horse. I have strength with my horse as my partner instead of being in a confrontational battle with a human being across the tennis net. I am a competitive, but not an aggressive, person. The experience and pressure of being a tennis star was good experience, but competing with the horses was a lot more fun— I'd still get very nervous in a show, but it's a whole different game from the stress of being a singles tennis competitor.

Diana highlights the difference between going up against an opponent and winning at your own game. The goal in most showing is to do your best as a single horse and rider team. Certainly there are other contenders in a horse show class, but no opponent—except yourself.

It's a lot easier to deal with a win than a loss. Perhaps that's why the "powers that be" have arranged that we get so much more practice at dealing with defeat: *The first world championship I went to in Italy, I was the favorite,* says Becky Hart. *It was the first time I'd ever been to Europe, and I was hounded by the press and had all this attention, which I'd never had before. This was supposed to be the big race between me and the European champions.*

Fifty-four horses started at 5:30 a.m. and thirteen finished—I came in at midnight. I finished, which was a miracle in itself, but I was dead last. Dead last. It was good that I'd completed, because with my finish the U.S. team got a silver medal, but I felt just horrible. It was a long time before I could let that loss be okay and I could talk about it without bursting into tears. That is hard to do—to find out how to live with defeat and to let it be okay. But simply put, competing has taught me to win and lose with grace.

I was once told, "A goal is a dream with a deadline," which is certainly true of competitive goals set by a schedule of singular events such as the Olympics. When the event calendar and your circumstances do not mesh, it can be very discouraging: *I really thought I had a very, very good chance for the 1960 games with Riviera Wonder, but he suddenly went lame in the games although he hadn't shown a thing before,* recounts William Steinkraus. *So I had that terrible disappointment—I'm expecting to be very competitive, and I'm nowhere.*

Then, in 1964, Snowbound had a terrific year, and I thought he had a good chance to win in Mexico City—if he could hold up—he was always a very delicate horse, physically. But I'd been down that road before, so I knew that expectations fall into a chance distribution curve.

There are times when you're doing well, you've been scoring well, your whole game is together…the sounder you are, the more experience your horse has and you have together, the more physical scope and all that…the better your chances. But nobody, especially in our sport of show jumping, nobody wins them all, so you learn to have a realistic expectation.

I'd say a terrific winning percentage for a year is maybe ten percent of the grand prix that you ride in, you win. That's terrific—that's horse of the year. So that means you don't win ninety percent of the time. To be a good competitor you learn to take the bitter and the sweet. As you grow up and compete, if you're reasonably mature, you learn to understand that for every time you win you're going to lose ten or twenty times. That's the nature of human existence: life, nature, and sport are very, very fickle…. Competition has taught me to take the losses in stride, then to build on them—to squeeze something constructive out of them. The wins? You learn not to let them go to your head…important things to learn.

The variety and nature of equestrian competition provide many opportunities for the disabled to participate in shows and gain the valuable experience and lessons available through competing: *A lot of children, particularly children with disabilities have never been in a competitive situation,* reports Octavia Brown. *They're held out of sports because they can't compete with able-bodied people. However, competitive nature is up and running in everybody; so often, part of our therapeutic training involves having to literally teach these children how to deal with success and failure. I think it's very important for the families, as much as anybody, to understand the nature of horse competition. To know the judge is looking at something that you may not be looking at. And if you feel that you should have won, you have to go and talk it over and figure out how to do better next time. Then you can see it as a continuing process rather than, "I didn't win, and I'm no good." Whether you're able-bodied or not, the same lesson holds true to teach competitors to handle defeat, and not winning, with a certain amount of grace and charm.*

For many, just making the decision to compete represents a personal victory that leads to tremendous growth and empowerment: *Shows for handicapped riders are judged the same way as regular shows, except that they do take into account if a rider can't post because they're paralyzed—the rider will wear a ribbon so the judges know,* explains Tracy Cole. *At a show, even if you think that you were really great compared to the rest of the class, you may not win. That happened to me this summer. After that class I asked the judge what I did wrong, and she said it looked like the horse was more in control than I was.*

So I entered the next class—same horse, same judge, but this time it was an obstacle course. My horse really had a problem with a couple of the obstacles because he got spooked by them—a visible spook—not just a hesitation. It was obvious he did not want to do them, but I got him to go over everything. I wanted that judge to see that I was able to control the horse. It did matter to me that I lost, but I felt redeemed after the obstacle course—"Yeah. We really do know what we're doing here." Tracy was able to turn her loss into a positive success for herself. Horse shows are competition, but even more importantly they are continuing education for each and every competitor.

Personal Best

Natural born competitors have an internal drive mechanism that constantly pushes them toward their personal best. *I'd say a good general prescription for riding better is to always be asking for a little something more—for something a little bit more perfect,* advises William Steinkraus. *Always work to refine the horse's response to the aids by developing more and more subtle finesse.* Such nuances of finesse often mark the difference between competent and inspired riding.

In equestrian sport, success is due to the performance of the whole athlete—the mind, body, and spirit—not just physical prowess. Equestrian contests reflect that need for wholeness, since it takes mental, emotional, and psychological proficiency even more than physical strengths to prevail: *Riding is more a psychological, emotional experience than it is a purely physical one,* notes Doug Lietzke. *People who do well in riding are emotionally tuned in, enjoy what they're doing, and get real satisfaction from it. Oftentimes there are minimal differences in skill between the person who wins and those who don't. Competitors at a particular level tend to have similar physical skills. Mark Spitz made an interesting observation after breaking seven world records and winning seven gold medals in swimming at the 1972 Olympics. He said at the higher levels of competition, physical differences are minimal; the winning edge comes with mental, psychological, and emotional strengths. That's very true in riding where the most memorable performances are highlighted by heart, presence, and spirit.*

If physical superiority were the only consideration in competition, the fastest or fittest horse would be consistently unbeatable. However, since contests are determined by a multitude of complex factors such as current conditions, attitude, strategy, heart, rider, and luck, in any given event, a long shot can win and a favorite lose. Such competitive caprice must be handled philosophically, not punitively: *In the cutting game, like in a lot of games, there's so much emphasis put on winning and losing that even a good horse suddenly becomes a "puke," as I've heard them called, if they don't win,* reports Larry Mahan. *I totally disagree with that. A lot of horses, especially in the name of competition, are pushed beyond their limitations, and if they don't reach the goals that man thinks they should reach, then all of a sudden they're no-good horses. To me, whether it be a horse, or a person, we all deserve the opportunity to reach our maximum potential, but just because we can't do some things that others can do, we shouldn't be discredited for that…or discarded.*

Running your horse into the ground in search of a win makes no competitive, economic, or common sense. A victory at the expense of your equine partner is never sweet: *I've learned through competition that when I've won by pushing my horse to perform above his means, I haven't felt real good about that,* admits Valerie Kanavy. *And sometimes when I've not won but have ridden a horse within its capacity—right to its capacity—and met all the challenges, it's better than winning. If I've had to overuse my horse in order to win a trophy, I don't like myself very much at all.*

One of my biggest lessons is that who I am, and what kind of person I am—how good or bad a person I am—does not revolve around whether I win a horse race. Winning a horse race has done nothing to save a soul or to make the world a better place, but being a good horseman—training a horse, riding it to its potential, then having the horse give back to you—is very gratifying. My horse has won some races with unbelievable runs to the finish that I haven't asked of him— never touched him with a whip—he just decided, "I'm going for it." That's an incredible high, an incredible feeling.

The line between competitive drive and exploitation can be a very fine one. When experience, knowledge, and sensitive horsemanship tell you your mount is "maxed out" and you should pull back, yet your horse continues to charge on, your horse is giving his personal best, and that gift is golden.

The only way to be a good rider and trainer is to win against your-self, states Helen Crabtree. *If you go in to a show thinking, "Last time I was sixth and Betty Jo was fifth, so if I beat Betty Jo now, I'm better..." that just doesn't work because now you're mentally riding two horses when you have enough trouble just riding your own.*

I put up a sign in the dormitory at our stable, "There is one word we never use on this farm, and that word is "beat." We don't beat our horses, and we don't beat other riders. When you throw horsemanship and sportsmanship out the window, things just get worse from there on. You forget yourself and your horse and the job at hand by constantly trying to wonder what somebody else is doing. That's up to them. The whole idea is to concentrate on your own accomplishments and do your best; that's all you can do—but do it—don't cheat yourself.

Best efforts do not always result in wins, but they offer rewards of personal pride and satisfaction, while slacking off and doing less yields only personal disappointment: *When you know you've done your best, there's nothing more you could have done,* notes Richard Shrake. *But if you come out of the ring knowing that you were late and really didn't get him warmed up, or you forgot to get his tail combed out, or you showed up with the wrong bridle or improper dress...that's when you really feel bad because you're only half-way trying, and that fifty percent effort will make you sick.*

We have a little saying that I tell the kids, "When it's time to ride and compete, it's too late to prepare." When you're in the middle of taking that test, you'd better be ready and have all your ducks in order.

How many other sports do you see young people, when the gate opens at 6:00 or 8:00, they're there with their very best hat and shirt on, their hair's right—in other words, they feel good about themselves. You see what's happening in competition is these kids are getting pre-pared for life. They've got to be responsible about how they compete and that they're not out there doing dirt to other people. It's a big re-sponsibility that they've got to learn early in life. I see life lessons like that everyday as I judge or teach.

That same philosophy of diligent preparation, when applied to school or career, couldn't help but generate success and personal gratification. Those precious instances when horse and rider perform their finest together can transform a personal best into personal perfection: *Every year I look back on a couple moments of total perfection, where everything came together,* reports Macella O'Neill. *For me, that makes everything worth it—the harsh physical elements, the many unrewarding results, the impossible schedule, every single thing right down the line is worth it for those few rides that at the end of the year I can look back and say, "That was great! THAT WAS GREAT!" Those few perfect rounds are why competing is really exciting. Everything clicks; everybody is on the same page; everything is working. It commands the attention of the crowd; suddenly everyone stops what they were doing, gets quiet, and watches. That goes beyond physical performance. That goes beyond sport. That gets into art.*

Losing Perspective

In the heat of competition, humans may "push the envelope" to test their own potential or set a sports record. Horses, on the other hand, have no concept of "world records" and are incapable of such statistical hubris. Horses do, however, give their trust to humans and can run on heart alone until they drop. That is a sacred trust for a rider.

When horse and rider have trained for months or years to be in top form on a specific day for an important event, the human may lose perspective. The higher up the competitive ladder, the more there is at stake, and if the human ego flares out of control, the equestrian partnership is out of control. Even seasoned Olympic competitors such as eventer J. Michael Plumb have fallen victim to competitive compulsion: *Most of the injuries that I've gotten,* Michael acknowledges, *have been because I had overfaced either myself or the horse and had no business doing what I was doing. I really did a lot of damage in Lexington, Kentucky. It was my own fault in that I was riding horses who were not ready for that high a level of competition. One horse had a heart condition that I was not aware of. I found out at the ten-minute check before the cross-country when the vet said, "This mare's heart is not quite right." Being a macho, tough— and I would say now—ignorant person, I said, "Listen, this is the last thing I want to hear before I set out; I'm going anyway." He said, "Okay, it's not a serious thing, but you'd better monitor her."*

Well, the mare fell at the water and lay there. I let her get her breath. Then I got on her and went on. When she fell again later, I broke my shoulder. The horse was all right, but that incident highlighted for me a problem that a lot of competitors have—when the adrenaline's going, you don't see clearly all the time. I didn't. I learned an important lesson that day: when in a challenging situation, you need to be competitive, but you also need to be sympathetic with how your horse is going. That's a tough one because the urge to win, the urge to finish, the desire for all those things sometimes overshadow your common sense.

As in most professional sports, drugs and alcohol have a presence in the horse world—albeit an aggressively regulated and comparatively small presence. It's tough enough to compete on charged horse flesh while sober, let alone strung out on drugs. *In the old days they used to joke, "When you buy the horse, you have to buy the key,"* notes William Steinkraus. *The key was often some particular way of feeding the horse, or a specific piece of tack, or a special way to warm him up. In the sixties, however, the key got to be, "You give him three cc's of this and two cc's of that six hours before the class...." Fortunately, the AHSA [American Horse Shows Association] medication rule has controlled most of that. Although it appears there's an ongoing contest with some individuals who continually look for a pharmaceutical miracle that won't show up in tests. I have never been into the drug scene. I have, however, observed drug use in equestrian competition, but I've never seen it improve anybody's riding. Quite the contrary—I'd say, "What happened to so and so?"*

"Well, he's a little spaced out today...."

I can think of a number of outstanding riders, however, who have had enough falls that they can't seem to make their bodies do the right thing unless they've had a couple of ounces of whiskey to bring their confidence back. Professional riders who really were basket cases when they'd do it all in cold blood, but who could ride absolutely brilliantly and fearlessly with a little bit of help from the flask. "False courage" is what that particular practice has been called, going back decades if not centuries.

Pushing oneself in competition to the point of physical harm or pharmaceutical dependence knocks a rider out of balance and usually out of the contest altogether.

Sportsmanship

Most equestrian sport involves individual rather than team competition, so the outcome of the event rests on the shoulders of each competitor. Hence competition in the horse show arena deals with sportsmanship on an intensely personal level. You may blame the horse, or the judge, or bad luck, but ultimately you come to realize the onus of responsibility sits in the saddle with you: *One of the first shows that my daughter entered, she came out and hadn't won a ribbon and sulked, "This is a terrible pony." Then she slapped the pony and jumped off,* reports Phyllis Eifert. *So I said, "Okay, let's pack up and go home—now." I'd spent money on all of the entry fees so that was lost, but it was a valuable loss. I gave her a good talking to—I told her it's never the pony's fault; it's always the rider's fault, and if you think that way, you'll improve yourself and be a better rider. From then on she was a fantastically good sport—and a good rider—she went on to win the medal in the Maclay classes. But she learned her lesson through that one experience.*

This does not mean to say that hard luck can play a part in dashing dreams through no fault of horse or rider. Qualifying for a world championship is arduous, expensive, and challenging, requiring consistent success over a long series of trials. To make the cut is a commendable feat; to be disqualified due to bad luck is a tremendous frustration that tries anyone's sense of sportsmanship. At the 1994 World Equestrian Games in Holland, America's Valerie Kanavy won the individual gold medal, but the rest of the team did not fare so well: *In 1992 Drubin and I won the National Championship,* reports Stagg Newman. *In '93 we won the bronze medal at the North American, and in 1994 we were heading for the world championships at the World Equestrian Games in Holland. I thought we'd done everything right; then we get over there and Drubin gets hurt. The day after we arrived, Drubin was going beautifully, but when we checked him five hours later, he was stiffening up really bad in the rear. After a bunch of diagnostics and ultrasound, we found out he had a hematoma in his right rear...possibly from the shipping...though we're still not exactly sure what happened. It looked like we wouldn't even start in the world championship—something I'd worked so many years for....*

Fortunately, with a tremendous amount of physical therapy from all the great people there to help us, Drubin was going fine the day before the ride. The vet told me he would watch and give me the thumbs up or down, but if Drubin felt good, I should go ahead and ride my ride.

For twenty-five miles Drubin felt fine—we were actually setting the pace in the lead group—he was just going beautifully. At that time, the three of us in the lead all were Americans. It was going so well, I could literally picture riding into the arena first, winning the gold medal....

It was the pulse monitor that first told me something was wrong—it jumped about fifteen beats—and Drubin started wanting to back off. But then he also wanted to stay with the other horses—again that will of the horse.... At the first checkpoint I rode past one of the American vets who said Drubin looked good, but then he started shortening up in that right rear, and it was clear he wasn't sound, and that was the end for us.... My tremendous disappointment was shared with other team members who failed to finish, but then we all shared in the thrill of Valerie's victory.

After I got home, I received a letter from a friend in California who made the point that even though the disappointment is strong, if you don't risk, you'll never achieve anything. That helped to put things back in perspective for me.

Being able to accept the whims of fate—good and bad—with equanimity is the basis of good sportsmanship: *Many years ago I was riding in Germany with a very good friend, Michael Freund, re-counts Jimmy Fairclough. He said to me, "When it's your day, it's your day. When it's not, be smart enough to go home and start over tomorrow." The sooner you realize that in training and competition, the more success you'll have.* As simple as that sounds, it is not always easy, though it is truly the best option for improving your abilities.

Competition taught me that you never know it all; you can always learn more, notes René Williams. It's also taught me not to complain a lot, to be a good sport. I've had horses where, as a professional, I was sure I won the class, and then I didn't. Yet I never complained, because I knew I had the animal and at the next show we'd catch them, and invariably we did. In a lot of sports today—hockey, baseball, football— you see so much fighting and arguing, but riding isn't like that. Good sportsmanship is much more than a mere social convention; it is a mechanism of experience that strengthens character, coping, persistence, and perspective throughout life.

At a luncheon for me at Midway College last year, Helen Crabtree relates with pride, *Randi Wightman, one of my former students who was then president of the American Saddlebred Horse Association, said, "At the Crabtree's we learned sportsmanship; we learned that when we got off of a horse, we went over and sincerely congratulated the winner; and we did—every single time."*

Win or lose, those who come away from the school of competition wearing the banner of good sportsmanship have claimed the most valuable prize.

Friendships and Opportunities

Additional bonuses to competition are the good times, travel, and camaraderie of friends on the circuit: *Competition has given me a lot of life experiences that I would not have had without it,* observes Becky Hart. *I've been able to go to Europe several times to compete and also to do clinics and seminars. I've met a lot of people I would never have met otherwise. Now I can go to most any country in Europe and know somebody, which is really great. It's made the world a smaller, friendlier place.*

Like a party on horseback, even the most serious competitions can be full of fun, surprises, and great memories: *Once in the world championships, it came down to a workout between me and a good friend of mine from Toronto, Canada,* recounts Camille Whitfield Vincent. *While we were waiting for the judge's decision, we were at the far end of the arena talking and laughing. We never even heard the announcer call the winning number—my trainer had to yell, "Get to the winner's circle" because Abbie and I were just carrying on. That's what showing was about for me: having fun with friends and the love of the animals. The friendships I made in riding have been more important than winning, and more lasting.*

The circle of friends that riding encompasses is not limited to riders. The various ancillary jobs necessary to support a competitive team offer connections to many who share a goal, but not from the saddle: *The sport and the horses have enriched my life with a tremendous amount of friends who share the same emotions and the same goals,* says Valerie Kanavy. *The mere fact of working and racing as hard as we do requires so much physical output that it opens you emotionally toward people—you can't be a phony—it's too much work to be a phony. Even people who don't ride come to crew and want to be part of the family that way—and it is a family. My husband and I have gained an extended family in which we feel love and respect and admiration for a great many people. A lot of people look at riding as a very exclusive sport, and yet for me, it's been much more inclusive than exclusive.*

Yet another bonus is found in the satisfaction of helping others learn the ways of competition: *Showing is fun, but it's hard when you're first starting out because you get really nervous, and it can throw you all off,* explains student Amy Hubbard (p.208). *But after a while you realize that if you mess up on one thing, just go on to the next, and forget about that thing—put it out of your mind—think about positives for the rest of the class. It's also nice because after you've shown for a while, you can help other people who are starting to show. You know what the feeling is like so you can help other people to do the same thing.*

Since most equestrian competition is a matter of exhibiting one's best rather than beating an opponent, other competitors are not targeted as rivals. This distinction allows for an esprit de corps across the board: *The thrill of riding along with others in competition is an aspect of the sport I really enjoy; and I believe the animals enjoy as well,* notes Stagg Newman. *Horses were made to go long distances and love traveling with others because they're herd animals. One of the things about endurance riding is that even though it can be fierce competition, those competitors are your friends, and it's still very much an amateur sport.*

The United States Equestrian Team video made at the 1994 World Equestrian Games in Holland really captures the sport. If you look closely, you'll see the four of us who didn't finish on the verge of tears. But you'll also see the support and the sharing in Valerie's triumph in the end. That's part of it—you all compete; you do your best, and then you share in the sorrows, and you share in the victory. We all have disappointments, but we also have tremendous highs.

Perseverance and Spirit

One competitor who has lived at the top of her sport for more than forty years is Barrel Racing World Champion, Martha Josey, yet she is still looking ahead, planning to best her own record: *My record of going to the National Finals Rodeo for four decades...I'm thinking I might want to go for a fifth one in the year 2000.*

Throughout the interview with World Champion Saddlebred trainer, Tom Moore (p.208), there was one word that cropped up like mushrooms in a rainforest: consistency. In raising and training horses, in schooling students, in competition, in parenting, in life...Tom attributes his success to consistency.

Tom saw his first gaited horse in Chicago at age thirteen, and by eighteen, he was vying for his first world championship: *I was driving a mare I'd trained in the Two-Year-Old Fine Harness Class at the Kentucky State Fair World Championships. I thought I had done well, but I was just a kid, you know, and some of the top trainers in the country were in there. But my mare, Miss America, was super great...and after four workouts, I won it. Just lucked out.... I've been able to accomplish everything that I've tried to do, and so I just want to keep it rolling....* And he has. Since that initial surprise win in the early fifties, Tom has won many more world championships, as well as the prestigious AHSA Lifetime Achievement Award. In serious competition, you may luck out occasionally, but luck alone doesn't earn you a career at the top like Tom's—consistent excellence does.

Skills for Success

As a kid, riding gave me an identity that I carry to this day, observes Camille Whitfield Vincent. *Competition taught me to excel with perseverance and resourcefulness and also gave me a real sense of accomplishment. I gained a lot of discipline and responsibility through riding competition, learning the value of having pride in turning the horse out as well as myself—I couldn't pass that off on somebody else....* And no one else could give that to her, for such skills and success are only earned through doing.

From the tranquil beauty pageants of halter classes, to the surgical precision of dressage, to the exhausting trial of endurance, to the chaotic excitement of polo, to the cardiac intensity of the Kentucky Derby...the many, varied equestrian competitions all offer personal lessons of success, failure, and sportsmanship. And along the way, one learns to dream, to dare, to plan, to stretch, to cope, to explore, to assess, to listen, to accept, to share, to improve, to enjoy, to teach, to travel, to endure, to excel, and to care about others...all lessons and gifts of competing with *HorsePower!*

AMY HUBBARD, b. 1980, is a young rider whose winning ways helped her qualify for the U.S. Pony Club Championship Team in Show Jumping. Amy and her gelding, B.W. (Bretton Woods), clear a vertical during the Mark Phillips Clinic at the East End Pony Club at St. Croix, Virgin Islands.

TOM MOORE, b. 1934, is the winningest Saddlebred trainer of all time. Tom claims consistency is an important element in training and his record proves it. He won his first World Championship at age eighteen, is a founder of the United Professional Horsemen's Association and member of that organization's Hall of Fame, two-time winner of the coveted AHSA Horseman of the Year award and trainer of numerous World Champion saddle and driving horses. Tom and the Saddlebred mare, Spring High, enjoy their victory parade after winning the Three-Gaited World Grand Championship at the Kentucky State Fair in Louisville.

CHAPTER EIGHT

MINDING THE BUCKS

Prioritizing Time and Money

"Personal bankruptcy" is when you spend your money more carefully than you spend your life. —Maria Nieto

It started out innocently enough: two young sisters in Natick, Massachusetts, received a gift from their parents of ten riding lessons for summer vacation in the late 1950s; that was all it took to touch off eight-year-old Jane's horse fever. In ensuing years, while her sister's attention turned to diving and figure skating, Jane's heart and mind filled with horses. The family budget had no room for a horse of her own, so Jane rode school horses. Her equine fantasies were acted out by playing with pink and blue plastic horses won at the county fair's bean toss and training the family dog to longe over a jump course of lawn furniture.

When Jane was fourteen, the stable closed. Jane watched sadly as the school horses were sold off one by one and their paddocks subdivided into house lots. In the end, only one Welsh pony with a well-earned reputation for rearing remained unsold—Jane's dad brought him home. A few years later, when Jane's father died, the pony had to be sold.

While studying veterinary science at the University of Massachusetts, Jane began training under Linda Jaskiel Brown. In 1975, Jane groomed for Linda during an Olympic training session at Gladstone, New Jersey. The awesome caliber of horses and riders Jane encountered at Gladstone was inspiring. Suddenly, Jane's chronic case of horse fever blossomed into *Olympic* horse fever. Jane bought her first horse at Gladstone and her Olympic quest began.

Unfortunately, neither Jane nor her $500 Thoroughbred were Olympic material. Jane was a plodding rider, in marginal physical condition (overweight and smoking almost three packs of cigarettes a day), who became physically ill in competition. In addition, Jane was broke. All her savings had gone for her horse, and her waitressing salary could not support regular lessons let alone an Olympic bid. She had no truck, no trailer, and no training—she could afford only two two-day clinics a year. Her new horse was a racetrack reject with a bowed tendon who thought "canter" meant blast off for the finish line. The only thing this pair had going for them was the allure of the Olympic flame that flickered brightly in Jane's dream.

Jane knew she had to make some phenomenal changes in order to reach her lofty goal; she started by searching for a way to cope with her show nerves, and found Maxwell Maltz's book, PSYCHO-CYBERNETICS. This was a turning point in Jane's life, for she not only conquered her fear of competition; she discovered tools for redesigning her entire future. She came to understand that it's not so much what you have, it's what you *do* with what you have that makes the difference.

Over the years, Jane trained herself and her horse with surprising success, and focused in on the 1992 Olympics in Barcelona. To get there, Jane not only needed to continue winning, she also needed a talented horse and international experience with an impossible price tag of more than $300,000!

For most people, the Olympic financing challenge is the obstacle that makes them give up because it seems insurmountable, remarks Jane. *I could have easily said, "I can't get that amount of money, I can't get that quality of a horse...I'm licked."* Instead, Jane applied everything she'd learned about psychocybernetics, positive attitude, and imaging and programmed Olympic financing into her life. She first made a personal appeal: *It was hard because asking people to give me money made me very uncomfortable...very uncomfortable! But my goal was that important to me, so I made cold calls and wrote letters—and raised $250,000!*

In an effort to feel more comfortable in asking for support, Jane founded the tax-exempt American Dressage Foundation, to offer donors a tax benefit in return. (ADF has since gone on to help many deserving competitors.)

With her initial funding, Jane was able to get a competitive horse: Zapatero. The next challenge was international competition—they had to campaign and win in Europe—a very exciting, but extremely expensive proposition. Jane had no idea how much European campaigning would cost, but figured $30,000 sounded about right. She plugged that figure into her mental computer and began looking for opportunities. In the pre-Olympic year of 1991, grants were being awarded to top horse and rider teams: Jane and Zapatero had to win in order to go to Europe. They did. One of the requirements of the grants was to keep a record of all expenses. At the end of their three months in Europe, Jane's expenses added up to $30,000—that's what she'd asked for and that's what she got. (Savoie, 1993 Audio Tape 1: THAT WINNING FEELING!)

The uncomfortable things I had to do to raise money to pursue my Olympic goal took the same kind of persistence and determination that I needed for all the rest of the Olympic dream—it was just one more obstacle that I had to overcome, notes Jane. *It was all character building; if it was handed to me, it wouldn't mean as much, or the drive wouldn't be there. What it allowed me to do is to prove to myself how effective this mental training with psychocybernetics really is. Having so little to start with, the cards were really stacked against me, but I had a dream...and I believed that if I worked hard, I could do it.*

The proof to me that you can do this in any aspect of your life is when I look back at what I was and what I was doing twenty years ago and realize what I have been able to do in the horse industry...it's mind boggling! I am your average person in the local barn who took an idea and went with it—no exaggeration. I came from nowhere just by applying these principles.... I found a way to do everything I needed to do—nothing was gonna stop me!

In 1992, Jane's improbable dream was realized. She represented the United States in Barcelona, Spain, as reserve rider on the Olympic Dressage squad that won a bronze medal. That was also the year her book, THAT WINNING FEELING! was published. Since then, Jane has produced audio tapes on mental training and riding techniques, become a motivational speaker, and expanded her dressage training and teaching clinics. Jane Savoie was not born with extraordinary ability or wealth—she just learned how to program her life for success. As Jane has proven time and again: "If you can dream it, you can do it!"

Equestrian Economics

Horses can be done lavishly or modestly, but never cheaply. This chapter explores how some have coped with equine money and time demands. It is amazing how few riders are of the moneyed class nowadays. As opposed to the wealthy few who have horses simply *because* they can, there are many more like Jane Savoie, who work hard to create ways to keep horses in their lives. These people know that while keeping a horse can be expensive, riding doesn't necessarily have to be. It just takes determination, creativity, and prioritizing resources.

Begin by Borrowing

Unless you're born into an equestrian family, initial riding will probably be on a borrowed school horse. This is how some of America's greatest riders began: *The first couple of years I rode I used a club pony at the Wilton Connecticut Riding Club,* William Steinkraus relates. *The lovely lady who ran the riding program at my sisters' school also ran the riding club and set up a branch of the British Pony Club there. So I was a very early pony clubber—before there was an American Pony Club at all. She had a pony that I loved, which we eventually bought. When I outgrew that pony, I started to ride a whole bunch of outside horses. I managed to have a horse of my own until I went into the service, but they were all cheap horses. Most of the good horses I got to ride were for other people—I did a lot of catch riding. I was very lucky, some very nice people gave me very nice horses to ride.*

Barter

Bartering offers a valuable exchange rate for anyone wanting to be around horses. Work is plentiful around a barn or a show, so a trade of time, talent, or energy is often welcomed: *[Napa Valley's] Wild Horse Valley Ranch had a program for years where kids could clean out stalls in exchange for riding lessons,* recalls Dr. Patty Latham. *That was wonderful for a lot of kids I know. I did that on a ranch when I was a kid. Actually, my horse, Lillie, was a gift from the ranch I worked for.* It's amazing how hard kids will work for something they really want. The same youngsters who turn their noses up at a request to take out the trash, happily shovel manure out of fly-ravaged stalls in trade for a half-hour lesson.

Bobby Christian scavenged old buggy parts from barns in the Napa Valley, took over an abandoned barn, bought a couple of hackney ponies and has since been collecting youngsters like an equine Pied Piper in Calistoga, California. He's managed to breathe new life into the carriages, the barn, and the children he attracts: *I just started by going to stables and getting old rusty carts and putting them together,* says Bobby. *The ranch where I keep the ponies was abandoned when I asked if I could keep my horses there. The owner liked the idea because I could watch the place and keep the place up— I don't pay them a dollar. When he and his wife come up and say, "We're so happy to have you here," it's worth my keeping their place clean and working.* In this bargain, goodwill was exchanged instead of money, and everyone gained.

Bartering offers creative opportunities for many services: *When my daughter was showing we made a lot of concessions,* explains Phyllis Eifert. *We got an old horse van, learned how to drive it, and she transported horses in turn for lessons. She also did show braiding to make money for her showing, while I went into the horse show trophy and ribbon business to help cover expenses.*

Bank Roll

Borrowing and barter can help offset some costs, but a bottom line bankroll is necessary for the ongoing financial responsibilities of a horse: *It takes finances to care for horses,* Ron Harding concurs. *You may have that deep love, but if you don't have the finances to commit it's better that you stay away from horses because you can cause traumatic situations to the horse, yourself and your family.... These animals are very expensive—they have vet bills and shoeing care every six or eight weeks.... They need feed, grain, and if they need medicine, they don't have money, so you're going to make sacrifices.... One way to look at it is, if you can afford another child, you can afford a horse.*

Add to ownership the costs of competing: trailering, stabling, entry fees, show clothes and tack, plus lodging; and a bank roll can vanish faster than snow in July. *Competition takes a lot of dedication, not just in terms of riding, but in things you have to give up in order to do it,* observes Sarah Hafner. *It costs a lot of money to go to those darn horse shows. My husband is pretty supportive, but he does grumble sometimes, wondering, "So my salary is to maintain the household, and your salary is to maintain your riding?" I don't know if I'd be as kind and generous as he is if he had a passion, or hobby, that takes so much financially. Part of the reason I work is to pay for riding—I'd feel too guilty if I didn't—plus I value it more.... When I was a kid, I didn't have to pay for any part of my riding. I never knew how much it cost. I would have appreciated it more if my parents had made me pitch in and do my share.* A youngster who is personally invested in riding learns about expenses, savings, and spending. Furthermore, horses are a good incentive for learning to prioritize and budget both time and money.

Budgeting Money

Budgeting comes down to a matter of researching, planning, and prioritizing expenditures in concert with income. Many riders take on extra jobs as needed to help pay for their riding expenses; learning the value of earning, allocating their own money, and compromise: *You've got to be willing to compromise for things that are really important,* states Kelly O'Boyle. *I drive a very old car and I don't own a house; those things aren't really important to me for I don't measure my success by an address or make of car. I don't know if I'm just that way and that's what allows me to compromise, or if riding is so essential to my life that those things are just less important. I suppose having a house and settling down will eventually come to be a top priority, but I can never imagine a time in my life not having a horse. Again it's a matter of balance: I don't go without clothing, I don't go without gas in my car, I don't go without eating—those things won't ever happen because I know I'm employable. I can go from industry to industry and get a job. I would take on extra jobs to supplement my income before I'd seriously consider selling one of my animals. I've had offers for Zodiac, and it was hard to turn down ten thousand dollars in a lump sum. But there are benefits from owning Zodiac: he's still got things to offer me, and I think he'll be a good school horse five years from now.*

Sixteen-year-old student Adrian Arroyo (p.235) contracts with her parents regarding major expenses: first she had to pay off the price of her horse, then in order to get a driver's license, she must earn enough for car insurance. With so much of her time invested in her riding, Adrian figures she'll be nineteen before she gets a license. To defer such a vital symbol of passage for *three years* seems inconceivable for most teens, yet Adrian believes having a horse in her life now makes the wait well worthwhile.

When a horse is a top priority for a person, the means can be found: *To have my horse, I've had to make some priorities,* observes Pat Lawson. *I can't go out and buy expensive dresses anymore—I have to buy something within budget. If you are going to own a horse, you have got to have the money for it because that horse needs board-ing, bedding, it's got to be shod...certain bucks that you can count on to be used. If you can't afford it, sooner or later, you, the horse, or both, are going to come up lacking, and that lack of necessary money can take the joy out of a lot of things. Riding in the Northeast, as I do, is a seasonal activity that's paid for monthly. Unless you have access to an indoor arena, you only get to ride for five or six months but have to pay for twelve. I estimate that within the last ten years I've spent close to $60,000 on my riding. Being a single mother and paying for my college, law school, my kids' colleges, and a horse, money's always tight.*

Even during the toughest of financial times, caring parents manage to provide what is important for their children: *I started riding in 1934,* recalls William Steinkraus. *What was remarkable was that during the Depression, my mother was able to contrive out of what was not a big family budget, riding and music lessons for me, music and drama lessons for one of my sisters, and music and vocal lessons for another sister.* Such luxuries as those extra-curricular lessons could have been quickly cut from a tight family budget, yet by procur-ing that training, Mrs. Steinkraus provided her son with the foun-dation for priceless riches: his stellar riding career and his lifelong love of music as an accomplished violinist.

Budgeting Time

Horses require a solid commitment of time as well as money. To be used most effectively, time, like money, must also be budgeted: *I have about thirty horses in training on the farm: hunters, jumpers, and driving horses,* notes Jimmy Fairclough. *When it comes to the driving, I train all my own horses. In a year's time, if I get somebody else to drive my horses once, so I can watch them, that's a lot. Ninety-nine percent of the time I'm behind my horses every day, seven days a week. I physically can't do it all for the horses, but I do oversee everything from feed to cleaning of the stalls. Horses are my hobby/second job; I also work in our family heating oil business. You can catch me at a quarter of five every morning on the way to work.* Jimmy has worked out an efficient and effective schedule that permits him to cover all his bases: family, business, training, and competing at driving's highest levels. Such a full schedule highlights how budgeting time differs from budgeting money: while everyone has varying income levels, we all are allocated only twenty-four hours each day. How differently each of us expends that common commodity of time!

It's also important to prioritize our time to accomplish that which we desire: *Over the years, I've heard lots of people say, "I don't have time to ride, or I'd do this better,"* says Buck Brannaman. *Now, they do have the time, it's just not a priority for them. But I know if someone walked through their yard dropping hundred dollar bills at 6:30 every night, they'd be out there like clockwork at 6:30. Pretty soon their whole life would revolve around being in their yard at 6:30—and if it took them ninety minutes to get all the hundred dollar bills picked up—they'd stay ninety minutes. Well, they could be riding their horse then; it's all just priorities. So when someone says, "I'd ride more if I had more time." What they're really saying is that riding's not important enough for them to make the time. They really have no excuse for inadequacy since it all comes down to priorities. Luckily, no one's sent to hell just for being a sorry rider.*

The very nature of priorities leads to compromise, but not necessarily sacrifice: *I never minded being there twice a day everyday to feed my horse—that was one of my requirements,* says Dr. Patty Latham. *If I wanted to go to a family party, or other big deal, I wouldn't go if it meant I would be late to feed. If you have an animal, you have a commitment to take care of it. And if that means doing without, or not going away unless somebody's there to take care of your animals, that's fine with me. Financially, I have always budgeted: if horse expenses mean not having something else, that's okay too. I don't consider any of it a sacrifice; it's just my way of living.*

Since horses can be time-intensive, riders have to blend many schedules with their own: family, job, chores, school, study, riding, and competition. In establishing such blended-time priorities, it is prudent to consider how others are affected. In his sports counseling practice, Doug Lietzke has witnessed many relationships threatened by the time constraints of horses: *Time is as important a consideration as money—more important really,* Doug cautions. *The rider has to decide how much time he has to devote as well as how much money. What are the time costs and are they worthwhile? And that decision shouldn't be made in isolation, but discussed with the significant people in that rider's life: a spouse, children, parents, even friends.* Time and attention are valuable assets to be shared with many in one's life.

When Mary Mansi began riding, lesson times affected her home and work schedules. Since her husband was also her accounting business partner, his support was crucial to the scheduling adjustments: *Taking on riding has forced me to organize my time better and learn to be more flexible; I'm managing to fit more into my life than ever before,* Mary observes. *Since I'm not in the office as much during the day, I have to work later and have evening appointments for my clients. My husband, Steve, supports my riding very much. He's taken on extra work since I'm gone more, so he's had to sacrifice to support me in this, yet he's never complained—ever. We've* both made adjustments, but all have been worth it.

I used to be totally governed by the clock. My very first riding les-son was set for 11:00 a.m. I thought that meant I'd get on a tacked up horse at 11:00, have my lesson, and then someone would put the horse away. Well, I got there at 11:00, filled out a release slip, then we walked down to get the horse, the instructor tacked him up...now it's about 11:30. I had an appointment at 12:30 and I'm getting nervous realiz-ing I'm never going to make it! My first thought was, I don't like this: it's dirty, it's cold, and I can't stay on time. But Steve had given me ten lessons, and I realized that first day: for the remaining nine lessons, you, Mary, are going to have to come to this barn with a different atti-tude. Part of that means you're not to schedule things so tight, and the other is to become more flexible.

Now, if I have a tight time-line, I let the instructor know and she honors that. There have been days when I came to ride, but my horse was off so I wasn't able to. I used to not be able to make that adjust-ment because I was so set in what I had to do. I've learned to let go of that, which has been very good for me because people considered me rigid and inflexible. I've become more flexible having to accommodate the horse, and I have learned to accommodate people as a result. I needed that lesson because I've always been very driven to accomplish.

As Mary discovered, time is relative—a weighty statement and a basic tenet in a life with horses: *There's Eastern Standard time and Rocky Mountain time; well, in the Southwest there's this thing called "Indian time": the meeting starts whenever everyone gets there,* ex-plains L.D. Burke. *You have to know and accept this or you'll go nuts. This has been a great lesson for me: that the universe is not ruled by the clock and calendar. The Indians have taught me a lot—they're great—they have a really beautiful energy. I've since learned that horses have their own time, too.*

While L.D. may have learned his lesson in relative time from his Indian friends and applied it to horses, horses are well known for teaching riders about horse time: *There's the old cliché,* remarks

William Steinkraus: *"If you don't wait for them, they'll make you wait for them."* There's a limit to how fast horses can make progress, so if you want to train them to grand prix—whether jumping or dressage—it's going to take some time—years usually. And you have to do it through building blocks a step at a time. If you're in too much of a hurry, you spoil the horse, so you learn not to overface them too early.

Taking the necessary time to do a job well is an important lesson young riders learn early on: *Shortcuts never work out,* states Tina Schuler. *I tried to groom my horse without tying him up, but he kept turning in circles, so it took me* longer. *And you can't just quickly brush a horse because a bad job could lead to saddle sores—you have to make sure that everything you do is complete—no cutting corners in the ring or in the stable.* No cutting corners—a valuable ethic for a everyone.

Perhaps the most compelling reason for investing your time in horses is found carved on a wood plaque that hangs above Jack Huyler's front door at The Thacher School: "Time spent on the back of a horse is not deducted from one's lifespan!"

Buying In

Choosing a horse is much like choosing a car: you can go for the top of the line, knock 'em dead, current luxury model with all the options and pay top dollar; or you can buy a good used model, within budget, and improve it through renovation, adding options as you go. A flashy, fit, finished horse with an impressive record will be expensive; while a common, cute, competent horse can be had reasonably. As with a car, no model is perfect; the flashier they are, the less dependable they tend to be—repair and maintenance are expensive; and resale rarely brings bluebook. Like cars, horses can be rented (at a public stable with each lesson), leased (from an owner with you paying some or all maintenance costs), joint-ventured (share expenses and upkeep with another part owner), or bought outright (you pay for the horse and full upkeep).

While buying in at the top is easy (it just takes cash), finding a good deal at the lower end takes knowledge, perseverance, creative skills, and luck. But it can be done: *We bought inexpensive horses, but that doesn't mean we didn't buy good horses,* declares Phyllis Eifert. *We got one navicular horse for $1,000 plus a pony. He was a good horse who had done it all, so he was something my daughter could go right on with. She rode him for two years and did well, he got her to Harrisburg and the Garden.... Then, about four years ago, I bought my daughter two horses: one was a makeover and the other a baby, so neither one was expensive. She qualified one for Harrisburg and won money with the other on the A show circuit. So you don't have to spend a lot of money on the horse because that's a drop in the bucket; it's everything else that goes along with it—stabling, showing.... But you can do it on a low scale—even get a gift horse, an old horse that somebody just wants a good home for—although you still have to feed, vet, and shoe him.*

These enterprising young horse lovers earned their first mounts in a joint venture: *My brother and I bought both our horses from our paper routes,* explains Lt. Carl Clipper. *My brother's the oldest, so we bought his first, and then we saved again and bought mine.*

So, horse ownership does not necessarily have to be the sport of kings: *In many cases horses can cost less than golf or tennis,* claims Jack Huyler. *You cannot improve and sell your tennis racket, but you can improve and sell a horse. But it's so varying depending largely on where you live and what kind of riding you do. It can be done as the sport of kings or as the backyard corral—which I'm all in favor of.... If you live in Greenwich, Connecticut and have a horse, it will cost a lot of money, but you can live in parts of Wyoming and have a horse for very little money.*

Buying the horse is the cheapest part of having a horse; there is no cheap way to keep a horse and do it right, says Patty Latham. *People who try to cut corners by sticking a horse in an eight-by-eight-foot paddock in the dirt with no cover and poor feed create problems: those are the animals that get sick and troubled.*

While horse ownership is never cheap, it is manageable if you prepare: know what kind of horse you need, have the appropriate place and know-how to keep it, have budgeted the necessary money and time for purchase and maintenance, and can accept the risk of losing the investment should something happen to the horse.

With proper planning, priorities, passion, and perseverance, almost anyone can own a horse: *People segregate themselves into haves and have-nots, which is terrible because it's a cop-out in the first place,* states Helen Crabtree. *They want to criticize somebody with horses—"Oh, those spoiled rich kids." That's not so! That is not so, and we have fought that image for years and years and years. A lot of people have no idea what's important and what isn't. Every once in a while a father would say, "Oh, I don't spend that kind of money on a horse." Then I'd remind him, "You're not spending money on a horse, you're investing in your child's future." And that's the common substance of it all: priorities.*

There are many people who, like me, had dreamed of owning a horse in their youth and were denied that, who come to it later in life as they gain control over their calendar, finances, and choices. Then they allow it for themselves: *I finally own a horse! Do you realize how weighty that phrase is?* asks Jenny Butah. *When I tell people I own a horse, there's an audible gasp—you do?* That incredulous response seems touched by envy from those who can imagine the outrageousness and magic of having a horse.

Business

There are many horse-related service and sales jobs for those who want to stay close to horses: *Long before I went to rodeoing full-time, I picked different jobs that I knew I might need,* Martha Josey explains. *I knew I'd always need insurance, so I got a job with insurance. Then I went on to a secretarial job, and that helped me with the organization, scheduling, and writing I need with the clinics and the schools. Along the way, I was always learning about quality equipment and now we have the tack business....* Martha consciously chose to learn business skills that would actively support her life with horses—that's living into your future.

Horses also offer opportunities to learn about independent contracting: *Many summers ago, my two oldest kids, who were excellent riders and pretty good horsemen, put an ad in the paper,* recounts Jack Huyler. *"We'll cure your horse of any bad habit for $5, and teach them new tricks for $5 each." ($5 was real money back then.) They'd teach a horse to work a gate, or cure a horse of pulling back, or whatever. Sometimes they couldn't cure them, and they didn't get the $5.*

Another horse-lover combined her therapeutic training with horses and created a valuable program for her local school system: *I believe that we can all make our passion our work,* declares Maxine Freitas. *I just kept saying, "There's got to be a way to combine the training and education I've had, and the love I have for horses into something that I can do consistently throughout my day." I created a job that incorporates it all by establishing a therapeutic riding program in the Santa Rosa school district, and now most of my life revolves around the horses. Since I've gotten back to horses, my mother, who hadn't ridden in fifty years, now rides and shows—and she's eighty-one!*

With the necessary talents, one can become a professional within the horse industry and gain time with horses, while minimizing or eliminating actual ownership: *At one time, I owned seven horses,* reports Mary Deringer Phelps. *When I left Willow Bend Polo Club, I was loading my trailer, and I kept putting my horses in. That's when it dawned on me: I have seven horses! Why do I have seven horses? And five of them are grey! Seven horses takes a lot of money—even as backyard horses—so I sold them. Then I started my training/teaching business, in which I gave lessons to clients on their horses. My first requirement was you had to board your horse with me, because I* *needed to get paid whether you came to ride or not. I never had any school horses, but I had good clients. Some clients had two or three horses and they'd let others ride them, so then I had more students, but I still didn't need to own the horses. Every bit of money that was made, I made; and every bit I made, I spent. We went on the top line.... We had the matching rig and the matching coolers.... Of course, now I wonder, "Why wasn't I in those IRAs [Individual Retirement Accounts] a long time ago?" "Well, I had it, but instead of buying that $2000 IRA, I bought that $2000 horse...and sold him for $800!*

Patty Latham supports her horse habit through her veterinary practice: *One of the reasons I became a vet is because I will always have animals—I can't imagine a life without animals. Luckily our horses don't get into disasters too often, but when they do, they seem to be big ones, so being a veterinarian has been a huge advantage.*

Elite equestrian competitors earn prize money and endorsements to supplement income from teaching, training, and trading: *Because I wanted to ride I didn't even go to college,* reports Anne Kursinski. *Most of us professionals do our own business stuff: on the side we're buying and selling horses, we're teaching, we're training...we've got to be so many things—much more than other top professional athletes. A professional basketball player, for instance, plays basketball while somebody else makes the contracts for him, and takes care of business. Because of their huge endorsements and salaries they don't have to teach; they don't have to buy and sell on the side—they might do some of that, but we **have** to do all that. In that sense we're a very different kind of athlete, since we have to be a business person as well. I don't really love the business side. I'm just a kid who likes to ride. But I've had to learn about money.*

Unfortunately, prize winnings for US equestrian events are not as rich as in many professional sports: *In driving you cannot win a lot of money, especially in America,* Jimmy Fairclough notes. *Since it's such an expensive sport, it teaches you to really care for your animals because you just can't go out and replace their ability, their tem-*

perament, or your training. You can't put a dollar value on it. It's almost like people in that respect: you just don't want to lose them. In the United States equestrians subsidize the sport; the sport does not financially support many athletes.

I never figured I could have horses unless I could afford them, says Irving Pettit. *Anytime they were too much for the family sacrifice, I didn't keep them. In good years I had a couple broodmares, so I'd sell a couple colts every fall at the yearling sale. I had pretty good luck with them. My broodmares had good records, and I tried to pick good stallions, first year in service, so the stud fees weren't too high. Once I paid $500 for each mare and got a filly and a colt. The colt sold for $9,000 and the filly for $6,000, so I got $15,000 for a couple that I'd only paid $1,000 in stud fees. I sold one or two colts every year for several years with the cheapest sold at $3,300. I made out better with the ones I sold than with the ones I raced, because I always sold the best ones to race and kept the others myself.* Breeding Standardbreds for harness racing proved to be a lucrative business, yet Irving never relied on that income; it was a venture he pursued only as family security allowed.

As in any market, the goal is to buy low, sell high, and the bottom line often requires selling stock even if you've become attached. *I constantly have to stop myself from thinking about the fact that we can sell these animals like slaves,* hunter/jumper trainer Macella O'Neill laments. *It goes against my grain, but it's part of my business. One of the horses in training with me now, Barney,…there's no reason that Barney should be anywhere except with me, because that horse loves me. He loved me the first time I ever touched him; Barney will do anything I ask. That horse loves me, and I love that horse, but I can't keep him. He is going to have to get sold. There's nothing right about it. There's nobody else that should have that horse. We get along perfectly, but his owner doesn't want to keep him, and I can't afford him, so he'll get sold….*

In the business of horses, if animals are simply thought of as commodities to be bought, bred, and sold, human avarice can bring tragedy: *We attend an annual hunter pace, where teams of three go out cross-country,* Sam Savitt explains. *It's usually about a ten-mile course, with thirty-five to forty fences, and the winning team is decided by averaging the fastest and the slowest times. One man had a horse that he was trying to sell. He rode that horse with his customer on another to show him what he could do. Well, his horse was not fit, and a ten-mile run is pretty demanding on a warm day, even for a fit horse. Along the way, a number of competitors told him, you'd better pull that horse up; he's having trouble. But he thought he'd luck it out and hopefully sell the horse. Well, the horse died.*

I went over to see him the next day and said, "You know, you killed that horse yesterday. All you had to tell your customer was that he's not fit and pull out when he began to fade." He was indignant, "What do you mean?" he said, "I lost fifteen hundred dollars!" I thought, "Oh, hell!" Some people just think of these animals as some kind of commodity—the horses mean nothing to them. If somebody can do that to a horse, he can do almost anything. Of course, he'd say, "What's a horse? Just an animal." But losing the $1,500—that hurt him!

In the sport horse trade, knowing when to sell can often prove difficult. Traders who endure are those who can prioritize economics and emotions appropriately: *"There's something about the outside of a horse that's good for the inside of a man,"* quotes Michael Plumb. *I had that feeling for the outside of a horse I had last year. Such a horse! I could count on him to cheer me up—that's a rare experience. Well, I had to sell that horse. If I'd had more money I would have kept him, but I just couldn't afford to. That horse made me feel good inside and outside. He was called Above All. He's now ridden by Anne Kursinski. There's another saying: "Sell the best and ride the rest." So, I sold the best to the best…and he might just become a very famous horse.*

Financial concerns are not the only issues that can force a sale.

When life becomes too complicated or stressful, adjustments may need to be made: *I had one horse, Trooper, that I totally regret having to sell*, says Genie Stewart-Spears. *But because of personal things in my life, I had to get rid of some horses. My husband had cancer. It was even hard to feed the horses then because my attention was so focused on my husband. In life everything changes and I had to let Trooper go. Thankfully I still have my husband!*

As difficult as selling a horse may be, buying the right horse is also a challenge, especially in the mercurial world of Thorough-bred racing: *Years ago I bought a horse for a person and we named her Silent Screen*, recounts René Williams. *She was small, so no one wanted her, but I liked her breeding and saw some possibilities. My father always said "some horses look small, but they have room to grow." He likened it to a young girl who had room to grow up to be a good looker. Well, this horse looked like she had room to grow.... I stole her for $14,000, and she wound up winning almost $350,000. That's when you can say "By God, I do have an eye!"*

As with any venture, the business of horses carries the risk of loss as well as a promise of gain. However, when done well, it of-fers access to riding and horses with financial support, attracting those whose happiness is found with the horse: *If you get good horses, breed them right, treat them right, and train them right, you can make money*, claims Chris Hawkins. *But don't go into horses expect-ing to make a bundle. If you go into the horse business, you'd better know what you're doing, and it helps to be a little bit hard-hearted. I'll never make a million off them simply because I'm not hard-hearted, but I live very comfortably. I'm happy with myself, I'm happy with my horses, and they're happy with me. And after all, happiness counts for a lot.*

Backers

The higher up the competitive ladder an equestrian climbs, the more expensive it becomes. Rarely does an athlete have the personal finances to support national, international, or Olympic campaigns. Thus, top equestrian competitors find themselves having to line up sponsors. For such competent self-reliant spirits, asking for help—especially asking for money—can be disturbing: *A really hard part of my sport, show jumping, is finding people who will put money into a horse,* observes Anne Kursinski. *Financially, I can't do this myself, so I've had to learn about going to people and asking for help. That's been very, very hard. Why should someone put money— a lot of money—into a horse that's **maybe** going to the Olympics? It's sharing—being brave enough to share my dream. My approach is honest, I don't tell them they'll sell the horse for a million dollars. I ask them to join me, share my dream, then come watch the horse in Palm Beach, or Rome, or wherever we're competing—perhaps even the Olympics. That's fun. If they agree, fine; and if not, that's fine, too. Some owners and sponsors have been around for years, and others are here for a while and move on. I've enjoyed getting to know people on this level; I've met some dear friends, plus a lot of very wonderful, interesting people from doing this. And I'm getting better at it. I like the people, the team feeling, and the support system. Being able to ask for help, accept help, and meet new people in this way has allowed some of my walls and my defenses to come down. This has been a tremendous life lesson for me: seeing that it's really okay to ask for help. After all, that's what we're here for—to help each other.*

I, too, have always hated asking people for money—even in the name of worthy causes—because I felt like I was begging. Then a friend said, "It's not begging; it's an invitation to participate. If a person wants to contribute, they'll appreciate the opportunity; if not, there's no obligation." Well, that attitude adjustment made a huge difference and I am now an effective fund-raiser. Like Anne Kursinski and Jane Savoie, I discovered that many do enjoy contributing so they can help others—and share the dream.

Bankruptcy

Many years ago, at the Circus Club Horse Show in Menlo

Park, California, a gorgeous chestnut gelding entering the arena was introduced as "Chapter Eleven." Laughter and knowing smiles swept through the crowd as everyone agreed this was a perfect name for a show horse.

In reality, however, neither a cowboy nor his horse are much fun when flat broke. The horse business is tough, and requires a level head, sound instincts, and prudent management. There are actually two types of bankruptcy in life—financial and emotional. Both indicate serious imbalances: financial bankruptcy is an affliction of the bank book, while emotional bankruptcy is an affliction of the soul: *When I first quit cowboying and struck out on my own with my clinics, I went for three months living on nothing but Krusteaz pancake mix, recalls Buck Brannaman. I didn't even have money for syrup. I had a pickup, but couldn't afford the gas, so I'd ride into Gateway, Montana, late at night on one of my colts, and I'd hobble him behind my apartment building. Then I'd get up early in the morning—in the dark—and ride back out to where I was keeping my colts. I couldn't afford to drive my truck, and it was against the law to keep a horse in town.... I remember being hungry, real hungry. So, when things started to really roll for me, I appreciated making a good living. But it wasn't too long before the novelty of making a healthy living wore off and if I wasn't doing something I genuinely loved, I'd have walked away from it. Because you can only get so many good saddles and bits—those are the things that always meant a lot to me—having good gear and some nice clothes. Well, I've had that for a long time now, so the money's not as important to me as the quality of life is. When work is play, life is good.*

Through financial destitution, Buck found his personal wealth: leading the life he loves. In that, Buck has realized that money is not the only measure of riches: *I went to college for a while and tried to do the business thing, adds Buck. It'd scare you how much money an uneducated person—just a ranch cowboy—can make when you're not concerned about the money. But if you're in it for the money only, you're going to fail and you're going to be broke besides. There's a guy I know up in Montana who has more money than God on account of having huge interests in Coca Cola. But you know? That poor guy spends millions of dollars just trying to have half as much happiness as I have just in a few hours every morning. It's amazing! He spends all this money and he never really gets it pulled off. Never gets it—yet it doesn't cost me a damn thing.* Buck saw firsthand that even extravagantly wealthy individuals can be emotionally bankrupt: when you are unhappy in your work and in your life, cash isn't the prescription.

Irving Pettit's son Fred tells this story of how his father sized up his fast track career choice: *I had just graduated from Princeton and University of Pennsylvania Law School, and got a job offer from First National Bank's International division to work in Europe,* recalls Fred. *I went home to tell Dad. We were walking behind his house, where he had his horses and his chickens and his hound dogs.… We used to go back in there and kick up quail and rabbits and what not. I told him, "I've got a job with First National City Bank."*

"Oh," he said, "You pleased about that?"

I said, "Yeah…I'll be going to Europe and things will be pretty exciting." I described what I would be doing and he thought a bit and then said, "Well, it seems to me like you're going to work your ass off forty-eight weeks a year so you can live four weeks a year like I live all year around." And he was absolutely right—except I never got the four weeks off! Fred freely admits today that he still hasn't found the daily enjoyment in life that his father has. But Fred continues searching—in the world of finance.

Some, like Fred, desert the country life in pursuit of fortune, yet pass others on life's highway heading in exactly the opposite direction: *I really got serious about horses and riding after I'd been through college and was married,* John Lyons reports. *I was twenty-five or six. My wife, Susie, and I lived in Kansas City where I had an orthopedic implant business—surgical implants—total knees and hips, and other orthopedic equipment. I worked with doctors, went into surgery with them, and actually did some different parts of the surgery. (I had minored in medicine in college and majored in education and philosophy.) I was doing pretty well financially, so I bought five acres where we planned on building a house. I figured anybody that had that much land should have a horse, so I bought a horse before I built the house. Pretty soon I had four horses and decided I needed a barn, so I built a real nice barn—and still hadn't built the house yet. Then one day I was in the barn cleaning out stalls and decided I liked that better than running the orthopedic business I had. About eight months later, I sold out and bought a ranch in Silt, Colorado.* John took his skills—medicine, education, and philosophy; and reapplied them to what he truly loved: horses. Since then he has built an international reputation with his training clinics, tapes, and books.

I came to California with $26,000, but by 1977 it was all gone, Rex Peterson reports. *I was so broke that my pickup was repossessed and I was on the verge of renting out the trailer I was living in. I'm not saying I'm wealthy now. Yeah, I got sixteen head of horses but I also got a feed bill that I have to hustle every month to pay. Right now I'm waiting for checks from the studio that I have to have this week. Very, very few—one out of ten thousand, or one out of a hundred thousand, maybe—become rich training horses. And they're not always the best— just maybe the luckiest. Glenn Randall was one of the best, bar none. He trained horses for every discipline under the sun, and yet he was never a very wealthy man. He had enough to get by on all the time, and he always said, "Money doesn't mean anything to me." Everyone who knew Glenn said that if he got to where he can't get to the barn, he won't last six months—and he didn't. Within a month of being told he had cancer, he was bedridden half the time. Within five months, he died. He'd devoted his life to horses, and never became a wealthy man.* Glenn Randall may not have accumulated wealth, but he was rich, and I believe he knew it. That's why money didn't mean anything to him—money is only legal tender—an artificial exchange system invented by man. By successfully living his passion, Glenn achieved true wealth. It was only when his passion was no longer available to him that he succumbed.

Benefits

While I still maintain that "investment horse" is a financial oxymoron, there are many valuable personal returns from an investment in horses: *The money part we don't even want to think about, because if we did, I would probably sell all the horses,* chides Genie Stewart-Spears. *I could sure be making money doing other things, but this is so important in my life that if I don't have my horses, if I don't have the riding, I become hard to live with. I'm miserable. I start getting crotchety and my husband goes, "You know, tomorrow's going to be a really nice day, why don't you just pack up the horses and go for the day?" He always knows when I need to go. Then I come back happy, and refreshed, and ready to work.*

That enhancement of one's state of mind—our very state of being—for some, that benefit is as basic a need as shelter: *I've put in twenty-two years of riding—that's a lot of time,* remarks Tracy Cole. *I ride once a week, except in the winter because there's no indoor ring. We're planning an indoor ring in a couple of years, then I will be riding more—I hope, I hope, I hope. I hate winter because I can't ride. I pay for all my riding, now. It doesn't seem like I'm setting the money aside—it's riding time, it's like, okay, here's the money, let's do it. My riding is more necessary than rent. I know rent is important, you have to have a place to live, but I think having a place to live isn't as important as having a horse to ride, if you can understand.... When I don't ride, I'm a mess. You can tell in the middle of the week at work.... It's like, "Wow, she didn't get to ride last weekend." I get very grouchy. I try not to let it affect me so much, but it does; it feels like something's missing.*

Such a deep need as Tracy describes for riding is difficult for non-riders to comprehend: *When I was in Washington D.C. on a press tour for the movie,* BLACK BEAUTY, *a reporter—a really sweet guy from the* BALTIMORE SUN—*said to me, "I am so happy to talk to you. I'm trying to understand my thirteen-year-old daughter and her horse and I just can't. Maybe you can help me,"* recalls Caroline Thompson. *Parents probably look at this as an incredible sinkhole in their pocket book. Money is an issue for everybody. I keep my horses at home, not for the economics of it, but because I want them with me. It's an incredible expense and it is the best money I've spent.*

Recognizing the benefits, yet constrained by money and time, this mother *expanded* riding to include her entire family: *I have a daughter who's twenty-seven, one is going to be twenty-three soon, a son that's fifteen, and they all ride,* reports Pat Lawson. *My grandson has been learning—he's seven—and my granddaughter is four. I've included the children in all of this. As a family, we could not go in opposite directions. We couldn't be tap dancing and riding a horse at the same time, so they all learned how to ride.* Tight money plus tight time equals a tight family unit: a successful equation for the Lawson clan.

Although it may not add up on paper, Mary Mansi appreciates the rewards of riding in her balance sheet of life: *As an accountant evaluating my riding expenses, I'd say, "You should be investing that money in retirement or something practical,"* she says. *For as much as I spend on riding, I could create a pretty good nest egg in twenty years. But for the way it makes me feel about myself, and about life, and the satisfaction that I get from it—it's worth every penny that I put into it. It has added so much to my character: how I relate with people, how I see things, and how I enjoy my life.... Not just riding, but how I enjoy everything else because of riding. It's added so much. If people knew how much I paid, they'd drop in their tracks and say, "You are nuts!" But it has enhanced my life so incredibly, that for me, the money's well worth it.*

Many committed riders consider that if they weren't paying for horses or riding, they'd be paying a psychiatrist or a doctor to treat them for the stress-related ailments that riding combats: *It really doesn't matter what riding costs, it's the best possible investment I could make because of the pay-offs: peace of mind, tranquility, well-being, and the connection,* agrees L. D. Burke. *Horseback riding is a lot more than the actual physical activity: the mental activity, spiritual activity, and emotional activity are the richest parts of it. Anyway, we're not here to make dollars; we're here to make sense.*

It is evident that for many, the economics of horses are measured on the *quality* of living scale, as opposed to the cost of living scale. As Winston Churchill advocated:

> And here I say to parents, especially to wealthy parents, 'Don't give your son money. As far as you can afford it, give him horses.' No one ever came to grief—except honorable grief—through riding horses. No hour of life is lost that is spent in the saddle. Young men have often been ruined through owning horses, or through backing horses, but never through riding them; unless of course they break their necks, which, taken at a gallop, is a very good death to die. (Churchill 45)

ADRIAN ARROYO, b. 1978, has been an avid rider since she was seven. Adrian enjoys jumping, competing and caring for horses, as well as helping and training other riders. She's shown on her Thoroughbred gelding, 4 Point Oh, crisply clearing a jump at the 1997 Santa Rosa Horse Show.

CHAPTER NINE

FROM TRIALS
TO TRIUMPHS

Breakdowns as Breakthroughs

Tragedy either makes you bitter or better. —*Dale Evans Rogers*

The good lessons come hard and cost dear. —© *L.D. Burke III*

As a youngster growing up in Washington, D.C., Bob Douglas learned to ride at Rock Creek Park Horse Center, but drifted away from horses as college, the military, marriage, and a career as a research biologist took precedence. He distinguished himself at the National Institutes of Health by helping develop a vital screening test for rubella in women. Then, in his late thirties, Bob was ambushed by multiple sclerosis.

Hand tremors and failing eyesight soon made it impossible for him to work with the delicate equipment and microscopes in his laboratory. Eventually, he could no longer walk and was consigned to a wheel chair. This progressively degenerative disease was robbing him of his sight, his strength, his legs, his career, his hopes, and his promising future—he was confused, depressed, and *ANGRY!* He cursed God and the universe for some time: "It's not

236

FAIR!" "Why ME?"

Finally, Bob asked a question he was able to answer—what *is the point?* He came to realize the point is, like it or not, fair or not, "This is your life, Bob Douglas!" This is what you have to deal with for the rest of your years—living with multiple sclerosis.

Once he was able to surrender to that state of his being, Bob began to move forward again, for the disease had not yet robbed him of his spirit. He was determined to learn to adapt to his unchosen, unexpected, but all-too-real new life. Bob was now ready to redirect his focus from wrath to work.

Logically or not, Bob decided—although he was paralyzed from the waist down, had hand tremors, and was intermittently blinded by M.S.—that he should get back to riding. So, in 1972, at the age of thirty-nine, he purchased the Rock Creek Park Horse Center, built a wheel chair ramp, trained a Tennessee Walker to stand patiently while he hoisted himself and scooted onto its back, and began his own program of physical therapy: The National Center for Therapeutic Riding was born.

As a research biologist, Bob understood that riding at a walk mechanically approximates human ambulation. Thus, a horse is an excellent alternative to human legs since the action of the equine walk automatically works the voluntary and involuntary muscles of the human diaphragm and lower back.

Bob also understood that receiving therapy on the back of a horse gives physical therapy exciting new dimensions: a degree of independence with a big shot of accomplishment thrown in. Riding not only works muscles, it gets the adrenaline flowing, tunes up the sense of balance, and forces the brain to keep up with new sensations and a whole new vocabulary. Riding expands the horizon of experience and ability, so self-esteem blossoms, and most importantly, the imagination soars. On the back of a horse, an individual is no longer merely a patient being worked on by a physical therapist; he/she is suddenly a *horseback rider!*...a cowboy...a barrel racer...a knight in shining armor...a beautiful princess on a noble steed...an Olympic Champion! Riding launches a whole new set of dreams, possibilities, and goals.

At the time Bob started the National Center for Therapeutic Riding, there were only a few other such programs in the United States. They were not well known in therapeutic or education circles since the benefits of such fledgling programs were not yet quantified. Thus, Bob found his biggest challenge was still ahead— that of convincing local schools of the benefits inherent in his program. It took him more than a year to get his first group of students, for Bob wanted entire special education classes—including the teachers—to come out to the stable for instruction. He wanted the group, as a whole, to have a shared experience, and then he wanted to be able to measure their progress as a unit. The evaluation results were astounding: a sharp increase in educational test scores, marked advancement in physical abilities, obvious growth in self-esteem.

Miracles happen every day now at the National Center for Therapeutic Riding. More than eight thousand students have been helped over the years, with about five hundred currently enrolled in the program. They are all flourishing physically, mentally, emotionally, and spiritually, just by sharing their lives with the wonderful Riding Center equine therapists.

As a result of the time, effort, and discipline he has invested in riding, Bob is no longer restricted to a wheelchair. He only occasionally needs crutches now, because his legs have learned to walk again from the back of a horse. And Bob has learned what the point of his life is—to share his program and his example to help others develop their own strengths and inspire new dreams—with *HorsePower!*

Bob Douglas's story may be unique, but its outcome is not unusual. Major breakdowns in life often result in empowering breakthroughs. At one time or another, everyone finds himself forced to alter his life's path due to unexpected and unwanted obstacles suddenly thrust in his way. Since working with horses presents daily breakdowns, horse people get lots of practice taking change in stride, and being creatively flexible and accepting of unanticipated impediments.

When I started jumping, I was surprised to discover that successful jumpers do not focus on the fence as they take it. Instead, they assess the jump from a perspective of distance, viewing the obstacle in its entirety. Then the rider makes a conscious plan on how best to approach the jump, deciding what he needs to do, and how to direct his horse in order to get past the obstacle successfully. By the time an effective jumping team actually arrives at the jump, they have mentally surmounted it and are already focused on the path they want to follow beyond it.

It struck me that this strong, positive assessment of jumps would be valuable when applied to the obstacles so often found in one's own path in life. When an obstacle, or "breakdown," appears in our way, we often focus so intently on the problem itself that we spend little time planning how best to handle it and dispatch it. The more we focus on the actual obstacle, and the closer we get to having to finally deal with the problem, the larger it looms in our eyes, and the more intimidating it becomes with each unplanned step we take toward it. On the conveyor belt of time, we are relentlessly pulled toward the obstacles barring our way. We can either resist and go along kicking and screaming to a wreck of a breakdown, or we can create a strategy for successfully clearing the obstacle so that we experience an empowering breakthrough.

If we would only view our own problems as merely individual hurdles to clear, then analyze and plan our approach to them, communicate what help we may need to get past them, all the while looking beyond the obstacle itself to the new course we've devised, our life's journey would be easier, less stressful, and much less intimidating. In this way, the detour from breakdown to break-through becomes a deliberate avenue of strategy, strength, resilience, insight, and growth.

Being Open to Change

It's easy to slip into habitual routines and often discomforting to change them, even for something as innocuous as a trail ride: *A while ago I was on one of our regular trails with my Saddlebred, Steve, and a fallen tree was blocking the way,* recounts Camille Whitfield Vincent. *We couldn't get around it, so we were forced to find a different route, which I had never done before. This was a blessing in disguise because we discovered new trails that I thought were too rugged for a fancy show horse, but Steve just cruised right on through. That was the most fun ride we'd had in ages—we ended up in a field full of wildflowers, totally by ourselves, just galloping through wildflowers—it was fabulous! I came home and told my husband that ride was a great lesson for me to get off the same old track—it took a downed tree to force me to venture out.*

While Camille expanded her horizons with that small change in routine, Rex Peterson discovered that change also expands the mind of man and mount: *Years ago, in our trick-riding days, my dad would never let us do anything on our trick-riding horses except trick ride. Dad was always worried that the horse would become confused. He felt they should do one thing and not change, so they'd know their job—run straight—not duck, not zigzag down the arena. A trick horse would last us one or two years before they burned out or learned bad habits.*

In the early seventies, the whole family went on our first really big Wild West show. Right off the bat my utility horse (the one that I rode in the grand entry, the wagon train scene, the Indian attack, and the cattle drive) got hurt. I had nothing else to ride except my trick-riding horse; so I had to use him for everything. He became the only horse we trick-rode for over ten years. After that we started using other trick-

riding horses more and more and more. Suddenly my dad's telling me, "Son, you'd better start using that trick-riding horse for other things." You see, we found out the more you do with a horse—the more you educate and open up their minds—the better they become. Being forced to use his trick horse showed Rex and his dad that the singular routine was actually ruining, not reinforcing, their horses.

At times the fates charge in and tear up a life's plan as callously as if it were yesterday's newspaper. Yet in the wake of that devastation lies the fertilizer for personal growth. As Pat Lawson notes, *Change is never 100% negative—there's always a positive in it.*

Since resisting reality is futile, perhaps the best course is to accept our new circumstances, then search for the positive surprise packages hidden within: *We can't always predict what our life changes might be, for there are outside forces involved,* notes Bob Douglas. *Sometimes changes are made for you by God so you'll move on to something new; I think this was certainly my case. Over the years I've come to understand what happened to me was really meant to happen. I had another life to live to help others; and the vehicle for helping was to be horses. Now I'm out of the wheel chair; I teach; I ride; I compete; I've come a long way.*

I often boast that I have the best job in Washington, D.C.! Whether or not tomorrow will bring even greater happiness, I don't know. But at this point, right now, I'm extremely happy with myself and my life, and that's a nice place to be...very few people get there. Bob found a number of positive surprises along his path altered by M.S.: teaching, riding, competing, and the best job in Washington—not bad!

Sometimes we need to be shut down to a point of meditative isolation before we find what we want for ourselves rather than what someone else envisions for us: *Our family was in the rodeo business; my brother and I did rope tricks for a living,* says Buck Brannaman. *We kinda had the perfect little life; my mother made our fancy outfits, and in the summer our family went all over the United States going to rodeos, where we'd spin ropes. Remember the commer-*

cials in the 70's with the Sugar Pops kids? That was me and my brother. That's what life was like when we were little. But then my mother passed away when I was eleven.

My dad so loved my mother that he just didn't want to live without her; so he went to drinking, and within two years, he'd become an alcoholic. Dad never really drank before that, even though he had had a pretty damn rough life long before Mom died. He'd been a prisoner of war in World War II, and when I was just a little guy, he had a bad accident on a job in Alaska—he got hit with seventeen thousand volts of electricity and fell from a ninety-foot tower onto frozen tundra. So he'd already had lots of heartaches that took a toll on him, but losing Mom put him over the edge. I think alcohol was just the weapon he chose to do away with himself.

Pretty soon he was abusing my brother and me to the point that we were sure he was gonna kill us. Looking back, it was really kind of morbid, but my brother and I had a two-mile walk home from school, and our discussion every day was whether we were gonna be alive the next day to walk home from school again. Every day for two years we'd talk about that. Then it got so bad that the law came and took us away. If they hadn't, we wouldn't have survived…we would not have lived.

So that's how we ended up in a foster home on a ranch near Norris, Montana. With my foster parents I felt like I was living in a dream, not having anybody hollering at me or beating on me; but all I really wanted was to be left alone. For four months I never spoke to anyone—that's when the horses and I became friends—it was like they understood.

I went for seven or eight years and didn't hear much from Dad, except for a threatening letter occasionally…his drinking continued…. Eventually, I did reconnect with him, and we had a decent relationship when he died a couple of years ago.

But that's where it really started for me—on that foster ranch I got the bug for being a cowboy. Prior to that I'd been with horses, spinning *ropes, but there's a big distinction between being a childhood celebrity in the rodeo business and wanting to be a real true-to-life cowboy—a Will James kind of cowboy.*

By stepping out of the expected and on to a new path, each of the above individuals successfully surmounted obstacles in his way and discovered exciting new adventures on the far side. So often it's just a matter of being open to a new vision, and going with it, rather than fighting to stay on a familiar old road.

Different Visions

As difficult as it may be to try alternate routines, plans, or perspectives, the very act of refusing to consider other visions can blind us to valuable potential and possibility: *I've been breeding horses a long, long time, and there was one filly that was simply the ugliest foal I've ever seen—just terrible,* recalls Chris Hawkins. *The poor little thing had a bum that looked like you'd use it for a ski slope—no buns at all, and her right ear flopped down over her eye. When I saw her, I thought, "Damn! As much as I paid for your mother? And as much as you've got in your background—being a King mare, from Depth Charge and Jesse James?" As a breeder of fine Quarter Horses, I was deeply ashamed of her.... Hell, a breeder of inferior mules would have been ashamed of her!*

I didn't want that thing in our barn or on our property where clients might see her; so I asked our next door neighbor, if I paid him three hundred dollars, would he take her over and feed her? Well, he agreed; but you know something? That husband of mine stopped it. He said, "Nope, you bred her. By God, it's your responsibility—you take care of her."

And I tell you, within three weeks, I'm saying, "Oh, thank you, Lord! My God, she's gorgeous!" When that four-legged ugly duckling grew into the swan, honey, there was no stopping her! Her looks and her attitude are those of a natural born champion. She is fully aware that she's a champion. She knows that the silver and gold belt buckle with rubies and diamonds, that's so big you can't bend over it, is hers. Yet I missed the mark entirely when she was first born—I just didn't see any possibility in her. So you see, even an educated first impression can be very wrong. I've learned a lot from that mare I bred, Zan— don't judge too soon.

When Zan did not match Chris's "foal template," Chris could not see any positive possibilities. This is a valuable reminder that some become champions precisely because they aren't typical— they are *exceptional*.

Another horse owner failed to see any potential when his horse proved to be less than stellar on the track. Rather than considering a different discipline for her, he sentenced her to years of pitiful neglect: *When I first found Lady, she was head down at the far end of her stall,* Kelly O'Boyle relates angrily. *She'd been stuck in a stall for two years—just left in a stall! She wouldn't turn around to see who was coming into the stall; she wouldn't turn to see what food she was getting, and she only weighed about six hundred pounds as a three-year-old. The guy who owned her didn't care about her because he didn't see her as a success on the track. I started taking her out of her stall for walks.... A quarter-mile walk broke her into the biggest sweat I've ever seen on a horse. But something about that horse made me want her—I paid him one dollar for her. Something about her made me work a little longer, work a little harder, spend a lot more time, and my gut feeling paid off. Lady now weighs a more normal Thoroughbred twelve hundred pounds. My local vet, who's an Olympic team vet, and another [equine] leg specialist have had a look at her and both of them said she can go grand prix. Not bad for a buck! I may take different risks than other people would, take harder routes sometimes, but when I listen to my gut, I'm not necessarily wrong!*

Lady's first owner's lack of vision cost him dearly: not only did he lose the potential sales price of a healthy young Thoroughbred, he lost a great deal more on a personal level by his inhumane actions. By taking a chance on a broader vision for that mare,

Kelly not only saved Lady's life, but found a talented dressage prospect and a beloved partner.

Traditionally, a bowed tendon would mark the end of a racehorse's career due to outright lameness or a general weakening of the leg. Yet a group of individuals willing to risk a new vision successfully treated a talented runner and found a way to save the athlete rather than retire her: *There was a Thoroughbred named Lassie Come Home that was in training with me,* reports René Williams. *She had a bowed tendon, and I think we were the first ever to surgically replace a tendon. The operation was done at the University of Pennsylvania. They took out the extensor tendon, which is a useless tendon in a horse, and transplanted it. For six months after we brought her back to the farm, I hand walked her on a flat floor and took care of that leg every day. Then we put her back in training and sent her to Florida, where she won six straight races. She won the Jersey Futurity, too. As it turned out, the fellow who was training her there ran her on the dirt, and she broke down—on the other leg—not the one that was transplanted, so then we bred her.* Instead of following convention and simply giving up on the animal's breakdown, René took a risk that resulted in a miraculous veterinary breakthrough.

There are times in life when plans, direction, and visions are devised by more than one individual. In marriage, it's important that some visions be mutually acceptable, for if they are too divergent, the marriage itself suffers: *I married Dick Phelps in 1964, had twin daughters, Brooke and Courtney in '66, and we welcomed our third daughter, Devon, in '69,* Mary Deringer Phelps recounts. *Over the years of our marriage, I'd been riding regularly at a variety of stables. In 1970 I joined the new Hickory Hill Hunt.*

One cold day at the Hickory Hill Clubhouse, one of the pipes burst under the sink. As I reached under to turn the water off, my knee slipped out of joint (an old basketball injury) and stayed out. I didn't hunt that day, but went to the hospital instead. When the doctor came in, Dick asked him, "What happens if you leave her like that?"

That was my first clue that things were not happy in Camelot. The doctor replied, "She'll walk like this"—leg totally stiff. Then Dick said, "Well, at least she'll be home." Can you imagine? He wanted to hobble this girl!

Well, I had a knee operation and Dick's sitting with me in recovery, staring at me, when he says, "You're going to drop out of the hunt; you're going to move the horses to the house; you'll ride only on the weekend, and you will continue your volunteer work at the hospital...."

I looked at him and wondered, "Who is this man? Where'd this side of him come from?" Then I thought, "I don't think so," and I filed—I went and got a lawyer, filed for divorce, and really shocked him. Dick wanted me hobbled and branded; but I refuse to wear a brand, so I got divorced.

Horses and riding are my life. The only thing that I wanted to do is to be around horses. It's a gift and a need so deep that others cannot understand how I can care this much about a horse—any horse!

My need for the horses definitely broke up my marriage. When I filed, Dick asked me, "How are you going to support yourself?"

"I'll go back in the horse business." It was that simple. I will go back in the horse business: I will teach; I will train; I will compete—I have my horse.

I moved up the road about three miles, put down two years' rent, and opened "Over the Hill Hunt Farm." After that, I moved to Denton, Texas, bought a big farm and really took off in the business. In 1975 I went to the Willow Bend Polo Club as the head instructor, barn manager, and trainer and did that for ten years. I've never looked back. Dick remarried within a year and has two more lovely children. I stayed in the area because of our girls being young and their father being there. Dick and I are still close as far as our three children; he gave Devon away at her wedding....

But if I had stayed with Dick, I wouldn't have been first in the state [in Amateur Owner Jumping]; I never would have been fifth in the nation; I would never have climbed Pike's Peak.... There's just so many things I never would have been "allowed" if I had stayed with Dick. I might have done other things with him, but it wouldn't have been my life. This has been my life—every mistake and every success....

Mistakes

"Mistake," the very thought of that word can turn a grown adult into a mass of raw, frazzled nerves, while a young child—blissfully unaware of the humiliating overtones—calmly treats a mistake as the integral part of the learning process that it is: *I'm a big believer in sport psychology, which indicates that the best frame of mind to be a great athlete is childlike,* states Anne Kursinski. *To have less fear and clutter, to get out of your head and proceed on a simple, honest, intuitive level where you're not afraid of making mistakes. There are many things that are so right about being childlike to suc-ceed. A little kid falls off, dusts off, gets back on, and goes at it again, like who cares? They haven't yet fallen under the power of peer pressure and embarrassment that you start learning when you become a teenager.*

Teachers quickly discover that mistakes are not only an inherent part of learning, but an effective teaching aid as well: *One time I was taking my Appaloosa stud, Zip, over a jump, bridleless,* relates John Lyons. *Well, I didn't give him enough room to set up his strides before the fence, so he popped the jump, and I went up and over the front of him. As I was going off, I grabbed on around his neck and was able to land on my feet, so it all came off pretty good. I got back on, made a few jokes about it, and jumped it right the next time.*

A few weeks later I get a letter from this guy who'd been at that clinic and was all excited about my going off. "It was so neat seeing you fall off, because if you could fall off, I knew it was okay for me to fall off—it wasn't the end of the world." After going through all this he ends the letter with, "You didn't plan that, did you?"

Over the years, my horses and I have made a lot of mistakes in front of audiences, but that's actually made people feel better—that we weren't perfect. They want to see how I handle situations when my horses aren't perfect, so our mistakes have become an important teaching tool.

When mistakes multiply, it's easy to throw in the towel. But William Steinkraus learned a critical lesson from his mount by staying the course: *In 1952, Democrat and I were just starting off together. All I knew about Democrat was that he was old and crotchety and not very sound. He was nineteen at the time, and I considered him well over the hill. Our first competition together was a speed class in Harrisburg, Pennsylvania. Due to some bad communication with a ground jury, all the spread fences were doubled in size: instead of 4' to 4'6" heights with 6' spreads, the course suddenly reached world-class proportions of 4'9" to 5' fences with 7'-8' spreads!* (Steinkraus 101–104)

I wouldn't have entered Democrat if I'd realized this kind of a fence was going to be in there. I figured his chances of winning that particular class were one in five hundred. As luck would have it, we were the last to go and watched as everyone came to grief—especially at the last fence—a real killer! I didn't think Democrat could jump that big a fence—no way—even if he got there right!

*Our round went incredibly well; we went clean to the last fence, but then I unwittingly put Democrat into a very bad spot. It turned out that he handled that bad placement and we sailed over that jump as if jet propelled. Democrat's performance was comparable to an ancient ballplayer stepping up to the plate in the last of the ninth and hitting a four hundred fifty foot home run. It was such an impossible long shot that I was just **startled**! That was really a thrill—a thrill's thrill! Not anything that anyone could have calculated—just sudden surprise—entirely unexpected....*

So, one of the important things I've learned from riding is to hang in there—never give up. Keep jumping those obstacles and who knows? Every now and then you catch the brass ring. But you have to stay in there—in the game—ready to play.

Irving Pettit recounts a comparable story from harness racing: *In the early fifties, at Harrington Raceway in Delaware, I was driving in a harness race when one of the other drivers ran up over my wheel. I fell clear out of the sulky, but landed on my feet and held onto the lines; so I jumped right back up on the cart and finished—third. The people in the grandstand had never seen that happen before! Goes to show that you should never give up in competition—we ended up placing rather than quitting.*

The anxiety surrounding mistakes may actually compound an error if we allow it to control our response rather than quietly regrouping: *Usually what I find when a horse is making a mistake, the rider will go ahead and push, push, and confuse,* observes Martha Josey. *That's when I'd stop, start over, and go back verrryyy slowly. I've always said, "Slow and right is much better than fast and wrong." The same works for me when I make a mistake in my life: I just stop, start over, and go back slower....*

Take one, take two...take seventeen—there are times when it seems that all we're doing is getting really good at making mistakes: *You can go on and on with unsuccessful schooling, and suddenly something good happens, and you think, "Finally some good luck." But it isn't luck,* says Phyllis Eifert. *It's the result of all your trying and failing; you just had to work through that process of trial and error in order to find what works.*

That maddening process of experiencing, repeating, and finally mastering mistakes is ultimately productive: *People talk about "accidents," and certainly there are such things,* Macella O'Neill acknowledges. *But even accidents have causes—not that you can always figure them out—but they do have causes. Anybody who's in my job of riding, competing, training, and teaching better be able to get some kind of rhyme and reason from every accident; then try to make them fewer and farther between. Like any mistake, you have to learn from accidents and move on.* Trial and error and accidents can stimulate education and innovation, which in turn generate progress; so mistakes are actually valuable motivators for improvement.

Getting Smart the Hard Way

The horse world is a productive proving ground for learning to cope with the inexplicable, since it's fraught with dramatic events and unfathomable accidents: *My dad was a horseman, and his dad was a horseman, and my great-great-grandfather was a horseman, so horses have always been part of our family,* remarks Richard Shrake. *I have pictures of me as early as two years old on a little pony. It was just part of living and breathing in our family. So, you bet, riding's important to me. I've done it all my life. I don't know anything else. My wife asked me to hang a door the other day, and I couldn't even do that…. Horses have been a total focus; I've never done anything else but been in the horse business. About ten years ago, I won the All-Around at the Quarter Horse Congress, and had a good show at the AQHA World Championship Show. I said to my wife, "We'll never have better shows than we're having this year." Later that same year, a horse turned over on me, and I cracked my hip. That's pretty well stopped my riding—if I ride every day now, I can't get out of bed in the morning.*

I've always felt that the guy who does his best is going to be okay and that I've got a pretty good plan for my life. Since that accident, things kind of fit together. What that accident did was made me focus my gifts a little narrower and said to me, "You love to teach." I'd been giving seminars before, but since the accident, I can't get on and fix somebody's horse like I did most of my life. Not being able to do that has made me realize that when I'm teaching someone, and I get on and fix their horse, they see that they don't have that touch, and that steals a little bit of confidence from them. They maybe get to thinking, "I'll never be able to do that." What I do now is be very visual, and listen, and help that person and horse from the ground. I am now transferring my talent to them so they can fix their horse. So, that accident really was a good thing—it has made me a better horseman and teacher.

Successful horsemen quickly learn to turn mistakes into effective knowledge: *There's going to be horses in your life that will leave impressions on your mind—some good, some bad—but you'll remember them your whole life,* declares Rex Peterson. *We had a horse at home we called Tailgate because he had a severe kicking habit. He kicked and hurt several people—he kicked me—and to this day, Tailgate's why I won't put up with kicking horses. I'll put a stop to it. Because of Tailgate, I can train the kick out of most any horse—it's a piece of cake. I really attribute that to that horse, and if I live to be 100, I'll never forget him, 'cause he left an impression on my mind.* Tailgate may have left an impression on another part of Rex's anatomy as well, but by having to deal with Tailgate's problem, Rex learned a valuable new skill.

Impressive "problem horses" may not command a high market price, yet they can be worth their weight in educational gold as Buck Brannaman also discovered: *I've started thousands of horses, but I've got a gelding now, Biff, that I'll never sell,* reports Buck. *The ranch I bought him off had a reputation for having real "bronc-y" horses, and doing a real sorry job halter-breaking them, to where they got most of their horses really fighting them. This outfit halter-breaks their young horses by trapping them inside a stall barn; then they muscle a halter on them and leave them tied in there for two to three days without feed or water. On the third day, one person tries to drag or lead the horse to the creek while another person stands behind whipping or beating on them. The horses are supposed to associate getting a drink of water with leading. It's pretty primitive. These people have been doing the same damn thing for forty years!*

Well, some of the foals have a little more substance and a little more grit, and they'd end up fighting. They'd flip over backwards and strike and kick. They'd kill themselves before they'd ever get to the creek.

Biff was one of those fighters. They threw him down, castrated, and branded him; but they never did get him to the creek. They just finally kicked him out and let him soak on his experience with man until he was a five-year-old. I was across the river on a different ranch when I heard about this man-made hellion, so I trotted over to take a look. He was a big horse: sixteen hands, thirteen hundred and fifty pounds, and ugly as homemade sin. I bought him because I knew he was gonna be a huge challenge. It's one thing to have a bronc-y little mustang—some of them can be kind of treacherous—but this horse was big and strong and treacherous! A different deal. When you get a saddle and a full-grown human on top of a little bitty horse that wants to buck you off, they can't buck near as hard as what they look like. But when the animal weighs thirteen hundred and fifty pounds and you put a full-grown man on him, it makes no difference to him—he can buck—hard! I'd say Biff was in the top five "bronciest" horses I've ever worked—he'd buck, strike, bite, kick, and break down the corral!

The first time I started working him, I just tried to drive him around the corral without anything on him, just like you'd herd a milk cow. I spent ninety minutes before he took one step forward. I worked with him for about three hours just to get him to a place where I could pet him and get my saddle on and off a few times without getting kicked. Biff was very dangerous to be around and I learned a whole lot about getting around a horse like that without getting hurt.

Well, now I've ridden him a long time. I've roped thousands of colts on him in my clinics, and he's never bucked a step. But of all the clinics and training I've done, I've never had a horse come through as touchy as Biff was when I got him. Biff helped convince me that no horse is impossible. I've been doing this a long time, and I've yet to see the impossible; I find it pretty unlikely that I'll see it now. For all I've learned from Biff, I could never pay him back. He will have a home with me forever. Thankfully Buck was up to meeting a career challenge the size and temper of Biff, for that success saved Biff from slaughter and gave him a fresh start with man. It also provided Buck with a tremendous educational experience, greater confidence, and the conviction that no horse is a lost cause.

Professional rodeo saddle broncs, with reputations that precede them, represent yet another measure of impressive horseflesh: *Andy Riggy was a great ol' cowboy who'd been around forever,* relates Larry Mahan. *He was a champion calf-roper back in the thirties, and I had all the respect in the world for him; but he was kind of a cranky old guy. Andy had the J Spear Rodeo Company in Newhall, California, and in his string Andy had a little ol' bronc called Sailor Boy.*

Now with the luck of the draw in rodeo, you could draw a bronc that was really hard to get out on—meaning that he'd developed the habit of rearing up and falling over backward in the chute. Climbing on was a real tense time if you happened to draw that kind of an animal. Sailor Boy was really hard to get out on. He'd fight the chute like you couldn't believe. At Long Beach, California, I drew Sailor Boy....

The first time I got on him, he flipped up and fell back into the end of the chute. When that happens, you usually have to reset your saddle, so we went through all the re-adjustments, and I got on him again. This time he really tried it. He reared up and back as far as he could go and when he came down, he jerked the restraining rope out of the guy's hand. Luckily, Sailor Boy didn't fall all the way over; he got a little bit of a mash on me, but then he fell forward—right down on his belly. So now he's lying there in the chute, on his belly, with me still in the saddle. Most normal people would jump off and start over again. But I figured, "He has to stand up now. He has to stand up and turn out." So I had them open the gate with Sailor Boy laying on his stomach. With the gate open, he scrambled up and turned out.... I rode him and won something on him.

The next week I was at another of Andy's rodeos and somebody else drew Sailor Boy. They're in the chute and that cowboy's looking a might nervous about it. Then I hear Andy yell, "Get outta there, kid! I saw Mahan take him lying on his belly last week!" I bet Andy told every kid in the world that got on Sailor Boy that story—obviously Andy got quite a kick out of it. By keeping cool and being open to a new approach, Larry's unnerving and unorthodox depart became an impressive winning ride.

Pat Lawson related another incident where success resulted from potential disaster: *A few years back the Ebony Horsewomen were invited to the Tournament of Roses Parade in Pasadena. There was a show at the Equidome (a big arena with spectator seats all around) prior to the parade; so we worked out a routine for that show. The Equidome entrance ramp takes you underground into the arena. Well, our horses didn't want to go down that ramp, and I did something that I should have never done.... Star and I were to lead the troupe in, so I just forced him down that ramp. Well, we got half-way down when he decided, "Okay, since I have to go, watch this...." He suddenly raced into the arena and all the Ebony Horsewomen horses followed!*

That little routine we had worked out? Well, we did it, but it turned into a rodeo act. Horses were reeling and bucking and just going out of their minds! The audience thought it was supposed to be a rodeo act, so they were standing and applauding.

There was one segment where our names are announced and we were supposed to wave individually. Well, the horses were ripped, but the riders were waving.... It was wild! At one point, I saw my daughter fly past me, and I thought, "Oh my God, I can't help her! I can't even get my horse under control."

Finally, I was able to get the bit back from Star, and we tore out of the arena just like we went in. We were all dazed and looked as if we'd been in a fight: hats askew, shirttails pulled out, we were covered in dust—but nobody fell off. It was amazing! We all did things we'd never thought possible, but we all went with it, survived; and put on one heck of a show.

Our trainers cracked up exclaiming, "We have never in our lives seen anything like that." Everyone else thought it was planned; only the trainers knew that we'd all lost our minds.

In addition to surviving their acclaimed rodeo routine, the Ebony Horsewomen discovered they could endure more equestrian chaos than ever imagined, precipitating a "post-traumatic pride" and an unexpected shot of confidence.

Sally Swift had to cope with a deforming disease throughout her life, but this enabled her to accumulate the knowledge and insight that became the basis for her innovative approach to riding: *I have scoliosis—lateral curvature of the spine,* explains Sally. *Since I was seven, up until my twenties, I worked with Miss Mabel Todd, who wrote,* THE THINKING BODY. *She took me off all right-handed sports; I couldn't play tennis or baseball, all those things that you play in school. When she discovered I was horse crazy, she encouraged that and had a brace made for me so I could ride. It turned out to be good for me because it strengthened my weak legs and lower back. Although there was no such thing as "therapeutic riding" back in the thirties, that's what it was. Miss Todd taught me a certain amount of physiology— not fancy at all—but there was always a skeleton by the table for reference. She talked a lot about the concentration of power in the bottom of the body...about the mast (the spine) being in the step of the boat (the pelvis). When I rode, I used to imagine that I'd dropped a ball through my body into the pelvis, and it would land with a sort of thump—like landing in mud—then I felt secure and could do anything.*

I rode and taught riding for twelve years in a conventional way. Then I went to agricultural college and did other things for thirty years. Through all that time, I still taught friends to ride, and when I retired, I decided I'd go on teaching and travel a little.

It was then that I began playing with the stuff I'd learned from Miss Todd and it worked like a charm. I was getting all kinds of nice results, and it developed like topsy. We've gone up into high levels in the last two or three years—we still teach the basics—but we can take high-level people now and make them fly!

My work with Miss Todd really was the basis...she didn't call it "centering"...but as I wrote CENTERED RIDING *I realized that that was what we'd been doing—going to the center. So, you see, this whole Centered Riding method really developed from my therapy for scoliosis.*

When faced with challenging situations, the above individuals had the vision, courage, and wisdom to glean new techniques and confidence from their experiences; they all got smarter—the hard way.

When the Worst Becomes a Personal Best

In assessing a personal challenge and its outcome, attitude is a defining factor in any lesson learned. Personally, I think Pollyana has been given a bad rap, for I'd much rather have her optimistic outlook than a self-defeating negative one. Consider the following setbacks that turned out to be opportunities for discovery and growth: *In Germany in 1983, I was loading a difficult mare in the trailer at the end of a very hard two-day clinic,* relates Linda Tellington-Jones. *I was really tired, and there were about eighty people very close by; when I turned to ask them to allow room, she struck me, breaking my ankle really badly.*

The following week I had a presentation at the Spanish Riding School in Vienna. Even though I could not do the presentation, I decided not to cancel, for it was a big thing to be invited to present at the Spanish Riding School. I asked one of my teachers, Annagret Ast, a dressage instructor in Austria, to do it. Annagret had only a couple of years' experience and would normally not have presented the work to such a prestigious group, but she did, and it was very, very successful. She wound up heading TTEAM in Europe. Had it not been for that unplanned presentation I would not have realized the degree to which she could present the work.

I remember thinking at the time, isn't it interesting how something that seems to be a real disaster can turn around for the better? So, now when anything in my life triggers "UH OH!" I now think to myself, "Hmm? I wonder how this is going to bring a turn-around? What is going to come out of this?" Usually, what appears to be a major disaster turns out to be an unexpected surprise package of opportunity.

After all, much of the Tellington TTouch and the TTEAM programs are oriented around problem solving. Many of our clients are led to TTEAM by what seems to be an unsolvable problem, and as a re-sult of that breakdown, they often end up with the breakthrough of learning a whole new way of being with horses.

Certainly Linda could have brooded over the fact that her in-jury deprived her of the honor of presenting to the famed Span-ish Riding School, but instead, she appreciated her unexpected opportunity to discover and promote Annagret's exceptional ability.

Another understudy became a star when Anne Kursinski un-expectedly lost her lead horse: *After Star Man's retirement, Can-nonball was my up-and-coming horse,* reports Anne. *He had been my Olympic horse at Barcelona, and we were slated to do great things to-gether, but then Cannonball's owner took him back. At the time I thought it was a real tragedy, and a lot of people wondered, "What's she going to do without him?"*

We had this one horse, Suddenly, who had been kept on the back burner because he was a little hot and a little crazy. Suddenly, Sud-denly became important in the line and showed me that he could do bigger and better things than we ever imagined. He got to do a Euro-pean tour and was just fabulous. In the end he was better than Can-nonball, yet he never would have gotten the chance, and I never would have known, had Cannonball not been taken back by his owner.

Going up against your boss can be a costly and unnerving battle of confidence and competence: *A while back, I was training horses for the mounted patrol and was given a horse to work that was there on a trial basis,* recalls Laura Bianchi. *He was a Standardbred from the track and used to different training, so when the Sergeant said to me, "Take this horse out, ride him on the trail, and see if he gets used to stuff." I told him, "I don't know if he has any foundation work and I'd like some time to work with him in the ring, as a safety valve before going out in the park." (It's very busy in Golden Gate Park—more like riding on a freeway than a trail). But the Sergeant said, "No. I don't want you to do that." He had his reasons, whatever they were…and he outranked me, but I told him, "I'm sorry, I can't do that."*

That's when my training career ended. I put my uniform back on and went back out on patrol.

The interesting thing is that after I left, the Sergeant went to another trainer who told him you shouldn't even get on a horse's back until you know what that horse knows or is capable of doing. Then it sunk in. But by that time, I'd realized that I really like patrol better than training—it's the same amount of money and a lot less headaches. So it worked out fine for me. By sticking with her professional instincts, Laura was ignobly forced to relinquish her position, yet ultimately realized greater respect and job satisfaction.

When an innocent baby suffers a debilitating congenital defect, it seems so unfair that many simply cannot accept it. Yet, it is through challenges such as this that true strength of character is manifest: *I was born with a congenital defect—I was missing an ear and part of my chin,* notes Macella O'Neill. *Since two inner ears are what give you equilibrium, my parents were terrified that I wasn't going to have any balance. The doctors encouraged them to have me do lots of things that would promote balance and coordination. So they bought me a donkey, Sultan, and I started riding at age three, and I've been with horses ever since. Over the years, I had seventeen operations to correct the defects. As a result of gearing up for all those surgeries, I have a pretty fearless outlook on the world. But finally, I just told my parents that we'd gone far enough with that—please no more operations—could I just use the money for a horse?*

Being born with a couple of physical defects could give a person cause to pull back from life—not Macella! She charges ahead with an energy, enthusiasm, and work ethic that would exhaust Hercules. Macella is clearly one of the most capable, directed, talented, balanced, and personally fulfilled people I know. Her single ear is so keen, I swear she's developed radar, and as for her sense of balance, she rides with the ease and supple grace as if she were a natural extension of the animal itself.

As we've seen, some of the trials we face are a result of bad luck or bad judgments beyond our personal control. Yet, many tough trials in life are actually self-inflicted by bad choices. There's not a much bigger breakdown one can have than to be convicted of a crime and sent to prison: *The Bureau of Land Management had a contract with the state of New Mexico to supply horses for inmates to halter-break and gentle so they can be adopted out,* reports Curtis Steel (p.271). *I was the supervisor for the program at Las Cruces from 1989 to 1992. We had twenty-five to thirty minimum-restrict inmates (anybody who didn't have a violent crime) working at all times. We halter-broke on average thirty horses a month and shipped a lot of horses to the Eastern states for adoption. We had real good results; it was successful…I don't know what the percentage rate was, but we helped a lot of boys!*

We had to spend a lot of time training them, but once they got the hang of it, well you couldn't make 'em miss work. Once an inmate got interested in working with the horses, his whole attitude changed. There's an old saying, "You never see a boy in trouble leading a horse."

Occasionally we'd get letters back from some of the people saying that they wanted to thank the inmate who trained their horse. Getting that kind of letter gave an inmate a lot of pride. I'm satisfied that we helped a lot of them enough that they stayed out of prison.

There was one inmate from Lubbock, Texas, who I'd had trouble with the first time he came to the program, so he transferred. But he came back one day and wanted to learn training. Then he really came around and was a great, great help. He kept the guys organized and made the program a whole lot better and became a real good horseman. He'd never been around horses before, but he became my lead trainer at Las Cruces.

This guy had never done anything that amounted to anything in his life before, but he really took an interest in the horses. Through the horse program he learned a lot more responsibility and behaved himself a lot better. He was a good leader who kept an eye on everything and everybody, and the other inmates respected him, which helped a whole lot. He proved to himself that he could be successful. I couldn't have gone out on the street and hired anybody better.

When I was in Lubbock this past Christmas I called him. He was working on opening a record store and was having trouble getting a business license in his name on account of having a felony, so I wrote a letter of recommendation for him. The empowering lessons gleaned from working with horses are wonderfully egalitarian—they can be learned by a prisoner as well as by a princess, and both can find strength in them.

At times a person may create his very own personal prison. In Michael Plumb's case, it was built out of avoidance, dependency, and denial, ultimately hampering his talents and potential: *Back in the old days, horsemen were known for their drinking; I got in on the end of an era and kept that tradition going,* explains Michael. *For years I had an alcohol problem. Like most alcoholics, I wasn't "aware of my problem" until it got me down so bad that I **had** to do something about it. It's only been recently that I could see that there is absolutely no place for it in our business nowadays. I've overcome it, and that's opened up a whole new thought process for me. I feel much stronger in lots of ways now being rid of it. In other ways, I feel weaker—because of the time missed and all the reality that is thrown on you right away. Having to deal with reality twenty-four hours a day and **no cheating**. I've got to face up to it. In using the escape of alcohol, I managed to eliminate a lot of things that I didn't want to deal with…that got to be a habit, then it got to be a problem. I made excuses and kept it going for a long, long time—twenty years. I think a lot of people didn't even know it was a problem, but it was; it has held me back from some of the talents I have. It may be a little late, but it was time I grew up. As of this November I will be two years without alcohol and recovering....* Even with all his Olympic and eventing success, perhaps the greatest triumph for Michael was in finding the strength to finally tear down his alcoholic fortress, and face life straight on—with no cheating.

Through strength of character and a positive attitude, each individual calamity we have looked at was transformed into a personal victory. Such personal resiliency is developed almost as a requisite defense in working with horses. In order to successfully cope with the daily frustrations of being a horse owner, you learn to reframe setbacks to discover the beneficial aspects of them, then continue on in a new direction—with *HorsePower!*

Resilience

The ups and downs of international endurance competition are an arduous testing ground for mental and emotional resilience: *At the North American Championship, I was told that I had to finish sixth or better to have a shot at going to the World Equestrian Games in Holland,* explains Valerie Kanavy. *We did finish sixth, but Cash got a cramp in his chest and jogged out lame, so we were pulled at the finish line. That was total devastation. Our goal was to go to Holland, and we'd started years before, preparing the horse, showing a consistent record of doing well in high-profile races like the Race of Champions and Old Dominion. So this was like watching the work and the dream totally dissolve, with no control and nothing to do. As a matter of fact, I was so devastated that it wasn't until the next day that I cried. How could this happen? Why did this happen?*

But I have had things in the past that were major tragedies in my life that in retrospect turned out to be the best things that ever happened to me. And there was a little bit of that thought in the back of my mind, even though I could hardly think. I didn't know where to go from here. That was in August, and I didn't race after that until October and had bad luck again. We ended up fifth, and I thought, "Well, just forget it. We can't make it."

Although we'd come in fifth, Cash won best-conditioned horse, which to me is better than winning. In my mind that gave me a jumping point and restarted my thinking about how we could make the team. From that point on, my whole life was completely consumed with doing everything physically, emotionally, and mentally to prepare my-self and Cash for the world championships.

Cash had a consistent top-ten record, not a "win" record, but Cash always came through looking better at the end of a race than the begin-ning, because he was real busy about taking care of himself. He'd had three years of consistent, uninjured, uninterrupted work in a way that allowed him to become stronger with each competition. So now was the time to know, "Is this horse really slow, or is he just conservative? Does he deserve to go to Holland?" He had to be one of the best. He had to be worthy to justify taking somebody else's place.

We went to the next race in November, which was a sand race like Holland would be. At that race I actually said out loud to him, "To-day you will win, or you will hit the wall; I have to know what kind of horse you are." Cash was never a horse that ran at the front from the get-go, but I told him, "Today your position is in front." Any time he wanted to slack back behind the other horses, I said, "No." And he got the message real quick; he figured it out, "Oh, my place is to be just ahead of the other horses. Now I get it." And he won! In February he won again on sand—two hours ahead of the course record.

But I don't believe that either one of us would have gotten to that point of determination if we hadn't had the rug totally jerked out on us. If we'd made sixth and not gotten pulled we would have figured we were golden and probably slacked off a bit. Instead, Cash and Valerie were tested and came up World Champions in Holland, and they're still winning. Obviously, both were worthy of their place.

At times examples of physical resilience are truly inspirational: One year I was judging at the Cow Palace in San Francisco, and a young man by the name of Tim Whitney won the American Horse Show Stock Seat Medal Finals, Richard Shrake relates. *After he won, he walked over to me and said, "Mr. Shrake, this is a wonderful win. Someday I want to be the one who has coached a student to win the AHSA medal finals." I thought, well, that's a nice thing for him to say, and I didn't give it too much thought beyond that.*

But then I heard that that talented young man was in a tragic accident that killed a couple of people, some horses, and left Tim a paraplegic needing twenty-four-hour-a-day nursing—unable to even feed himself. When I heard he was hurt like that, I remembered him saying, "My goal in life is to train somebody else to win what I won." I thought sadly, "Well, that will never happen now."

Four years later, I'm judging an eleven-and-under pleasure class in Santa Barbara. I watched as some of the kids on the near rail were so wound up that they were almost in a wreck with their horses; then they'd go around the far end and come back the other side and suddenly have all the confidence in the world and their horses would straighten out. I asked the ring steward, "Who in the world is the trainer on the far end? He must be magic." The girl looked at me and said, "Why that's Tim Whitney." And there he was, sitting in a wheel chair—still dependent on twenty-four-hour-a-day care—but the guy's giving lessons....

Here's the best part of the story: so far, Tim has had five different students win the AHSA Medals Finals.

Rebuilding

There are personal tragedies that suddenly rip the very foundations of our lives out from under us. These are the impossible times when mustering our as-yet-untapped inner strength becomes as vital as drawing our next breath. That inner strength is built on upbringing and bolstered by personal spirit and faith. Those who spend time working with horses have an additional dimension of strength and perspective to draw from—the many empowering lessons of *HorsePower!* As a result of all these combined avenues of strength, the following individuals were able to face some of life's toughest trials and turn them into personal triumphs.

In 1984, I was thirty-nine and had been dealing with a lot of the tough stuff that life can throw at people, reports Jill Keiser Hassler.

But then came the crowning blow—my step-daughter was murdered by her husband in front of their children. That was the end. I fell into a "To-Hell-with-life-it's-not-worth-it attitude." I decided that life was unfair because my step-daughter was dead; her husband had ruined his life, the children's lives, and my life.... It was a very bad situation. Three or four days went by, and I never left my room. I was just unable to deal with anyone or anything in my life—period. All I wanted was to run away...I mean really run away—get in a plane and fly—not face another single human being.

For some reason, on that fourth day, something drove me that I had to teach this particular student. On the way to the barn, I walked through the woods, and during that walk, I realized I had to find some way to let go of my pain so I could teach the lesson. When I got in the ring I was committed to doing a good job in spite of my anguish, so I poured myself into teaching. At the end of that lesson I realized that I had succeeded in displacing all my problems. The problems weren't gone, but they no longer controlled me—I had been able to break the grip they had on my being for the time of that lesson. I felt completely energized, like a new person, and I could take on life again.

After that lesson, I went for a very, very, very long walk in the woods to try and figure out why I did feel better. How did that pain relate to my ability to function and not function? How could I deal with it? From the commitment to leave my room to the end of the lesson was only two hours, but in that time I learned one of the biggest lessons in my life. Those two hours got me out of that "runaway mode" into the "how can I learn from this mode?" What I learned about life-threatening soul pain and how to deal with it has truly changed my life.

Even with all that raw tragedy, I still ended up personally better off than I was before. I developed important empowering skills. I was able to take in my grandchildren, raise them, and help them work through their trauma as well. So when you ask about a breakthrough from a breakdown—I really was broken down, but I managed to piece myself together again—stronger. That single riding lesson showed Jill that not all of her life had shattered—there was a normalcy to reclaim through her work. Once she grasped that, Jill discovered she not only could go on, but that the bonding glue of tragedy actually creates a stronger framework for her life than her original untested fiber.

Another who found that scar tissue is tougher than unbroken skin is Buck Brannaman: *I'm on my second marriage right now. My first wife had a horse accident—a gentle horse stumbled and fell—my wife hit her head, sustained a closed-head injury, and went into a coma,* Buck recounts. *The doctor said she probably wouldn't live, let alone recover; it was just a matter of time. I sat beside her bed, twenty-four hours a day for four months waiting for her to wake up. When she finally did, we spent three more months going through rehabilitation, which is a nightmare. I can't even describe how horrific that experience is for the person who hasn't been injured—seeing your loved one like an animal—it's the craziest thing you can ever imagine.*

The hospital was good enough to reduce some of the charges to me for taking on a lot of her nursing care because I couldn't afford the hospital bills, and we didn't have insurance.

Now, I'm a person who's always been a little skeptical about the concept, but I can honestly say I've seen a miracle. It happens. Because not only did she live, but she started recovering from a situation that had been absolutely hopeless.

Unfortunately, due to circumstances he was unable to control, Buck's marriage did not survive. He recounts *After the divorce, I felt like I had my whole world taken away from me. I spent a couple of months moping, feeling bad. Then I started doing a few clinics here and there; within a couple of years it was full steam ahead, and it's just been a whirlwind ever since. Life doesn't stay bad forever; the law of averages says that.*

About a year later, one of my best friends called, and damned if the same thing didn't happen to his wife! It wasn't quite so severe with her, but pretty severe. I canceled my last few clinics of the year and went to be with him at the hospital in Colorado. I helped him through something that I don't think he'd have gotten through on his own. I was able to help because I'd seen it; I'd lived it; I knew a lot about it and I knew what kind of pain he was in. I was someone that he could lean on. He and I will always be friends.

So, all told, that tough time with my wife's accident also gave me the opportunity to spread some good out of it. Believe you me, I've gotten a lot of good out of it. I would never wish my hard times on anyone else, but I sure wouldn't trade what I got on the inside as a result of all my tough times. I wouldn't trade that away—it's made me what I am.

Just as Buck had taken on the challenge of an "impossible situation" with Biff, Buck mustered the nurturing abilities and dogged determination he'd gained working with tough broncs to cope with his wife's accident and recuperation. Then, as if delivering a personal clinic, Buck generously shared his hard-won lessons with friends.

In 1982, when bullets cut through President Reagan's entourage, tearing open James Brady's skull, his life changed forever. Although his miraculous recovery has not brought him back 100 per cent physically, his reinforced inner strengths not only support his current situation, but have allowed Jim and his wife, Sarah, to fight for gun control legislation and succeed with the passage of the Brady Bill. Because he credits so much of his resilience to therapeutic riding, Jim has also become a national spokesman for NARHA (North American Riding for the Handicapped Association). With his incredible strengths of character, determination, humor, and therapeutic *HorsePower!*, Jim has managed to turn his tragic twist of fate into tremendous good: that of protecting and inspiring millions.

One of life's most inconceivable tragedies is that of losing a child. Over the years, Roy Rogers and Dale Evans have had to face that time and again...and again: *It's devastating. We've lost three children at three different times,* says Dale. *Our darling baby, Robin, died just before her second birthday—she had Down's Syndrome and a defective heart. Then our adopted son, Sandy, died of alcohol poisoning shortly after he joined the Army. He was stationed in Germany and was so eager to be one of the guys.... He'd never done much drinking, but he was challenged to a drinking match and passed out. His buddies thought he was just drunk and put him to bed, and he died. Then our little girl, Debbie...we adopted her from Korea when she was three years old...she was a doll—a real Daddy's girl.... Just two weeks before her twelfth birthday, she was killed in a bus accident while on a church trip.*

That about killed both of us, added Roy. *That's why we moved. We just got away from down there to where we wouldn't see things that reminded us of her. That was hard...that was hard.... Humanly, there's no way to figure it.*

But as you know, continues Dale, *tragedy either makes you bitter or better—one of the two—according to your faith. Even with faith—and a strong faith—it is hard...there's nothing easy about it. But you can be healed in your faith if it's strong. If you can take your eyes off yourself and your loss and place your trust in a God who is infinitely merciful. God knows the end from the beginning...before you had your children, they were in the mind of God...it was His will that they be born. Therefore, there's a plan for them, a plan for their lives, and a plan for yours.*

Dale's faith in a plan was validated shortly after Robin's death, when Dale published her book, ANGEL UNAWARE, telling the story of Robin and the joy she had brought to their lives. As a result of that book, Roy and Dale noticed that handicapped children suddenly numbered in the audience at their appearances. This, at a time in the 1950's when retarded or emotionally disturbed children were often denied by families and relegated to institutions. To see such children in public was a rarity. Yet, as a result of the Rogers' loving endorsement of their own handicapped daughter (they had not put her in an institution as was recommended), doors were opened for many disabled children whose parents found a security in the Rogers' empathetic acceptance.

Roy commented with pride: *In addition to* ANGEL UNAWARE, *Dale wrote* SALUTE TO SANDY, *when Sandy died, and then she wrote a book right after Debbie was killed called,* DEAREST DEBBIE. *Those books seemed to minister a lot to people who had lost children.*

As America's most beloved western couple, Roy Rogers and Dale Evans have experienced many Happy Trails, and they have also survived tragic trials that have made them stronger, better, wiser...shining examples lighting the way for others.

To marshal the courage to mend your battered life, then selflessly share your experience to give others support and hope is one of the most difficult and noble lessons available to us; such individuals are truly heroic.

Skills for Success

Throughout this chapter we've witnessed some of the personal benefits from uncovering positive powers hidden within life's negative experiences. There are beneficial lessons to be found in all that we do once we are open to embracing change, different visions, learning from mistakes, and enduring calamities with courage and an optimistic attitude: *My book,* THAT WINNING FEEL-ING!, *is really an autobiography,* claims Jane Savoie. *It's not that I'm a big authority trying to tell everybody else what to do—I needed it myself. It grew out of my need to find ways to cut through my own shortcomings and self-limiting insecurities in order to achieve my goals. At my lectures I often hear, "Sure, it's easy for you; you're the queen of positive attitudes; everything's going so great...." But it's precisely when things are NOT going great that you need to hold that positive atti-tude more than ever. To deal with life's discouragements and not let them destroy you, but to use them as stepping stones of opportunity to learn from and to improve.*

Attitude is a matter of choice for each of us—we can choose to go after what we want, or be jealous of those who have it; we can surrender to adversity, or improve our lot; we can become bitter...or better. These are real choices...life saving or life limiting choices.

Obviously, for many of life's setbacks, there are no sure cures or antidotes, yet there is always the possibility of improvement: *After working with the disabled in therapeutic riding for so many years, I've come to the conclusion that there is no situation you cannot improve,* states Octavia Brown. *Clients have shown me that their very hardships brought out in them strengths that they just never had to tap into before. I believe such latent strength exists in everybody. We all have enormous powers of compensation that we normally never have to use—not super-human abilities—they're an inherent part of the human condition. Such inner strength should not be seen as any more admirable than it really is. The fact of the matter is, it's a normal human reaction to adversity: something that we should expect and encourage to find within ourselves. We all have that potential.*

I'm not saying people don't give up—some of my clients had—but we should gear ourselves to expect that inner wellspring of strength and build on that positive expectation. Octavia's professionally matter-of-fact assessment offers reassurance that although many of us may have yet to be seriously tested in life, the potential to ameliorate the worst of situations lies within each of us. Viewed in this light, adversity can be seen as a motivating catalyst for new life experiences. Then it's up to us to make the most of it and divine a meaning with which we can cope.

Disaster survivors often wonder or wail, "Why did this happen?" That is a critical question, for it is the first step to carving sense out of the inconceivable. The next step is, where do I go from here? We have seen how many of the above horsemen and women, like Buck Brannaman, Bob Douglas, Dale Evans, and Sally Swift discovered or divined answers to their life-altering experiences. Those answers allowed them a new perspective, acceptance, and committed direction. In addition, their ensuing teaching programs and books have helped thousands of individuals struggling with similar challenges. That's a resounding affirmation of the indomitable resilience of the human spirit to find the best in the worst, then turn trials into triumphs through the combined strength of character, spiritual faith, and the empowerment of *HorsePower!*

CURTIS STEEL, b. 1942, is a ranch manager and retired horse training supervisor for the New Mexico Corrections Department, where he managed the wild horse domestication program within the prison system. Curtis and his wife enjoy raising, riding and competing on the registered Quarter Horses and mustangs they train. Curtis and his Mustang, Jake, are shown in 1991 after winning the Champion Reining Horse competition at the New Mexico State Fair's Mustang show.

CHAPTER TEN

ON BALANCE

Psychological Well-Being

I've learned more about people from horses than I have about horses from people. —*Jack Huyler*

If I had my life to do over again, I'd probably add a few more horses. —*Mary Deringer Phelps*

I grew up in a house built by my grandfather and embellished by various family members for more than seventy years. The backyard, with its expanse of lawn, lily-of-the-valley rock garden, fish pond, bike shed, and apple orchard was the theater for my childhood imaginings. Most of those fantasies centered around horses.

My very first mount lived in the southeast corner of that backyard—in the shade of a tall pine stood a huge granite boulder roughly shaped like a horse's torso. It had a shallow swale at the saddle area, rising withers, and a swelling barrel that five-year-old legs could hug. I remember how hard it was to climb on, with only a tenuous toehold two-thirds up the near-side that served as a narrow "stirrup." Occasionally, my foot would slip as I struggled to mount in hard-soled shoes, and I'd come away with a bloodied knee—but never tears.

Over the years, as I grew, that huge rock horse gradually diminished in size to little more than a stone pony, but he was ever loyal and steadfast—always at the ready for a fantasy gallop. When I'd bring my children to visit their grandparents, they'd scramble onto his craggy back; and they, like me, never seemed to mind that our rock horse wasn't real. I still visit him when I'm back home.

Cornerstones

The foundation of *HorsePower!* has four cornerstones: simplicity, balance, spiritual nourishment, and personal growth. Simplicity allows us to slow down, relax, focus, learn, communicate, understand, and deal with the inherent honesty of nature. Balance is necessary for our physical, emotional, psychological, spiritual, and ecological well-being with horses and with life. Spiritual nourishment, derived from the individual give and take with horses, feeds our very essence—our soul—through enjoyment, relationships, adventures, risks, rewards, turbulence, and passions that produce enrichment, empowerment, and satisfaction. The final cornerstone, personal growth, is intrinsically connected to the other three, since it encompasses one's entire life process resulting from lessons learned and individual choices made.

Simple Pleasures

The uncomplicated existence of a horse underscores the value of simple pleasures that offer respite from contemporary complexity: *At the start of a four-day clinic in Grand Junction, Colorado, a lady of about forty came to me and said she'd just bought her first horse—a yearling that wasn't broke to lead yet—and she needed to move it to another stable,* recounts John Lyons. *She wanted to know what I would charge to break it to lead, put it in my trailer, and move it. Well, I really didn't want to do it, but for some reason I said, "If you're still here at the end of clinic, I'll do it." I figured she wouldn't stick around. Well, on the last day, she was still there, so I followed her to the corral where her horse was.*

The lady goes over and sits on this milk stool by a large feed bucket and sticks a halter down into the bucket—this is how she's been getting the halter on the horse—while it's been eating. The colt comes over and puts its head into the feed bucket, but finds no grain this time. The lady didn't even get the buckle snapped before the horse took off—with the lady hanging onto the halter strap over the horse's neck. The horse is dragging her around until finally she lets go when the horse steps on her. She gets up, kind of crying, with mud all over her face.

Now I'm watching this thinking, "Jiminy Christmas! This woman is greener than Kermit the frog! The combination of her with a yearling is going to be a wreck a day until she's killed." So I start explaining to her that this is just the first of many, MANY lessons this horse needs to learn. Even if I break it to lead now, and get it in the trailer, and haul it across town for her, she's still going to have to finish teaching it to lead…she's still going to have to get a saddle on it the first time…and a bridle…and learn to ride…. Now I'm going through just a super explanation of how, as a first-time buyer of a horse, she would be much better off with an older, broke horse and not this yearling with no training at all.

After I finish my whole lecture, she looks at me and she says slow and calm, "John…I have a very stressful job—really high stress…. On my way home I come here and I sit on this milk stool and I feed this horse and I watch him eat. And while I watch this horse eat his grain it seems like all my stress and all my problems just disappear. Then I can go home and be a decent mother to my kids and a decent wife to my husband. Now, if I own a horse…do I have to ride it?"

It was like somebody hit me in the head with a sledgehammer! I said, "Well, no, ma'am, you don't. In fact, I know a lot of people who'd be a whole lot better off if they never climbed on their horse."

What she was teaching me was that people have horses for different reasons and that horses fulfill different needs in people's lives. That helped me learn to ask, when people come to my clinics, "What is the

*need that you're trying to fulfill with your horse?" Then I can help
train the horse to fill their need; not just train the horse the way John
Lyons thinks the horse should be trained. Not every horse lover is a rider.*

The pleasure of just watching and being with horses strikes a
heartstring in many people: *A family up the road from us built a
house then bought horses: a black horse, a white horse, and two bays,*
recounts Dr. Robert Miller. *Every weekend we'd hear all four of
them wildly galloping down the road. After awhile, the son and father
quit riding, then the mother quit, and at sixteen, the daughter found
boys and quit riding. They still took dutiful care of those horses, but no
one rode them. After five years, they sold the two bays and only kept
the black and the white one—landscape horses. I've just recently learned
that term: "landscape horse," meaning a horse that's not used, just kept
for viewing purposes. Now that still fills a human need; horses fill a
wide spectrum of human needs.*

Simple Contentments

I've been collecting rocking horses for years and have one
adult-sized rocker that I jokingly refer to as my psychiatrist. Little
did I realize how close to the truth that is. When I'm upset, that
wood horse offers solace: the simple action of rocking, whether in
the arms of a caring parent, a rocking chair, on a rocking horse or
a quiet mount, evokes security and contentment and eases stress.

*When I get overly tired at clinics, stressed out, and tired of all the
questions, there might be a hundred people around the pen where I'm
working with a horse, but I can walk up to the horse and I can disappear inside that horse,* notes John Lyons. *I can literally not be there. I
can get so involved with the horse, it's just like walking out into a half-
mile meadow, surrounded by trees, with nobody there but me and that
horse. For me, like a lot of people, the horse ends up taking away a lot
of the world's problems and the stresses that we normally deal with.
There's nothing better than hugging a horse to alleviate tension.*

A number of people in this inquiry admitted that they love

going to the barn at feeding time and just sit there, listening, while their horses eat: *Not everybody feels on top of the world all the time— they have their disappointments and heartaches and deaths,* observes Phyllis Eifert. *I used to go down and sit in the stall and just watch my horse chew hay. It would be at night usually. I'd do my crying down there. When I cried, I'd put my head right on my horse's coat, hold on and just cry—get it all out. It was a meditation sort of a thing. Just watching the horse chew hay and sitting in the stall was real therapy. It was quiet, I felt comfortable with the horse. A real friendship.*

Sam Savitt concurs: *I could have our horses boarded out, but that would not appeal to me. I just love being at the barn with them. Even on a wintry night, the stable seems to stay warm because of the horses— they are hay burners. I go down just to be there, or take a horse out just to groom him; I love that. I had a neighbor who used to come with me when I was feeding the horses; he'd say, "I love to sit here and listen to the horses eat." And I feel the same way.*

Monty Roberts has even researched the phenomenon: *For me, watching cattle and horses eat is better than a fire in the fireplace. They're touching on some human nerve,* says Monty. *Thinking that I was probably the only one in the world who noticed, I did some study on it. I found that this business of horses or cattle eating is therapeutic for a lot of people. When animals, particularly flight animals like her- bivores, are eating, they cannot fear anything, or they couldn't eat. The instant they fear something, the adrenaline shoots up, and they have to stop eating—that's just nature. So, when flight animals are eating, you know they're tranquil and there's a cathartic effect that almost tranquil- izes you.*

Perhaps it's as simple as feeling "All's right with the world" at that instant in time: *There's a contentment that your soul really soaks up when you feed a horse, or groom him, or care for him,* notes Rich- ard Shrake. *You know he can't pick up the phone and order room ser- vice, he counts on you and when you deliver there's a contentment in that mutual trust.*

Simple Tempos

There's peace of mind to be found in the simpler rhythms of equestrian life: *When we went from horses to vehicles, the world got smaller,* notes Dennis Marine. *And when we went from vehicles to airplanes, the world got even smaller. The smaller it gets, the faster we go; I'm not sure we're going anywhere, but we sure are in a hurry to get there. Now, people have always worked hard, but they didn't seem to pack the stress level that they're packing today. Everybody's stressed out, going too fast. At that speed some basic things get lost—like basic common sense. There's a train of thought among people raised around livestock that that's where common sense comes from. You start working or being around livestock—and if your eyes are open—you become more aware of yourself and your relation to others and the natural order of things—that's where common sense comes from.*

The tempo of a barn is very different from the industrial percussion of a factory or the push-button staccato of a modern office. The orchestrations of a stable haven't changed much over the millennia: *I was really struck when my husband came to the barn the first time,* says Jenny Butah. *He said, "God! It's so timeless here!" It was like a revelation for him that he could come here and get stress reduction just by sitting here—not even riding.*

By decelerating from today's supersonic pace and settling into the simpler, synchronous rhythm of a four-beat fox-trotting walk, a two-step trot or three-beat waltzing canter, riders find more tranquil tempos in life: *Riding is a total escape from the rapidity that we have to live in this day and age,* says Larry Mahan. *I'm such a lover of music that I ride with music a lot. I plug in a walkman and ride to instrumental pieces that help me get in time with the horse— rhythm is so important—just like dancing. If you're dancing around without music, you really don't have anything to relate to. The music helps me to get into the rhythm, then I try to get the horse into the rhythm of the music.*

Simple Joys

From dance rhythms to the simple joy of an outing, horseback riding has value above and beyond the parameters of work: *One thing I do now that I didn't do when I was younger is ride just for recreation,* Dr. Robert Miller reports. *When I first started my veterinary practice, I was baffled by people who kept horses and didn't do anything but go out for a ride. If I was on a horse, it was to be doing something. I spent all my summers working ranch jobs, packing for the Forest Service, or driving teams. During World War II, there was quite a resurgence of draft horses, so I drove farm horses. Even my recreational riding had purpose: I was crazy about roping in my school years. So, I'd always worked horses and I'd rope off a horse for fun, but to get on and just joy ride—I found that slightly incomprehensible. But I wasn't in veterinary practice too many years before I discovered the tremendous therapeutic value and escape from stress that riding brought in and of itself.*

The simple joys of equine give-and-take put the kick into Rex Peterson's life and career: *Many years ago, when I was going to college, I worked for a man whose grandson was into drugs. He shook his head and said to me, "Son, don't ever get into drugs. Get high on life, because it's going to be there everyday. Drugs are a high that you get for a little while, but when you come down, life is still there: get high on life!" My greatest highs come from the things I can get my horse to do. People say, "Well, sure... you're in front of the crowds—that's a high." Well, the crowds don't mean as much to me as the horse giving something I've asked for.*

Balance

A scale is constantly dipping back and forth; balance isn't static— it's not something you find and keep. It's something you're always moving into and out of, observes author and trainer Vicki Hearne *(p.297). That is why when you're learning to ride you have one day when you really think you've got it: you're sitting up there right with the center of the motion of the universe and all the stars are circling around you—just like they ought to—being propelled by angels! Then the next day you can hardly stay on the horse because you forgot what you had to do to make that happen. You always have to do something to make balance happen.*

Learning to work with our own inner scale helps us to maintain balance: *If you try to micro-manage horses by saying, "I have to control everything," you're doomed to failure,* notes William Steinkraus. *If you say, "I'm not going to control anything, I'm going to be cooperative no matter what, you're equally doomed. You have to find a balance. Riding, like life, is a question of finding the right balance.*

Physical Balance

Working with physical balance highlights a basic fact of nature: nothing's perfect—no human, no horse, no life. The sooner we accept that we will be making concessions, adjustments, and compromises throughout life to compensate for our own as well as every other being's inherent imperfections, the sooner we will master balance—physical and otherwise. As Buck Brannaman explains: *A lot of times people ask, "Why don't you teach more equitation in your clinics?" It's because I believe that when you get your horse to where he operates as if he's your legs, you can't have bad equitation. When you move as one mind and one body the equitation cannot be poor. One problem with human beings' physical balance is that we're not even on both sides: we're not as handy with one leg or one hand as the other. You'll see this imbalance in horses, too. I spend my whole life talking about it because people are so, so far out of balance physically in terms of their coordination and their skills, that you just can't believe how much they get in the horse's way and inhibit a horse from being able to do what he ordinarily would do well. That's a huge problem.*

Successful compensation also requires balance, since overcompensation causes new problems: *Often times the more a rider con-*

centrates, the less communication there is with the horse, Doug Lietzke notes. *The individual becomes so focused on what he's trying to accomplish that he's not picking up on what the horse is saying. The paradox is that trying softer often works better than trying harder. I think of it in terms of "a window of effort." In medicine there's a window of optimal medicine: if you give too little, it doesn't work; if you give too much it doesn't work. And with riding, the rider has to stay within that window of effort: too little effort doesn't work, likewise, trying too hard doesn't work either. Often trying softer works better than trying harder.*

Improvement may come from trying softer and simpler: riding bareback—the oldest riding method—is still the most effective: *At the core of physical balance is the center of gravity,* says Caroline Thompson. *I did a lot of bareback riding when I first moved to Burbank since it's so hot in the summer. I learned to find the center of the horse. When you find his center and work your center with his center, it all goes right from there. Yet when you lose your center it all goes berserk—and probably the horse will lose his center because horses do not come perfectly balanced either.*

In addition to coordination, compensation, and centering, physical balance also involves successful management of lifestyle and all that entails: work, family, calendars.... *I'm very focused and very absorbed in the horses and in riding, but I make sure there's a balance in my life,* says Jane Savoie. *I'm an early riser and as far as I'm concerned, if you want to call at five in the morning and talk business, that's fine, but come six-thirty or seven at night, I will not answer the phone. I'm married, I have a husband, and I want to have another life. My husband is very supportive of the horses, but he's not a horse person, and I'm not going to do horses twenty-four hours a day—twelve or thirteen hours is enough. Evenings are my hack time.*

Emotional Balance

As we've seen, many have found they can trust a horse with their innermost secrets long before they establish that kind of trust with another human. A horse has wonderfully strong, warm shoulders to cry on. They offer two attentive ears to listen to your thoughts, concerns, hopes, and dreams without dashing them. They are patient counselors who don't argue, give unsolicited advice, or judgments. Even though they do not speak out, (or perhaps *because* they don't) communication with an equine friend often leads to discovering solutions within oneself. *When I'm riding Freckles, I'm constantly talking to her—she's my ear,* explains Tracy Cole. *They laugh at me at the barn, because we have these long trail rides once a year and everybody else has a leader and a side-walker, but I don't have anybody since I'd been riding for so long. So I'm sitting there talking to Freckles for the entire five miles. She's just my ear, if I have a problem, Freckles will listen. She may not give me an answer, but she'll listen. Sometimes there are things that I can't talk to anyone else about because they're personal. I just need somebody to listen who's not going to answer back and not give me an opinion. I just want to work out how it sounds. So I talk to Freckles and it's fine.*

Horses can provide stable companionship: *Riding keeps me alive; it keeps me grounded,* claims Caroline Thompson. *In my business, people either treat you like you're the Queen of Sheba or like you're a heap of shit. The horses and me—that's a pretty steady thing—for the business I'm in, it's great to have that grounding. If I get tense about something when I am on a horse, all I have to do is breathe back down into my chest, my heart chakra, instead of operating out of my head. I'm not talking about the center of physical balance, I'm talking about emotional balance. To me riding is a completely emotional experience, and when the emotions I am acting out are coming out of my emotional center—that's where it all works for me.*

Horses can provide a healthy distraction: *When I was first divorced, there were a lot of things going on inside of me emotionally,* Pat Lawson admits. *I needed something to take my mind off my own problems; to have my mind engrossed with something other than "woe is me" and all that's associated with that. The horse did that for me.*

When I bought Star, he needed so much attention…that horse would not let me touch him in the face for a long time because he'd been beaten in the face. He was also afraid of small places and wouldn't go into a two-horse trailer. He wouldn't do a lot of stuff. But Star saved me from myself. Riding is almost a necessity now; it's a stress reducer for me. There are times when the walls come in on me, my problems come in on me, and I would run—out of the house, into my car, go to the barn, and just putter around—just do anything. I'd find my mind was taken off my problems because every time I would go to see Star, there was something to do, something I had to attend to. That gave me time out. At times when I was very upset, Star would pick up on that and be really sweet: he'd allow me to do things he normally would not have allowed. He'd chill out and decide he would be easy that day. We have come a long way. Star has become a crucial piece in my life. I guess he's a friend. He still challenges me; he's thrown me a couple of times and done some silly stuff, but he's really saved some things in my life. He's pulled me back from some real bad times.

Horses can provide love: *As a young man, I had a home life that had a lot of conflict—really a lot of conflict to the point that I had migraine headaches and stuff,* reports Ron Harding. *So, what did I do? I went out to the horse corral. Because I had that trouble early in life I turned my love toward horses and that's made me ask a lot of questions about love. I knew that I knew how to love horses, but I didn't know how to love people. So learning how to give and take with the horses taught me a lot about how to give and take with people. Horses taught me to care for my fellow man. To me, it's like it says in the scriptures: when all else is said and gone, love will remain. That's the biggie.*

Psychological Balance

Many contributors suggested that an hour at the barn is more productive than months on an analyst's couch: *Some days I take my driving as therapy,* says Jimmy Fairclough. *I've come home, had a beer and said, "I'm taking the horses for a nice long walk." I know that's a day that I'm not in the mood or in the frame of mind to train; I have gotten tired of people. I've gotten up at five-thirty in the morning just to be with my horses because they're better than people. They fill that need for companionship that I have and I don't need the people around me. They don't talk back and they give to me every day. That's the reason I do all this, they give to me and I get something out of it—daily.*

When you're drowning in work, riding can feel like surfacing for fresh air: *Riding is incredible psychological therapy*, agrees Mary Mansi. *My husband and I are in business for ourselves in a profession where there's a lot of liability, responsibility and a requirement for detailed ongoing education. We are in a three-person office eight to ten hours a day and I was going crazy. I needed to get out. Riding has opened up a world of getting out in the country, being out in the fresh air, and meeting other people of all ages who like to do what I do, so we have a common bond. And it's so different from my accounting work. It is psychologically very beneficial to diversify my activities and interests. It's detailed in a different way and I'm not behind a desk. If I had my druthers, I'd live on a big ranch, and I'd work my butt off all day long.*

Changes of pace and scene are important to everyone's psyche: *I see clients at our clinics who are high-powered attorneys, high-powered CEO's, and for three days never think about their work because that horse has a magic that gets them totally away from what they do in everyday life*, says Richard Shrake. *You can go work out at the gym, but it's not like going for a ride. You can run a marathon and it's not like being able to go out and just brush a horse. That horse is one of the absolute perfect stress-relievers of all time. An exercise bike doesn't come close, nor do skis, or the race car with a motor. The horse is alive—he's living—and he's like a psychiatrist: he doesn't talk back, he just listens.*

Rege Ludwig supports Richard's point: *The wife of a New York student of mine was telling me that since he's taken up polo it's the first time he's been able to sleep well at night. He plays polo on Friday night, exhausts himself, and sleeps like a baby. As a result, their relationship is better and his business is going better; that is definitely a psychological therapy for them.*

Even young people realize the value of a time out: *I know I need an outlet from the stress at school,* Tina Schuler admits. *If I didn't ride this fall, I don't know how I would have survived. Riding is the one thing that makes me happier than anything else. Riding gives me more confidence, it refreshes me, and I just like being with a horse— another living creature that I don't have to speak to and to worry about saying the right thing, or doing the right thing, or being judged by…. I know whenever I get back from riding I'm more ready to see people, more refreshed…. It always makes me feel better.*

Balance is everything, Anne Kursinski reiterates. *Everything in balance—for sure with horses. They tell you when you're doing it right and when you're not. It's like balancing a broom in the palm of your hand—it's that elusive—but when you get it, it's great. You can't do too much or too little, that's what it's all about—balance—mentally, physically, psychologically, everything. The better balanced one is inside, the better balanced your riding will be, and probably everything else in your life. Most all successes or feeling good comes from inside. The bottom line is that balance really has to come from inside yourself. A lot of people don't get that. When I'm feeling good about myself and feeling balanced on the inside, my results are better, my teaching is better, my riding is better, my everything is better. But it does have to start on the inside—with that broom being balanced inside—then everything else is much easier.*

As Tracy Cole points out, almost everything seems better when viewed from the saddle: *Even if I'm having a rotten day, when I'm on the back of a horse, everything isn't as rotten as it seems. It's like the bumper sticker: "A bad day on a horse is better than a good day at the office."*

That simple change of perspective can be the remedy: *I told a friend of mine who's going through a divorce, "If you're having a bad day, come up and ride; the day may not turn out as bad as you thought it was,"* reports Rex Peterson. *Horses are one of the best non-prescription medicines you can buy…not cheap, but effective.*

Environmental Balance

Humanity's trend, especially over the last hundred years, has been to increase protection against the elements and life by gradually disconnecting from nature and one another. Like circled Conestoga wagons, our homes are tightly clustered and reinforced against various enemies: animals, insects, fire, storm, earthquakes, and man. Interiors have deadbolt locks, electronic surveillance, smoke detectors, and panic buttons wired directly to police. Communities erect miles of sound walls, form neighborhood watch groups, and create legislation on everything from smoking to outlawing pets. Through civilization, urbanization, and legislation we willingly abdicate self-reliant awareness for contracted protection, insulating ourselves more and more from nature and instinct.

Horses provide us with living, breathing, instinctual lab animals that are ecologically friendly vehicles into nature: *One of the greatest gifts that riding has given me is being able to experience riding in all parts of the world,* notes Camille Whitfield Vincent. *I love to travel, and riding makes for such special experiences all over the world. I've ridden on the Parker Ranch in Hawaii, ridden jumpers across the emerald fields of Ireland and shown Elation before royalty in England. One of my most memorable rides was galloping up Mt. Kenya with zebra running along beside me—talk about a rush! I kept thinking, "I've got to pinch myself—I'm on this horse surrounded by zebra and gazelles and giraffe—everything right there. To this day I still remember that feeling of "I can't believe this! I cannot believe this!" It was just awesome! But I never would have been able to do that if it wasn't for riding. The fact that I was on a horse was non-threatening to them. I could never have connected that way if it wasn't for the ability to ride.*

Technology has been slicing away the traces that once tied man to beast, by eliminating man's dependence on animals. Carriage horses, oxen teams, and watch dogs are all headed the way of the carrier pigeon. It is imperative that we maintain our connection to animals, for they are a crucial part of our world and our psyche: *People often say to me, "Oh, you don't have any children, your animals are your children,"* recounts animal communicator Penelope Smith (p.297). *But I say, "Love is love." Frankly, to be complete you need to love all beings—human, children, adult, all animals—to be connected with all of them because underneath we are the same spiritual essence. We all have the same source. We are all spirits. Our form makes for the variety: we all have different senses, different ways of looking at and appreciating the world. Humans need to be connected with everything, for we are the species that needs the most compassion, the most education and the most connection with other beings. Native peoples have known that throughout the ages. Otherwise we lose our way: we get lost in our heads, we become psychologically off-balance if we don't connect. So, I would say in our modern society, riding horses or being connected with other animals is absolutely essential. We need to be connected much more with the whole earth and horses do that. When you are with animals, particularly a thousand pound or more animal, who has four feet on the ground, you suddenly feel a solid connection to the earth. Energy actually grounds, goes down to the earth. Instead of being up in your head and in your thoughts or in your computer, you are right here on the earth, solid. Your energy goes through your body from your feet all the way up your spine when you are with a horse. You can't help that. Whether you are standing next to them or whether you are riding them, you are more grounded: connected with everything around you and your whole environment, rather than just mental ideas that are society-oriented.*

Mankind must remain concerned, knowledgeable, responsible, and respectful of other species. We must share the planet in a way that allows for their unique natures in natural and authentic cohabitation.

One big lesson for us in this era of ecological crisis is that human beings aren't the only form, or perhaps the most important form of life, notes Dr. Elizabeth Lawrence. *The horse shows us that we can live in harmony with other species without destroying them, being antagonistic, or dominating them. We must give and take and consider ourselves as a part of nature if we are to save the planet.*

Horses have been mankind's silent partners for ages, contributing much and asking little in return: we owe them a tremendous debt. Safe, accessible public trails are needed within a variety of living centers: from wilderness to rural, to suburban, to metropolitan. The rails to trails program is one obvious resource for this.

Legal liability and appropriate responsibility must be limited so that riding academies can give lessons and lease horses without punitive insurance costs or fear of financial ruin should an accident happen.

Compassion and common sense must be balanced to manage a healthy existence for the feral horse and burro herds within current habitat restrictions: *Now I love horses dearly, but I disagree with people who say, "I could never put a horse down, I can never send a horse to be made into dog food,"* states Rex Peterson. *Because there's another situation that well-meaning people have caused with the mustang herds. Do you know why the wild horses in the New Mexico desert are starving to death? Because what I call "bleeding hearts" will not allow the government to thin the herds the way they need to. It is no longer an area of total open range like it was two hundred years ago, so these horses only have a certain area to live in, and that area has drought some years. The BLM (Bureau of Land Management) was controlling the numbers by sending horses to slaughter, which was the kindest thing they could do for them. Now they are watching whole herds die slowly because people won't allow the horses to be thinned as they should be. In some ways we have helped the animal and in some ways we have hurt him very badly. I hate to say it, but sometimes a bleeding heart is the worst thing for the animals because they want no control, no restrictions put on them; yet we live in a whole society of restrictions.*

The Wild Horse and Burro Protection Act saved feral horses from extermination by barring helicopter shoots and mustang round-ups. Due to that act's success and culling restrictions, herds are now threatened by overpopulation on limited lands: over-crowding, drought, and starvation make for slow, stressful deaths. Man-made control mechanisms—adoption and contraceptive programs—are complicated and expensive, while culling by slaughter is spurned as heartless. Until America's wild horses become a political and financial priority, their future will remain clouded. The wild horse dilemma illustrates that to sustain a reasonable quality of life—and death—population control must be considered in light of limited resources and financial considerations.

While horses are not an endangered species on this continent, the American equestrian is. Preserving equine habitat and the equestrian way of life is important because both are treasures of our American heritage.

Spiritual Nourishment

Throughout their historic partnership, man has recognized the horse as a prize beyond its obvious economic value. Classical mythology attributed poetry, prophecy, and military prowess to the horse, as did other cultures.

Mohammed said of the horse:

Kindness and good fortune are found on the back of a horse. These are precious treasures that mankind shall strive to keep. (Jeschko)

In the Koran, the description of God creating the horse reads:

I have made thee without equal. All the treasures of the earth lie between thine eyes. Thou shalt stamp thine enemies under thine hooves but thou shalt carry my friends on thy back. This is the seat from which men shall pray to me. Thou shalt take precedence over all other creatures: The masters of the earth shall love thee. Thou shalt fly without wings and win victories without the sword. (Jeschko)

Native Americans held the horse in high spiritual regard:

The famous Absaroka, or Crow, chief, Plenty Coups, described a special bond that often existed between a Plains Indian warrior and his horse. 'My horse fights with me and fasts with me, because if he is to carry me in battle he must know my heart and I must know his or we shall never become brothers. I have been told that the white man, who is almost a god, and yet a great fool, does not believe that the horse has a spirit. This cannot be true. I have many times seen my horse's soul in his eyes'. (Josephy 362)

Horses bring us closer to nature, to our Creator, and to our own souls.

Spiritual Balance

Americans are accomplished at training the mind and attending to physical and material needs, yet we often neglect our spirit—even though spirit fuels our mental attitude, personal endurance, and creativity.

One hears, "Know yourself, love yourself, understand yourself, control yourself," relates Jill Keiser Hassler. It's great to hear those words, but to really succeed with horses, you need to do all that. With a horse, you have an opportunity to develop your inner self, your inner balance, your inner harmony through the aid of their feedback. A horse will give you immediate honest feedback once you learn how to listen.

As difficult and demanding as a lifestyle built around horses is, many find it richly fulfilling: When my daughter was born I was working for Hobbs Cattle Company, a large outfit back in Nebraska, recalls Dennis Marine. I had to mow hay, fix fences, and all the rest of the time I was riding. I really enjoyed that outfit, but the job didn't pay much and when you have a baby you start putting expectations on *yourself about what you need to provide. I've looked back at those times a lot and look at where I ended up. Maybe I'd have made more money by doing something else, but I'm not sure I'd have gained anything in the long run. I might have wasted a good percentage of my life doing something that I didn't enjoy. Now, I don't enjoy every day of ranching either—there's always things that I don't care for and there are things in nature that I can't control, but a lot of the rest of the situation seems like I can. And as far as the lifestyle…it's a good lifestyle. Here it is twenty-five years later, and the bank ain't full of money, the body's broke down…yet I keep working back towards the ranching life.… Now I do a bit of day work on my days off. I still don't make any money at it, but it's jobs for the horses, and it pays the fuel. Ranching's a tough way to make a living, but it's a pleasurable way of making a living. I can be plumb whooped and tired at the end of the day—but it's a better tired—I'm not a stressed out trembling mass that can't go to sleep. I don't know if it's roots, or heritage, or what…but there's definitely an attraction.* Many consider the life of a cowboy a national privilege: *It's quite a country where you can make your living just working with horses,* notes Buck Brannaman. *It's real humbling to even think of doing something like this for a living when you consider the challenges some people have living in other parts of the world. All I've ever wanted to be is a good hand with a horse—a good cowboy. I've dedicated my whole life to working with horses. For me, the term "cowboy" carries a lot of pride with it. Some people think "cowboy" is a nasty word, but they haven't been around much if that's their attitude. Where I come from, for someone to call you a cowboy—"Old Hank, he's a cowboy"—that's a mark of honor.*

Part of the attraction exists in the fact that horses aren't about meeting deadlines, time tables, and civilized perfection; horses are about challenge, freedom, spirit, accepting life as it comes, and honoring the natural world: *I'm a different rider: I don't ride in the ring, I don't compete…I like to ride the trails,* says Zaven Ayanian. *My horse Jeramy is a very free-spirited horse. He is like me. I like to be on top of a mountain, in the valleys, in the woods, all by myself with my horse. I enjoy the freedom tremendously and I cherish it very much— it's very important to life. When I'm riding I feel great. I feel free. I don't worry about my business, politics, or world problems. I disconnect from all that when I'm on the horse. I just have a great time with him.*

Another attraction is as basic as Buck Brannaman notes: *The biggest part of working horses is in matters of the heart.* And Mary Deringer Phelps agrees: *I don't ride horses because I have emotional problems, or I'm trying to overcome something or have anything to prove. I do it just because I love it. Horses are a great love, and it's a deep love…and they've given me tremendous peace of mind. Haven't you ever laid down beside a horse when he's laying down and talked to him? And just looked at him? He's soft and he's sweet and his breath smells good and his nose.… Then the nice thing is you can get up and leave! I like all of them—I like the way they feel, I like the way they breathe, I like the way they smell.…*

Dr. Elizabeth Lawrence adds her vote to equine companion-ship: *You can never be lonesome when you're around a horse. Never ever. They just provide a wonderful friendship even if you don't ride them.*

Horses keep us in touch with our inner child: *When I'm on a horse I feel transported,* Mary Fenton reports. *I feel joy. That's when I laugh the most. Sometimes when I'm riding, and it's going well, I just laugh like a little kid.*

Beauty, love, friendship, youth, and great times—a veritable banquet of spiritual nourishment—is it any wonder people keep horses in their lives?

My whole life is built around the passion of horsemanship, adds Helen Crabtree. *It's the source of my life. The anticipation that you have—which is almost greater than realization—knowing that there is no ceiling on what you can do or what you can think. I'm a perfect example of that: three years of encroaching blindness and advancing age, yet here I am, ready to jump over the moon with the excitement of*

*my new horse projects: the college program, writing my new book....
These are new challenges that can keep me young and learning forever.
If you stop looking forward, stop learning, or stop analyzing things,
you're dead—you're brain dead—you may be here physically, but
you're gone otherwise.*

Personal Growth

Most horses don't allow us to go brain-dead; they constantly
challenge us to maintain balance of one sort or another: *As we
move through each stage of life, horses and riding fill different needs,*
notes Diana Thompson. *As a child, riding was everything for me—
the joy of being with my horse and all the caretaking; the exhilaration
of riding bareback, swimming with my horse, galloping up hills...the
freedom and power that comes with riding. I had a fairly strict childhood and a pretty unhappy mother. I'd come home from school, change
my clothes, and get out of the house—to the horse. Emotionally, riding
kept me alive into my twenties. Getting out in the woods and the wilderness with my friend the horse—that really fed me. The strength I
got from the horse was how I stayed emotionally healthy, and okay in
a fairly intense environment. Some kids start smoking, or get into other
stuff to divert their stress; I played with horses. That's where I went to
feel good about myself and have some control over life.*

Kids who meet the challenge of horses get a leg up on life:
*Kids who have the opportunity to deal with horses have a real special
experience,* says Larry Mahan. *There's just so much to be learned from
it. I wish all kids could enjoy that experience.*

That experience is so rewarding because when you're working with horses, you're really working on yourself. As L.D. Burke
observes: *Horses help us get in touch with ourselves and help us understand ourselves. We have to expand as beings to communicate with a
horse. No question, the horse is a great teacher.*

Mary Deringer Phelps attributes a great deal to her equine
teachers: *Horses have just taught me so much that I guess they've made*

me what I am today. That's why horse people are a breed apart.

I think it takes special people to own horses, claims John Lyons. *Most people who have horses don't have other people take care of them. It takes a real giving person to own a horse. They have to give of their time, their money, and a great deal of themselves to own a horse. That's why I like horse owners—they all have a heart.*

Role Models

In Europe, accomplished equestrians and their mounts hold star status. Just like our national sports heroes of football, baseball, basketball, and tennis, European riders are followed closely by the press and sought after for autographs by admiring fans. In America however, equestrian athletes and trainers are given very little national coverage or recognition. This is an untapped source of inspiring role models who do our country proud on the fields of competition and in their daily life.

HorsePower! has introduced you to many well known and lesser known cowboys, equestrians and trainers who are heroes in both their sport and in life. Beginning with my lifelong idols: Roy Rogers and Dale Evans, and continuing with Buck Brannaman, Helen Crabtree, Martha Josey, Becky Hart, Larry Mahan, Jane Savoie, Bob Douglas, Sally Swift, William Steinkraus, Anne Kursinski, James Brady, Macella O'Neill....

The list goes well beyond this book's contributors to individuals such as show-jumping star Michael Matz, who was chosen as flag bearer for the entire United States Olympic contingent at the 1996 Atlanta Games. Matz earned that honor not only for his sportsmanship and riding talents, which have won him three trips to the Olympics (winning a team silver in Atlanta), but also for his selfless heroism following the 1989 crash of United Airlines flight 232 when he rescued several children. (Jaffer 32)

Others such as David and Karen O'Connor, Robert Ridland, Jim Shoulders, Margie Goldstein-Engle, Ty Murray, and D.D. Matz are also worthy of recognition. If many of these names are not familiar to you, that's the point. All are accomplished athletes and admirable role models, yet most Americans do not know of them because their sports do not gain consistent national coverage. As a parent, I would rather see my children aspiring to be like these individuals than many of the media "sports heroes" who exhibit disdain, greed and even outrageous lawlessness in their sport and private lives.

Yet another advantage of role models from the equestrian field is the fact equestrian competition is equally available to both sexes and includes a wide spectrum of ages, from teen-age superstars of rodeo to the mature masters of dressage and the senior rodeo circuit. Hence, there's a maturity factor within the equestrian disciplines that is missing in sports restricted to youthful athletic prowess.

By seeking out the cream of America's varied equestrians, corporate sponsors have a wealth of opportunity for endorsements and role models in sportsmanship. As decades of Budweiser Clydesdale ads have proven, *HorsePower!* pays off in advertising.

Skills for Success

Of course, the true heroes of *HorsePower!* are the horses themselves. It is through them that one harvests the many strengthening, enlivening, and inspiring lessons and skills that set the cornerstones for success: simplicity, balance, spiritual nourishment, and personal growth. Even measured amongst all his life's momentous accomplishments, Winston Churchill recognized the impact of *HorsePower!*: "I was pretty well trained to sit and manage a horse. This is one of the most important things in the world." (Churchill 45)

As I mentioned at the start of this chapter, I still check in with the rock horse of my childhood. No longer in the backyard, it now stands proudly with our family name branded on its side, in

Sleepy Hollow Cemetery, a silent sentry at the graves of my father and mother. To me, that rock horse remains a stalwart symbol of my family heritage and the earnest endurance of *HorsePower!*

Landscape horses, miniature horses, rocking horses, stone ponies, steeds of literature, art, song, and poetry—sirens of the human imagination—there is something about the very idea of horses that is romantic and captivating. Although it is evident that one need not ride to catch horse fever, to experience the full impact and range of values of *HorsePower!* one must connect with the real thing: *There are a lot of people who are only with horses for a while to learn what they needed to from the horse, then life takes them elsewhere,* notes Buck Brannaman. *But they'll always take with them what they learned from the horse because it applies to so many other things in life.*

Buck's point was dramatically illustrated for Helen Crabtree recently: *Last year the phone rang and a woman introduced herself to me and said, "Mrs. Crabtree, you won't remember me because it's been a long time. You taught me to ride on your little five-gaited horse, Tommy Tucker, in St. Louis in 1946. I'm vacationing in Kentucky and had hoped to visit you, but I'm having to return home sooner than expected. I still wanted to call and tell you this.... I haven't ridden for years now; but I wanted you to know that what I learned from those lessons—not just about riding—but what I learned as a person has made me one of the happiest and most fulfilled people in this world. I just know if it had not been for those lessons, I wouldn't be the happy person I am today."*

Isn't that wonderful? asks Helen. *I nearly dropped the phone! After fifty years, here's this lady saying that.... You just don't realize...some people go through life and never realize their opportunities with riding; they think it stops at the saddle, but obviously it doesn't.*

Sally Swift concurs: *People often tell me, "You haven't just given me riding lessons—you've changed my whole life."*

"It doesn't stop at the saddle," "riding lessons as living lessons," "you've changed my whole life," that's *HorsePower!* in a nutshell. The old horse-powered age where horses were slaves sacrificed to work and war is gone. We are now in an exciting new age where horses—as partners and teachers—offer lessons of personal empowerment and skills for unbridled success to those wise enough to reap the benefits of living and winning with *HorsePower!*

VICKI HEARNE is a philosopher, poet, and award-winning author, and renowned trainer of horses and dogs for almost thirty years. Her books, ADAM'S TASK, BANDIT, and ANIMAL HAPPINESS offer unique perspectives on animals, pets and humans. Vicki is pictured with Bandit.

PENELOPE SMITH, b. 1946, shown with one of her favorite Afghan companions, is an acknowledged pioneer in the field of animal communication. A popular speaker and author of a number of books and audio tapes on interspecies communication, Penelope also holds workshops and seminars throughout the United States and the world.

In Gratitude

Dear Lord,
Thank you for their generous spirit,
Thank you for their beauty and versatility,
Thank you for their strength that supports us,
Thank you for their patient, constructive partnership,
Thank you for their thrilling, competitive heart,
Thank you for the exciting joy of their dance,
Thank you for their power to heal,
Thank you for the lessons they teach,
Thank you for the wisdom they provide...
Dear Lord, thank you for the horse.

—Rebekah Ferran Witter

Bibliography

American Horse Council, *1996 Horse Industry Directory*. Horse Industry Statistics: 4.

Churchill, Winston. *My Early Life, A Roving Commission*. New York: Charles Scribner's Sons, 1930.

Crabtree, Helen K. *Hold Your Horses*. SADDLE & BRIDLE, 1997:16, 17

"Events & Athletes: Equestrian." *Olympiad—Atlanta 1996: Official Souvenir Program*. 1996.

Huyler, John S. *The Stamp of the School: Reminiscences of the Thacher School 1949–1992*. Seattle: Special Child Publications, 1994.

Jaffer, Nancy. "Michael Matz: Giving Riding A Leg Up." *Spur* March/April 1997: 32.

Jeschko, Kurt and Harald Lange. *The Horse Today—& Tomorrow?* New York: Arco Publishing Company, Inc., 1972.

Josephy, Jr., Alvin M. *500 Nations*. New York: Alfred A. Knopf, 1994: 362.

Random House Historical Dictionary of Slang. Volume 1, New York: Random House, 1994.

Rogers, Roy and Dale Evans with Jane and Michael Stern. *Happy Trails: Our Life Story*. New York: Simon & Schuster, 1994.

Savoie, Jane. *That Winning Feeling! A New Approach to Riding Using Psychocybernetics*. No. Pomfret, Vermont: Trafalgar Square Publishing, 1992.

Savoie, Jane. *That Winning Feeling!* Audiotape 1: *Choose Your Future*. No. Pomfret Vermont: Trafalgar Square Publishing, 1993.

Steinkraus, William, Ed. *The U.S. Equestrian Team Book of Riding*. New York: Simon and Schuster, 1976.

Photo Credits

Index